On the Move

On the Move

THE POLITICS OF SOCIAL CHANGE IN LATIN AMERICA

■

HENRY VELTMEYER

broadview press

Copyright © 2007 Henry Veltmeyer

All rights reserved. The use of any part of this publication reproduced, transmitted in any form or by any means, electronic, mechanical, photocopying, recording, or otherwise, or stored in a retrieval system, without prior written consent of the publisher—or in the case of photocopying, a licence from Access Copyright (Canadian Copyright Licensing Agency), One Yonge Street, Suite 1900, Toronto, Ontario M5E 1E5—is an infringement of the copyright law.

LIBRARY AND ARCHIVES CANADA CATALOGUING IN PUBLICATION

Veltmeyer, Henry
    On the move : the politics of social change in Latin America / Henry Veltmeyer.

Includes bibliographical references and index.

ISBN 978-1-55111-872-7

    1. Social change—Latin America. 2. Latin America—Politics and government-1980-. 3. Latin America—Economic conditions–1982-. 4. Latin America—Social conditions-1982-. I. Title.

HN110.5.A8V445 2007   306.2098'09048   C2007-902340-1

BROADVIEW PRESS is an independent, international publishing house, incorporated in 1985. Broadview believes in shared ownership, both with its employees and with the general public; since the year 2000 Broadview shares have traded publicly on the Toronto Venture Exchange under the symbol bdp.

We welcome comments and suggestions regarding any aspect of our publications—please feel free to contact us at the addresses below or at: broadview@broadviewpress.com / www.broadviewpress.com.

North America
Post Office Box 1243,
Peterborough, Ontario, Canada K9J 7H5

Post Office Box 1015,
3576 California Road,
Orchard Park, New York, USA 14127
tel: (705) 743-8990; fax: (705) 743-8353

customerservice@broadviewpress.com

UK, Ireland and continental Europe
Plymbridge Distributors Ltd.
Estover Road, Plymouth PL6 7PY, UK
tel: 44 (0) 1752 202300;
fax order line: 44 (0) 1752 202330;
enquiries@nbninternational.com

Australia and New Zealand
UNIREPS University of New South Wales
Sydney, NSW 2052 Australia
tel: 61 2 96640999; fax: 61 2 96645420
infopress@unsw.edu.au

Broadview Press acknowledges the financial support of the Government of Canada through the Book Publishing Industry Development Program (BPIDP) for our publishing activities.

Cover Design by Xavier Pompelle, Black Eye Design.
Interior Design by Michel Vrána, Black Eye Design.
Printed in Canada

10 9 8 7 6 5 4 3 2 1

Contents

INTRODUCTION 7

CHAPTER 1: NEO-LIBERALISM AND US IMPERIALISM 11
    Neo-liberalism in Theory and Practice 12
    Neo-liberal Policy and Politics: Socio-economic Impacts and Political Responses 15
    The Economics and Politics of US Imperialism 19
    Conclusion 27

CHAPTER 2: A NEW PARADIGM? 31
    Structural Adjustment with a Human Face: The Appeal to Social Liberalism 32
    The War against Poverty and the New Social Policy 37
    The Search for Alternative Development: A New Paradigm? 41
    The Neo-structuralist Pivot of Alternative Development 47
    International Co-operation for Development and the NGO: Civil Society to the Rescue? 50
    Conclusion 52

CHAPTER 3: SOCIAL CAPITAL AND LOCAL DEVELOPMENT 55
    The Local and the Social in the New Paradigm 55
    Making Democracy Work: Putnam on Social Capital 59
    Social Capital and Its Critics: Unrealistic Expectations or Political Demobilization? 62
    Social Capital, Poverty, and Development 67
    Conclusion 68

CHAPTER 4: PARTICIPATORY BUDGETING AND LOCAL GOVERNMENT 71
    Setting the Stage for Participatory Development: From the Old to the New Republic 72
    Decentralization and Local Development 74
    Decentralization in Practice: Municipalizing Development 75

Porto Alegre: A Model of Participatory Development? 78
Transforming Local Governance: The Challenge of Local Power 79
The Workers' Party in Porto Alegre: The Participatory Budget Process 81
Conclusion 83

CHAPTER 5: THE DEVELOPMENT DYNAMICS OF SOCIAL EXCLUSION 85

Neo-liberalism and the Offensive against Labour 86
Capitalist Development and the Search for Alternatives 95
Conclusion 103

CHAPTER 6: RURAL STRUGGLES AND THE LAND QUESTION 109

Landlessness and Rural Poverty: The Peasantry and the State 110
Three Paths to Reform 117
Social Movements in Latin America—Old and New 127
Conclusion 129

CHAPTER 7: FROM THE BARRICADES TO THE BALLOT BOX 131

Social Movements on the Rise 136
NGOs and Participatory Development: Solidarity from Below 138
New Class Movements in the Countryside 142
Conclusion 146

CHAPTER 8: MOVEMENT IN THE COUNTRYSIDE AND CITIES 149

The Road to State Power: Electoral Politics or Mass Mobilization? 150
The Dynamics of Social Mobilization and Electoral Politics 152
The Development Path to Change 161
Conclusion 164

GLOSSARY 169
BIBLIOGRAPHY 187
INDEX 201

Introduction

A left-wing current in the crosswinds of change is sweeping over Latin America. This current of change is a reaction against the political regimes that have been democratically elected to manage a process of adjustment to meet the requirements of a new world economic order. It particularly affects societies and economies in the region that have been reconstructed over the past two decades to integrate into this new world order. This process of integration, popularly known as globalization, has brought about epoch-defining changes in the way that these societies and economies are organized. These changes made to accommodate globalization have generated widespread discontent, particularly because they have led to the social exclusion of a large part of the population from any of the presumed economic benefits of the process, and they have increased the disparity in the distribution of wealth and income, leading to both new forms and widespread conditions of poverty.

This growing social discontent has totally changed the political landscape in Latin America. Today, this landscape is dominated by diverse political forces pushing for fundamental changes in the social and economic conditions of globalization—forces that believe it is possible and necessary to construct a "new world," a better world with less social exclusion, more equitable distribution of society's wealth, and a significant reduction in poverty and its associated misery. This book is an exploration of these political forces of social change in Latin America.

Throughout what historians have termed "the golden age of capitalism" but that we might well term the "age of development" (roughly from the 1950s to the 1970s), the primary agency for social change was the nation–state, via policies of economic development and social reform. Organized labour was another key factor, because it could negotiate collective agreements with capital to improve wages and working conditions. However, in the 1960s and 1970s, military regimes began to emerge in reaction to the political left and the slow but steady gains of the working and producing classes in the development process.

In the 1980s, these military regimes were replaced by democratically elected civilian regimes committed to the rule of law. During that time, debt and decreased economic production created fiscal crises, and the state retreated behind an emerging new world order in which the forces of "freedom" (the private sector, the free market, and democracy) held sway. The state's capacity to bring about social change was severely reduced, and organized labour's ability to organize and negotiate was decimated. In the wake of this process of democratization and the retreat of the state, a "civil society" emerged and was consolidated in a wide spectrum of non-governmental organizations.

Social movements emerged to mobilize resistance against the implementation of this new economic model of untrammelled free market capitalism, or neo-liberalism—a model brought about by introducing policies of stabilization and structural reform in macroeconomic policy. These new social movements emerged in the urban sector of civil society and took diverse forms—from political protests by the urban poor against International Monetary Fund (IMF) reforms to efforts to protect and advance diverse interests, such as the economic and personal security of social groups defined by ethnicity and gender or bound by a concern for the environment.

In the 1990s, new developments gave rise to a second wave of social movements that mobilized the forces of resistance and opposition to the neo-liberal agenda of virtually every government in the region. These movements, for the most part, were led by organizations of peasant farmers, landless rural workers, and indigenous communities. They were motivated by another round of structural adjustments that had deepened the reforms already made in countries like Mexico and extended them to countries that had not yet ridden the wave of neo-liberal reform—most notably Argentina, Brazil, and Peru. In addition, the World Bank and the other multilateral and United Nations agencies for development had tried to move beyond the Washington Consensus to redesign the structural adjustment program (SAP) to include a new social policy with a greater concern for forms of "good", that is, democratic governance to engage civil society in the public policy process and the construction of political order, and incidentally to stabilize the fragile democratic regimes in the region.

This book probes the dynamics of social change in Latin America in the context of all these developments in the 1980s and 1990s. The central argument is that the popular movement—the organizations constructed in the popular sector of Latin America's civil society in the 1990s and in the new millennium—confronts three options in the struggle for social change. One is electoral politics, or what in the 1960s and 1970s was conceptualized as the parliamentary road to social and political reform. The popular movement has taken this road to change with very interesting recent political developments in Bolivia, Ecuador, Peru, Mexico, and Venezuela. Ecuador presents a particularly interesting case. Not only did the November 26, 2006, presidential elections bring the left to power, but the president-elect will be the eighth president in a decade.

A second road to change involves mobilizing the popular forces of resistance by means of direct action taken against the holders of economic and political power. In the political lexicon of yesteryear, this was termed the revolutionary road to social change, generally taken by the social movements formed primarily in the countryside by peasant organizations and indigenous communities. In the political context of the 1960s and 1970s, the options available to the rural poor were encapsulated in this formula: Reform or revolution. In the current context, the formula might be recast: Democracy without social movements or the politics of mass mobilization.

The third option available to the rural poor is local development in the form of micro-projects to bring about improvements in people's lives. Rather than challenging the power structure with social mobilization, political confrontation, and direct action, the idea behind this option, formulated by economists and sociologists at the World Bank and its sister institutions, is to seek improvements in people's lives by acting within local spaces of the power structure.

HOW THIS BOOK IS ORGANIZED

Chapter 1 elaborates on the conditions that gave rise to these various dynamics of social change—conditions generated by the economics of structural adjustment to the requirements of the new world order. It also documents and reviews the search for "another development"—the diverse efforts to constitute a new paradigm able to account for emerging trends.

Chapter 2 explores the various efforts over the past two decades to construct a new paradigm of development theory and practice, a new form of development that is initiated from below and from within civil society, and that reaches beyond the state and the market into local settings and communities in order to promote development (alternatively defined here as improvements in living standards and associated changes).

Chapter 3 elaborates on various models and strategies advanced within the framework of this new paradigm. The chapter explores the thinking on and diverse strategies associated with the idea of local development based on the accumulation of social capital. This idea could be said to define international development in its most recent incarnation over the past decade.

Chapter 4 is a case study of Brazil, examining the role of local governments in the development process within the framework of the new paradigm. The focus of this study is the process of popular participation in the construction of the municipal budget in Porto Alegre. In the new way of thinking about development, local governments are viewed as having a critically important role in development as strategic partners of both the international and grassroots organizations in the poor communities. This chapter critically reviews the theory and application of this role, exemplified and repeated in what is widely perceived as a case of successful "best practice."

Chapter 5 focuses on poverty in Latin America, a problem that is widely viewed as a matter more of social exclusion than economic exploitation. The chapter includes a review of the social conditions of poverty as it affects urban labour and the dynamics of various strategic responses to it. Particular emphasis is placed on the international development community's strategic response, based on the United Nations Economic Commission for Latin America and the Caribbean (ECLAC) and the sustainable livelihoods approach (SLA) to social change.

Chapter 6 turns to social change in Latin America's countryside. While the previous chapter focuses on rural development, this chapter reviews the rather different struggles and political confrontations that surround the land question—the problem of landlessness or near-landlessness. At issue in chapters 5 and 6 are radically different approaches to bringing about social change.

With Chapter 7, the book turns to another political dimension of social change, namely the democratic electoral process and the politics associated with the rise of new peasant social movements in the region in the 1990s. These dynamics are analyzed as alternative political paths towards social change.

The political dynamics of these paths to social change are analyzed in more detail in Chapter 8. This chapter introduces the process that is involved in unfolding these paths in Latin America.

ONE

Neo-liberalism and US Imperialism

Latin America is at another crossroads. The region has been struck by the storm of a profoundly destructive and socially exclusive form of capitalist development at work over the course of more than two decades of neo-liberal reform. In the countryside and the cities, the landscape is littered with the detritus of this counter-revolutionary process. However, there are many signs that the economic model behind this process has reached its limits, having generated forces of resistance and opposition that are threatening to bring the whole system down.

In this chapter, we examine the conditions behind these forces for social change. First, we identify critical components of the economic model that governments in the region have used to implement the neo-liberal reform process that has brought Latin America to its present state. This climate of change has three dimensions. One is a series of structural adjustments to national macroeconomic policies made to align them to the requirements of the new world order—to what John Williamson (1990) termed the Washington Consensus—and thereby to integrate the economies in the region into an ongoing globalization process. Another is the social impact of these adjustments on different groups and classes in the popular sector (the working people of civil society). The third dimension arises from the diverse strategic and political responses to these changes, ranging from efforts to rescue neo-liberalism from an early demise by giving it a human face to attempts to overthrow it by social movements aiming to create "another world." These responses are reviewed in subsequent chapters: the systemic response of sustainable human development in Chapter 2 and the anti-systemic response of the social movements in Chapter 8.

The second part of this chapter turns from the new economic model (neo-liberal globalization and capitalist development) to the economic and political dynamics of US imperialism in Latin America. This process, together with neo-liberalism in practice, has generated both the objective (structural) and subjective (political) conditions of social change in the region. On the one hand, neo-liberalism and US imperialism have generated conditions that are, as Karl Marx postulated in a different context, "independent of people's wills, shaping their material circumstances and life-chances." On the other hand, the same conditions have given rise to forces of political opposition and resistance that are threatening not only the Washington Consensus but the very foundations of the system in place all over Latin America. The dynamics of social change in Latin America can and should be analyzed in this context, in terms of the specific conjunctures of these conditions, economic and political. This books attempts to do so.

NEO-LIBERALISM IN THEORY AND PRACTICE

Development as a political and intellectual project has its roots in the eighteenth-century idea of progress and its associated plan to modernize and industrialize the economy and to create a society of free and equal individuals. But the idea of development germinated in the immediate aftermath of World War II. This historic conjuncture included the following: an emerging cold war between capitalism and socialism, and conflicts between blocs of nation-states promoting one form of systemic development or the other; a series of anti-colonial wars of national liberation that resulted in independence for countries in sub-Saharan Africa and subjection to the yoke of European (and American) imperialism in Asia; and the institution of a world economic order organized on the foundation of liberalism and capitalism. The World Bank and the International Monetary Fund (IMF), both founded at the Bretton Woods Conference immediately after the war in 1944, and the World Trade Organization (WTO), founded 50 years later in 1994,[1] provided the institutional framework for this new world order.

Two paradigms were at play: one predicated on capitalism (private property, the state, the market, and wage labour); the other oriented towards socialism. Most of the ideas that surrounded the project of international development were advanced within the limits of the first paradigm, which allowed for two lines of thinking, liberal and structural, and led to the construction of two economic models. The first economic model, based on liberalism, promoted the idea of a free or unregulated form of market capitalism. The second model, structuralism, was based on the need for government intervention—the state as an agency of economic and social development (Wilbur and Jameson, 1975).

In the 1950s and 1960s, structuralist forms of thinking dominated the theory and practice of national development. The central proposition of this approach was capital accumulation—to accumulate capital by increasing the savings rate and investing these savings productively. Structuralist theoreticians advanced several ideas and models based on this theory of economic growth, with a number of permutations.[2] The mechanism behind this theory called for increasing the savings rate by extracting economic surplus from the traditional agricultural sector to finance the modernization of industry in the capitalist sector.

The state, viewed theoretically as an agent of modernization and development, availed itself of several economic and extra-economic mechanisms in the 1960s and 1970s (particularly in the newly industrializing countries [NICs] of Asia):

- the compression of wages by the political means of repressing working class demands and converting savings into capital;
- less transparent methods such as inflation and what we might call "financial repression" that impedes potential wage gains; and
- the transfer and appropriation of productive capital accumulated in other regions of the world system to achieve higher rates of profit and lower rates of labour remuneration.

From 1965 to 1980, Latin America experienced a fairly robust rate of economic growth—over 5 per cent and superior to the world average. But this growth, by virtue of its dependence on external financing (mostly from international co-operation, but in the 1970s through recourse to bank loans) had an exceedingly high economic and social cost. In the early 1980s, these costs reached crisis proportions, the debt owed to external creditors having climbed from US$28 billion in the early 1970s to US$239 billion 10 years later. The effects of the debt crisis (marked by governments unable to service these debts with interest payments) created a deep and widespread economic and social crisis, as large parts of the population were deprived of the financial resources needed to improve their standard of living. Indeed, the entire decade was "lost to development," with all but the richest parts suffering decreased living standards or sinking into poverty.

In the vortex of this crisis, politics and economics in the region gave way to a neo-liberal program of policy measures that introduced far-reaching reforms into the economy and society. A first round of experiments with neo-liberal policies of structural adjustment—liberalization, privatization, deregulation, and administrative decentralization—was undertaken in the 1970s by several military regimes in the southern cone of Chile, Argentina, and Uruguay. But in the 1980s, this structural adjustment program (SAP) was widely implemented in a new wave of democratic or democratizing regimes. By the end of the decade, only three governments were not hit by this second wave of structural reform, but these too (Argentina, Brazil, and Peru) would soon follow.

The central idea behind the SAP—formulated and imposed by the IMF, the World Bank, and other such International Financial Institutions (IFIs)—was Adam Smith's seventeenth-century notion of a free market whose operations, under competitive conditions, would invisibly produce an optimum (that is, efficient) distribution of society's productive resources and the benefits of economic growth. Theoreticians of neo-classical economics such as Alfred Marshall and Friedrich Hayek extended this idea as follows:

- the dynamics of the system derive from the utilitarian decisions (rational calculus of personal interest) made by each individual;
- the motor of the economic expansion process is the international division of labour (production) based on the law of comparative advantage;
- private enterprise is the best driver of this motor;
- prices create and maintain a balance between the demand and supply of commodities; and
- the free market produces the maximum social welfare on the condition of "getting prices right."

With these ideas, economists at the World Bank put together a policy reform package of stabilization and structural adjustment measures in the early 1980s. The basic elements of this policy package were as follows:

- a realistic rate of currency exchange (that is, a policy of devaluation);
- anti-inflationary measures and cuts in the public expenditures (a policy of austerity, elimination of subsidies, etc.);
- an outward economic orientation towards the world market through a liberalization policy of trade and foreign investment;
- deregulation of markets and economic activity;
- privatization of the means of production and state enterprises; and
- downsizing and the modernization of the state.

NEO-LIBERAL POLICY AND POLITICS: SOCIO-ECONOMIC IMPACTS AND POLITICAL RESPONSES

The impacts of the SAP become evident when the new economic structure is put in place. This new structure is based on the social relation of capital to labour: the capitalist class, which is composed of the large, medium, and small property and business owners, and the working class, which assumes different shapes but whose members share a dependence on wage labour. In the interstices of this structure, there is what Marxists term the "petite-bourgeoisie," a middle class traditionally formed by independent producers and operators of businesses (small and medium entrepreneurs). Like the working class, this middle class has several divisions that include professionals, intellectuals, and those who manage capitalist enterprises and provide several other services to capital.

The operating process of capitalist development is the concentration and centralization of capital: the fusion of many firms and a struggle to survive for the ones remaining.[3] In 1988 alone, innumerable fusions of the largest capitals were organized in what the United Nations Centre for the Study of Transnational Corporations termed "the Billionaire Club"—500 of the biggest corporations that together with their 35,000 or so affiliates control around 25 per cent of world trade, at least 40 per cent by transfers among affiliate companies. The United Nations Conference on Trade and Development (UNCTAD) (2001) further estimates that over 50 per cent of world trade, conducted for the most part by multinational corporations, takes the form of "internal transfers"; that is, transfers between the headquarters and affiliates of these firms, and thus do not enter the market at all. When this statistic is added to the sector that is monopolized by a few giant firms, the competitive market accounts for barely 25 per cent of total world trade. And a good part of this trade is not free, especially because developing countries have poor access to the markets of the wealthy industrialized and developed countries in the North.

As for the middle class, its productive sector (independent producers and the entrepreneurs) constitutes around 15 per cent of the economically active population but generates two-thirds of all productive enterprises and employment (up to 90 per cent of all net new employment over the last two decades).

The size and the shape of this middle class varies considerably, encompassing up to 25 per cent of the economically active population (EAP) in the developed countries or in countries developing like Argentina, but less than 10 per cent in many of the less developed countries. There are few studies on this issue (but see Portes, 1989), but the available data suggest that the general impact of the SAP on this class has been significant, particularly in the trend towards bankruptcies, bank indebtedness, proletarianization (dispossession of their means of social production), and, in many cases, immiseration and impoverishment. In many cases, in the countryside and in rural society, this class has been heavily hit by neo-liberal policies, such as economic opening, liberalization of imports, drops in prices, credit restrictions, elimination of subsidies, and decreases in purchasing power, among others. In Mexico alone, bank indebtedness affects close to 60 per cent of producers and entrepreneurs, driving hundreds of thousands of independent producers and entrepreneurs into bankruptcy.

However, the working class in its various forms clearly bore the brunt of neo-liberal policies, having absorbed most of their heavy social costs. The structure of this class and its socio-economic conditions—the relationship of labour to capital, its forms of employment, and conditions of work and organization—has suffered a serious deterioration in many countries. At the beginning of the 1980s, the working class centrally comprised the industrial proletariat: wage workers in heavy and basic industries (construction and manufacturing), as well as the public sector. After years of hard struggle and organization, the working class had won the right to decent work conditions, with wages adjusted to productivity gains.

In many contexts, workers had acquired, if not political and economic power, at least an organized social force. In the 1980s, all this changed in the wake of an offensive launched on several fronts by the capitalist class and the state in service of this class. Towards the end of the decade and into the 1990s, neo-liberal policies had radically transformed the working class, driving it from the factories and offices into the streets, and seriously weakening its organizational and political capacity. By the early 1990s, it was but a poor shadow of what it once was, exposed to conditions of economic and social insecurity, disorganization, and low pay, with labour often remunerated at levels well below its value and subject to precarious and irregular occupational conditions and forms of employment (short contracts and temporary or part-time work along with the formation of a huge reserve army of surplus labour in the face of this unemployment and underemployment). The dynamics of this transformation vary from country to country, but they can be identified in the north as well as in the south.

The impact of these neo-liberal policies, which have been in place in many developing countries for several decades, has been heavily debated. Although there is no consensus, most studies—including some commissioned by the IMF and the World Bank—have found no systematic relationship between structural adjustment and economic growth. What has been achieved in many cases, however, is macroeconomic balance; that is, relatively balanced current accounts and the control of hyperinflation (which in the 1980s had reached an annual rate exceeding 7,000 per cent in some countries, such as Argentina, Bolivia, and Peru).

As for economic growth, results have been mixed, although it is clear enough that the rapid economic growth experienced in a small cluster of developing countries in East Asia, Southeast Asia, and China has nothing to do with neo-liberal policies and everything to do with government intervention and state strategic development planning. Indeed, if anything, the connection between neo-liberal laissez-faire policy reform and economic growth is negative. The countries that have grown so rapidly over the past two decades have done so without a neo-liberal policy regime and its associated reforms, while the majority of countries in Latin America and sub-Saharan Africa have seen their growth rates dramatically reduced under the SAP.

According to the World Bank, the average per capita income in 1994 was US$4470, considerably more than in it had been in 1980. But the disparities in the distribution of this income strip this statistic of any meaning: 20 per cent of the world's richest populations appropriate 87 per cent of this income, while the poorest 20 per cent receive only 1.4 per cent. Seen in another way, 63 of the least developed countries (LDCs), representing 56.2 per cent of world population, receive 4.2 per cent of world income, while the richest and most developed countries (MDCs), representing 14.8 per cent of world population, receive 79 per cent of world income. The degree of income concentration today is such that according to the United Nations Development Programme (UNDP) (1992, 1996, 2005) just 385 individuals, all members of the Forbes 400, appropriate a total combined income equivalent to that received by the poorest 40 per cent (Korten, 1995: 108–09; UNDP, 1996). In fewer than 30 years, the degree of disparity in the distribution of world income, aggregated and calculated at the national level, changed from 30:1 to 60:1, a dispersion that reaches 100:1 at the extremes of the average per capita income. The gap deepened in the 1980s during the period of structural adjustment.

This issue—"the inequality predicament" as the United Nations (UN) (2005) describes it—has been seriously studied and heavily debated. The consensus among researchers is that social inequalities in the distribution of wealth and income have increased significantly over the past two decades of neo-liberal reform, resulting in an extension and deepening of poverty, and creating new forms of it. Neo-liberal policies affect the distribution of income (and concentration of wealth) by compressing wages through a variety of economic and extra-economic mechanisms. These mechanisms can be traced in the distribution of national income between labour and capital, and in a fall in the value of real wages for the working class. The connection between neo-liberal policies of adjustment and poverty is clear enough, an issue explored further in chapters 3 and 4.

More than anything, neo-liberal policies have produced a broad and deep division at all levels of society, polarizing it and procuring all sorts of benefits and wealth for "the winners" but subjecting "the losers" to conditions of exploitation and exclusion: social and economic insecurity, low returns on their labour, and, for many (2.4 billion, or 40 per cent of the world's population), conditions of abject poverty. In other words, the benefits of neo-liberal policies have been very concentrated, excluding the vast majority (see chapters 3 and 4). At least a third of the world's population is excluded from the system and its fruits, deprived not only of basic needs such as shelter, nutrition, and access to potable water, but of their economic human rights, decent work, or any form of employment. In the words of Ignacy Sachs, they constitute a "Fourth World" in the regions of South Asia, sub-Saharan Africa, and parts of Latin America, but they are also found in the underclass and, to quote Zapatista Subcomandante Marcos, the "*huecos perdidos*" (lost holes) of many cities in the North. Just as the privileged minorities of the Third World can be viewed as the presence of the North in the South, the growing underclass of poor families and individuals deprived from even the minimal standards of living constitute the presence of the South in the North. The North and the South, in effect, have penetrated each other (Ignacy Sachs, 1995: 168ff.).

THE ECONOMICS AND POLITICS OF US IMPERIALISM

The neo-liberal new economic model (NEM) has been advanced by the World Bank as a form of development; that is, a means of designing and promoting "pro-growth" policies. More generally, it is used to promote the process of globalization, a fundamental aspect of the new world order. However, a closer look at the dynamics of social change and development associated with the NEM suggests that rather than perceiving it in this way—as a form of development and a way of improving the socio-economic conditions and livelihoods of the population—it is better understood as a means of advancing the interests of the dominant transnational capitalist class and the nation-states that control the world system. The NEM is better viewed as a form of imperialism.

Imperialism refers to a project of world domination, a project pursued by various European states and led by Great Britain during the time of nineteenth-century global capitalism. Since the end of World War II, the United States has taken over as the leading imperialist nation. At that time, the US commanded a lion's share of the world's productive resources and industrial production capacity—at least 50 per cent of development finance (gold and monetary reserves) and an estimated 38 per cent of industrial production. Since then, the US administration has been possessed of the imperial dream—a belief in the right to global rule, rooted in a sense of superiority and an ideology not of divine right but of a "manifest destiny," a mission supported by an all-too-clear awareness of the economic and political power commanded by the state.[4] However, this imperial dream had to contend with diverse pressures to avoid the fate of the declining British Empire—and a widespread concern among allied capitalist states to prevent world domination by a unilateral projection of power. These pressures resulted in the formation of the United Nations and a system of multilateral organizations designed to prevent any one state from seeking and establishing hegemony over the world system.

The United States was a party to the negotiations involved in setting up this system. However, a number of foreign policy documents and subsequent events show that the US state actually never abandoned the imperial dream of Pax Americana and the political project to realize it. Indeed, US foreign policy and subsequent events point towards efforts by successive US regimes to secure a world order designed to support their own national interest. Agents of this project were diverse. They include:

- international co-operation for development—a project of multilateral and bilateral "assistance," ostensibly oriented towards the improvement of socio-economic conditions and a process of nation-building and capitalist development for those countries seeking to escape economic backwardness and European colonialism;
- support for US multinational banks and corporations in their search of profit and opportunities for capital accumulation overseas;
- foreign aid in the form of humanitarian assistance, disaster relief, and local self-development, designed (with the strategic assistance of private voluntary and non-governmental organizations contracted by the US government) to help subdue the fires of revolutionary ferment in the Latin American countryside;
- policies (via the World Bank and other IFIS controlled or dominated by the United States) designed to adjust the economies of developing societies to the requirements of the US-designed new world order;
- policies to secure the subservience of a series of satellite or client states, able to protect US economic and political interests; and
- the imposition of military force where possible or as necessary.

The dynamics of this process of empire-building are too complex to cover here (but see Petras and Veltmeyer, 2005). But to provide a backdrop for our analysis of the dynamics of social change, we will review two aspects: namely, the process of capital accumulation associated with the financial and production operations of US- (and European-) based multinationals; and the dynamics of US foreign policy in Latin America. These processes are summarized to provide essential or useful points of reference in the ongoing struggle for social change throughout the region—a class struggle as well as a fight for national sovereignty, democracy, and social justice.

The Economics of US Imperialism

In the 1960s and 1970s, the financial and production operations of US corporations were hampered by a series of restrictive regulations put in place by governments in the developing countries under the policy advice of the United Nations Conference on Trade and Development (UNCTAD). In the 1980s, however, with the Washington Consensus on "correct" (that is, pro-growth and pro-development) policy, governments in Latin America dismantled their regulatory controls over capital and the operations of the multinationals. As a result, private forms of capital began to flow at an accelerated rate. From 1990 to 1997, virtually every government in the region implemented policies of financial and trade liberalization and deregulation, as well as the privatization of public assets and state enterprises. As a result, the inflow of private capital in the form of foreign direct investment (FDI) and portfolio investment for Latin America multiplied by a factor of seven, twice the rate experienced by any other region in the global economy. The dynamics of this process, regarding both inflows (investments) and outflows (repatriated profits, interest, and royalty payments) are summarized in Table 1.1. The table shows that the operations of the multinational banks and corporations have been highly profitable [see also the related academic studies by Saxe-Fernández and others (2001, 2002)]. Over the course of the period, an inflow of loan and investment capital functioned as a mechanism of surplus outflow—a net transfer of US$100 billion in as few as 10 years, an enormous hemorrhage of productive and financial resources and a not-insignificant pool of capital accumulated, as it turns out, at the "centre" of the system.

The economic and social conditions of this capital drain are clear enough. They are reflected in the poor indicators of economic growth over the decade relative to other regions and countries such as China and India, where the corresponding dynamics of economic growth and development were all too different. They are also reflected in various developments discussed in chapter 3 related to the inequality predicament and what many studies describe as a deepening and extension of poverty in the region.

The statistics of surplus transfer and outflows are by no means the entire story of the scope and effects of US imperialism and its economic operations. In the 1990s, opportunities provided by privatization programs instituted by Latin American governments under the dictates of the NEM attracted a good part of FDI. It is estimated that as much as 40 per cent of FDI inflows over the decade, especially in the heyday of privatization policy (1993–1997), entailed the purchase of assets of lucrative public enterprises, requiring little input of new investment. That is, these investments were largely unproductive. Nevertheless, they entailed a significant increase in the stock, if not outflow, of accumulated capital, resulting in increased ownership of corporate stock and assets in critical sectors, such as banking and telecommunications. In the not atypical case of Mexico, foreign investors now own all but one of the country's banks, which were "restructured" to the advantage of these investors (privatizing their assets but socializing their liabilities so that even today, some 10 years later, taxpayers are still paying out US$3 billion a year to the new foreign owners of the country's banks).[5] These banks, as well as a number of other privatized enterprises, provide foreign investors and multinational banks and corporations a significant source of new revenues, not all of which are transferred out. Up to one-third of profits are ploughed back into the privatized firms, to either better capitalize production or increase market share. If we were to weigh the long-term benefits and returns to capital generated by the newly acquired ownership interests in corporate stock and assets, adding them to the mass and volume of repatriated profits and interest payments, then the Latin American operations of the multinational banks and corporations, as agents of US imperialism, have been (and are) profitable indeed. Obviously, most of the local population does not share in the booty of foreign investment. On the contrary, as discussed in chapter 3, this population continues to bear the heavy, supposedly transitional, social costs of pro-growth macroeconomic policies and US empire-building.

The Politics of US Imperialism

Many people attribute the invasion of Afghanistan and the Iraq war to America's geopolitical interest in capturing a larger part of the world's major oil reserves. Some (James Petras, for example) have understood the Iraq war to be a partial response to the power of the state of Israel and the US Jewish lobby over Middle East policy. Undoubtedly, both oil and support for Israel or Zionism provide motives for US military power in the Gulf region. However, an altogether more powerful explanation can be found in the concerns of a group of neo-conservatives who, under the presidency of George W. Bush, has captured the White House. Although this group perceives a need to improve access to, if not increase control over, the world's oil reserves, their greater concern is to reassert US hegemony over the world system—to re-establish the imperialist project of what Henry Luce termed the "American Century" as early as 1941. In the early 1990s, well before the Iraq war, Paul Wolfowitz (a key member of this White House gang and the lead author of the notorious "Project for a New American Century") proposed the unilateral projection of US political and military power in the service of empire—to help the US carry out its global responsibilities and its imperial burden, to free the world and secure the new American world order.[6]

Immediately after World War II, the United States commanded control over the world's financial resources and production capacity. With just 6 per cent of the world's population, it had over 59 per cent of the world's developed oil reserves, generated 46 per cent of electricity worldwide, and dominated world trade in goods and services. With this economic power, it had little difficulty designing and securing the stamp of US foreign policy on the proposed world economic order at Bretton Woods. However, faced with the challenge of the USSR and the socialist bloc, the US Empire and its project

TABLE 1.1 CAPITAL INFLOWS AND OUTFLOWS, LATIN AMERICA 1985-2002 ($US BILLIONS)

	1985-90	91-92	93	94	95	96	97	98	99	00	01	02
Capital Inflows	–	105	124	126	67	99	104	109	97	97	83	50
ODA (Official Development Aid)	38	10	5	6	6	6	-9	11	2	11	20	13
Private Flows	95	118	120	61	93	112	98	95	85	63	37	–
FDI	43	29	17	29	32	44	66	73	88	76	69	42
Portfolio[b]	–	45	74	63	5	12	13	-2	-4	02	1	–
Loans 642	127	28	24	38	33	27	11	10	-9	-6	–	
Returns to Capital	142	74	73	79	79	83	99	108	91	100	97	–
Profit on Assets	–	62	35	37	41	43	48	51	52	53	55	53
Interest[c] 211	76	38	35	36	35	33	46	54	35	43	42	
Royalty fees[a]	5	2	1	2	2	1	2	2	2	2	2	2
Net Resource Transfer (on assets)	-150	31	32	10	19	23	32	27	-3	-0	-5	-39

Sources: ECLAC, 1998; UNCTAD, 1998: 256, 267–68, 362; 2002; US Dept. of Commerce, 1994; World Bank, 1997. FDI stock 1999–2001 for US only (US Census Bureau, US *Direct Investment Position Abroad on a Historical Cost Basis*) (2002); (a) as of 1995—World Bank, *World Development Indicators*, 2002. (b) World Bank, *Global Development Finance, Statistical Appendix*, Table 20, 2002. (c) World Bank, *Global Development Finance*, 2000, 2002.

of world domination had to rely on multilateral action and a system of alliances, allies, and satellite or client states. The parameters of this system were established at Bretton Woods and consolidated from the 1950s to the 1970s, not without the exercise of military power when and where it was needed to secure dominance and control. As for Latin America, the US deemed it to be well within its "sphere of influence," and its heads of state as satraps of the empire.

For the United States, securing power entailed a series of invasions and other aggressive actions, some successful, others—for example, Cuba—not. The successful invasions of Guatemala and the Dominican Republic resulted in the ousting of less than fully compliant or recalcitrant heads of state. But US imperial rule was established in most of Latin America when countries drafted national security doctrines that secured massive military "aid" in the form of the training and indoctrination of leadership cadres of armed forces; the sponsorship and installation of military regimes; and a counterinsurgency strategy directed against the guerrilla armies of national liberation. Through the military regimes they installed, Washington also waged a dirty war of repression against "subversives": unionists, human rights and political activists, students, and other domestic enemies of the "forces of freedom and democracy." By these means, together with the Alliance for Progress—the soft glove and development arm of imperialism initiated by John F. Kennedy in 1961—the population was more or less subjugated, and a complex of client states, beginning with Brazil in 1964 and Chile in 1973, were installed throughout the region.

But in the 1980s, the empire began to fall apart as the United States experienced a series of losses in almost every region across the world, except its immediate backyard (Central America) and in regions of lesser importance, such as the Balkan states of Kosovo, Macedonia, and Serbia. Losing Vietnam was the catalyst for this decline, and the US state subsequently experienced a series of additional defeats and reversals, both in Asia and Europe and in the Middle East and Gulf region. Despite successes on some fronts in Latin America, the US failed to bring down the Castro regime in Cuba or to defeat the Revolutionary Armed Forces of Colombia (FARC).

These failures and the erosion of US military power brought about a conservative reaction to renovate the world order and restore the US Empire. In part, this reaction was a response to the fact that the erosion of US military power paralleled a similar loss of power at the economic level. In the 1970s, the "golden age of capitalism" had come to an abrupt end and the world economy was in crisis. The United States had lost dominance, primarily compared to Japan and Germany, but also in relation to western Europe and a group of emerging "tigers" in Southeast Asia—the first of several tiers of NICS that proved to be formidable rivals in the battle for the world market. By the end of the decade, despite its unilateral move to abandon the use of the gold standard to fix the rate of international exchange in trade, the United States had accumulated an enormous and growing balance of payment deficit, and its erstwhile dominant share of world trade continued to slide. In 1950, the US accounted for 20 per cent of world export trade, while Germany and Japan between them accounted for only 6.3 per cent. By 1970, the US share had been cut 25 per cent, while Germany and Japan's combined share of world exports tripled to 18.8 per cent (Brenner, 1998: 119). By 2000, notwithstanding the long boom of the 1990s, the US share of world production and trade continued to slide relative to its competitors both in the European Union (EU) and in Asia. China in particular, whose output was growing at over 10 per cent a year, more than doubled the economic growth rate ever achieved by the United States.

The US response to the loss of economic and political dominance was twofold. First, the state redoubled its economic and political pressures on the USSR, which coincided with other largely internal pressures to bring about the collapse of the USSR and the socialist bloc—eventually allowing the United States to claim victory in its war against "international communism." Second, through a network of international financial institutions under its control, the US designed and installed a new world order, dictating rules to client states to adjust their macroeconomic policies and open up their economies to the forces of globalization (privatizing economic enterprise, deregulating markets, and, above all, liberalizing trade and the flow of capital).

The result of this economic restructuring process is difficult to determine. However, the end is near, given that the neo-liberal model is in evident decline, rejected as economically dysfunctional even by many former advocates. Restructuring has been a mixed bag at best. Increased productivity of labour and profitability of capital along with a relatively sustained economic recovery in the US has been combined with growing resistance to the neoliberal globalization agenda, not only from some recalcitrant or reluctant states but from a global and regionally located civil society—powerful social movements that are challenging US power.

In Latin America, these forces of resistance have spawned powerful anti-globalization, anti-imperialist movements that have derailed the US agenda of a regional free market and generated a new wave of left-of-centre regimes disposed to bring about another world, if not an alternative system.

In this context of multiple, ongoing crises, the US state under George W. Bush and neo-conservative foreign policy has launched a counteroffensive, redoubling its efforts to restore US dominance and hegemony. This imperial counteroffensive has taken diverse forms:

- invading Afghanistan and Iraq, and other policies and efforts designed to re-establish the subordination of Europe to Washington;
- reasserting control in the Middle East and Gulf region;
- deepening and extending military penetration in Latin America and Asia;
- increasing pressures on, and military warfare against, FARC in Colombia;
- projecting economic and military power in the rest of Latin America;
- incorporating the private sector (profit-oriented and profit-making enterprises) into the development process and making a concerted effort to launch the war on global poverty with the assistance of strategic partners, including NGOs and local governments;
- attempting to repress protest and opposition against multinational corporations and IFIs such as the World Bank, the IMF, and the World Trade Organization (WTO), replacing democratic rights with dictatorial powers;
- spending on weapons; and
- supplying state subsidies for near-bankrupt US multinationals (airlines, insurance companies, tourist agencies) and providing regressive tax reductions to halt a deepening recession that could undermine public support for the empire-building project, particularly in the context of growing military expenditures against the war on terrorism (and on Iraq and other "rogue regimes" and "enemies of freedom").

Notwithstanding this onslaught of counteroffensive actions and the projection of its economic and military power, the United States has not managed to secure and consolidate its empire. In Latin America, the new millennium has seen a tilt towards the left and the emergence of a distinct anti–US (that is, anti-imperialist and anti-globalization) state alliance. At the level of trade and investment, Latin America is seeking to diversify relations, turning in particular to China, which Hugo Chavez notes is a "world power... [but] she doesn't come here with imperialist airs." More important, Chinese investors are willing to accept lower profit margins than their US or European competitors, strengthening the hands of governments seeking to tighten the terms of concessions in oil, gas, and other sectors. Brazil and Argentina, the two biggest economies in the region, also see China as a political counterweight to Washington, an ally in the WTO and other arenas, and a counterbalance to US imperialism in the region. Elsewhere in the world, the US Empire has proven to be equally fragile, infested with conflict and surrounded by growing forces of opposition and resistance. China and India have entered an alliance of sorts with Russia regarding the "big game" of Eurasia's massive reserves of natural resources. US geopolitical strategy to divide Russia from its erstwhile satellite states and gain access to the region's oil, gas, and other resources (see Vasapollo, 2003) is not bearing fruit; nor is its costly venture into Iraq and posturing about Iran. Despite the massive mobilization of financial and military resources, the US Empire in every area of strategic geopolitical interest is challenged or under siege.

CONCLUSION

Latin America in the new millennium is at a historic crossroads. On the one hand, the dominant system of neo-liberal globalization and capitalist development is in decline, if not demise, having exhausted its productive capacity or at least having exceeded the political limits of the inequality predicament (an excessive polarization in the distribution of wealth and incomes). On the other hand, the forces of "economic freedom" have by no means given up and are actively seeking to rescue the system from its internal contradictions and the active forces of resistance.

The social and political dynamics of the struggle between these so-called forces of freedom, concerned that the system be preserved and that governments in Latin America "stay the course," and the forces of political opposition and resistance will be explored in subsequent chapters. Chapter 2 reviews the dynamics of thought and the practice (the policy) behind the project to reform the SAP, to move beyond the Washington Consensus so as to save the system from itself. This project takes multiple forms but is associated with what we might term the search for "another development": diverse efforts to change the specific neo-liberal form of capitalist development and globalization—to create a more ethical, more sustainable form of capitalist development (another world). Chapters 3 and 4 review and critically assess the associated project to save capitalism by reforming it, but doing so on the basis of a new paradigm of social capital and local development. As we will see, the World Bank, the Inter-American Development Bank (IDB), and other international organizations engaged in this project have enlisted the support of NGOs in a revitalized civil society (the collectivity of institutions within society not controlled by the state). We critically assess and evaluate the role of these organizations in a project that, as we see it, was designed as a means of conserving the system in place, to limit the popular demand for substantive and radical social change. Subsequent chapters, especially 7 and 8, turn away from this project to examine the forces of resistance and radical, if not revolutionary, change. The political dynamics of these forces are associated with and mobilized by the anti-systemic social movements that have emerged in "the belly of the beast" (US imperialism), to quote Subcomandante Marcos.

These movements, we argue, represent the most dynamic forces of resistance and substantive social change. However, in the current context, these movements do not have an easy time of it. Far from it. They are, in fact, stuck on the horns of a dilemma: to seek social change via the road of electoral politics or to do so via the revolutionary road of social mobilization and anti-systemic class action. This book concludes with an analysis of this dilemma and its associated political dynamics of social change.

NOTES

1 At Bretton Woods, the original design of the liberal and capitalist world order, in addition to the World Bank and the IMF, included the International Trade Organization (ITO), an institutional mechanism for promoting free trade among member states. However, protectionist pressures within the US precluded it, leading to an interim arrangement in the form of the General Agreement on Tariffs and Trade (GATT), a free trade negotiating forum. It would take fifty years, and seven rounds of trade negotiations, for the stillborn ITO to emerge in the form of the WTO.

2 For a brief review of this theory, and later permutations of it, see the succinct summaries provided by Pritchett (2006).

3 For an analysis of this process in Argentina, a paradigmatic case of this development, see the studies by Apia (1996), Apia and Basalt (1999), and Basalt (2001).

NEO-LIBERALISM AND US IMPERIALISM

4   On this drive of the US for world domination and the imperial dream see, inter alia, McGowan (2000) and Petras and Veltmeyer (2005).

5   In the context of a major financial crisis, the Zedillo government created a special fund, FOBAPROA *(Fonda Binaries de Protection al Horror)*, to provide a rescue package for the 14 private banks with financial problems—to prevent them from going broke. This fund, through which the government insured 100 per cent of bank deposits, turned a private debt into a public debt—privatizing ownership of the banks' assets but socializing their liabilities. The bailout was so large that 10 years later, the accumulated public debt had grown to US$60 billion, requiring annual interest payments to these same banks (but new owners) in the order of US$2–3 billion a year, constituting a significant drain on the public purse—and a huge ongoing scandal. The enormity of the bailout and scandal is reflected in the fact that annual interest payments to the foreign owners constitute a drain on the public purse larger than the budget for UNAM, a public university of more than 120,000 faulty/employees and 250,000 students.

6   The document "Project for a New American Century" was drafted eight years after the Wolfowitz Report. It draws much of its inspiration, and its policy recommendations, from this report and like it is saturated with the belief in the moral and military supremacy of the US.

TWO

A New Paradigm?

The idea of development has permutated over the years in response to changing conditions. Since 1945, when it was purportedly "invented" (see, in particular, Wolfgang Sachs, 1992), there have been a number of important changes in development thought and practice in association with historic events, such as a crisis in global production in the early 1970s, the opening of an extended class war between capital and labour (see Crouch and Pizzorno, 1978; and Davis, 1984), and a conservative counter-revolution that gave rise to a new epoch of capitalist development and globalization. A significant if indecisive shift in both the mainstream and several side streams of development has emerged (Parpart and Veltmeyer, 2004). This shift is aligned with a search for alternative ways of thinking about development and new ways of putting it into practice: a new paradigm, or "another development" (AD), as it's called. This shift has been caused in part by a theoretical impasse and an attack on the diverse forms of structuralism in social and development analysis and associated ideologies (liberalism, socialism, modernization, etc.). However, a deeper explanation for the ubiquitous search for a new world view can be found in the material and political conditions of capitalist development itself, such as a growing divide in incomes and wealth, the exhaustion of the dominant model of state development pushed to and beyond its limits, and the dynamics of global capital, including the formation of a new international division of labour and a system of global production. In the 1970s, the need for a new paradigm was but an idea. By the mid 1980s, it was a global movement. By the end of the 1990s and the turn of the millennium, AD was on the agenda in all manner of development organizations, both intergovernmental and non-governmental.

On the Move: Two

STRUCTURAL ADJUSTMENT WITH A HUMAN FACE: THE APPEAL TO SOCIAL LIBERALISM

Two decades of neo-liberal policies have had a devastating impact on Latin America, polarizing society between a small minority of extremely rich capitalists and a large mass of proletarianized individuals forced to subsist on the margins of an exclusive economic and social structure. Between these two extremes, most social classes have experienced deterioration in their material and psychological condition. On the one hand, individuals within the upper middle class have managed to derive some benefits from the process of neo-liberal development by servicing the interests of the propertied and capitalist class and the political elite. On the other hand, the bulk of rural producers and indigenous communities, as well as the urban and rural working class, most of whom live and work in the interstices of the burgeoning informal economy on the streets and in the urban slums, have experienced neo-liberalism as a degradation of their social existence (see, for example, Davis, 2006).

Within most cities in Latin America, a divided social world has emerged. About 15 to 20 per cent of Latin Americans living in the cities share a First World lifestyle: They are waited on hand and foot at home and at work by functionaries and servants; send their children to private schools, abroad if possible, and to the best universities overseas; belong to private clubs where they swim, play tennis or golf, and do aerobic exercises; get facelifts in private clinics; travel in luxury cars on private toll roads; and communicate via private courier services. They live in gated communities protected by privately contracted police. They frequently vacation and shop in New York, Miami, London, or Paris. They enjoy easy access to influential politicians, media moguls, celebrities, and business consultants. They are usually fluent in English and have most of their savings in overseas accounts or in dollar-denominated local paper. They form part of the international circuit of the new imperial system of globalized capital. They are the audience for the neo-liberal discourse of global prosperity, and of course, they are the primary, if not exclusive, beneficiaries of policies designed to create the new world order.

The rest of the population, or most of it, lives in a very different world. Cuts in social spending and the elimination of basic food subsidies have pushed peasants and rural workers to the city in search of informal work at very low pay, or towards malnutrition and hunger in dismal living conditions. The large-scale redundancy of factory workers has pushed them into the streets to eke out a precarious existence on the margins of the urban economy, dependent on the extended family, community-based charities, and solidarity (soup kitchens) for survival. Slashed public health and education budgets require people to pay more for deteriorating services, leading to greater social exclusion. Cuts in funds for the maintenance of water, sewage, and other increasingly privatized "public" services has led to the resurgence of infectious diseases. Declining income and living conditions is the reality for two-thirds or more of the population, many of whom find themselves in what Mike Davis (2006) has described as the not-so-new but growing "planetary slums" in which crime, social disorganization, and poverty is the order of the day.

Neo-liberalism has been a clear and abundant failure, a far cry from the promised land of prosperity for all. The impact of neo-liberal policies, however, is also evident at the political level in that the people that make up the popular sector of civil society have not taken neo-liberalism lying down. In fact, from the beginning, the neo-liberal agenda has spawned cycles of political protest against IMF-mandated austerity measures. (For example, in Mexico in 1996 alone, I documented over 380 acts of protest.) It has also generated several waves of social movements in resistance (Walton and Seddon, 1994; Veltmeyer and Petras, 1997; Petras and Veltmeyer, 2005).

In neo-classical theory, the high social costs of neo-liberal policies reflected in these acts of protest and social movements, are viewed as a bitter medicine to be swallowed by the patients to assure that their health eventually improves. The problem is that these "patients" have not been content with their treatment or willing to swallow the bitter pill of SAPs at all costs, particularly regarding the grossly inequitable distribution of resources. In the wake of this disillusionment, discontent, and protest, those who have prescribed the neo-liberal medicine and monitored its effects—the "witch doctors of the IMF," to use an expression of former president of Mexico Lopez Portillo—have clearly become concerned, even frightened. The acts of resistance are threatening and dangerous because they point to the possibility that the discontent might be mobilized not only against the "medicine" and its providers but also against the entire system. This fear is expressed at the global level (for example, Kapstein, 1996) and, in many contexts, at the domestic level, creating a critical response from the very institutions that elaborated the SAPs in the first place—the World Bank, the IMF, and other regional and international financial institutions such as the IDB. This concern has translated into the search for a new development paradigm, a more decentralized, participatory, and sustainable form of development, and a new more humane form of capitalist development.

A host of intergovernmental and non-governmental organizations have taken on the search for a new development paradigm, resulting in what is nothing less than a global social movement—a movement that at times has connected to the more overtly political anti-globalization movement. One of several institutional expressions of the anti-globalization movement is the World Social Forum (WSF), which, since 2001, has been extended from Porto Alegre in Brazil to a number of regional locations and events (on the dynamics of this process, see Patomäki and Teivainen, 2004). The hundreds of organizations that have come together in this anti-globalization movement and the associated search for "another development" do not always see eye to eye on their various programmatic statements and reflect the diversity of civil society organizations engaged and mobilized by the movement. Nevertheless, they can agree on certain principles, although the issue of whether or not these principles constitute a new paradigm is unsettled (Atria, et al., 2004). The role of the international organizations and the International Financial Institutions (IFIs) is also a concern, given that "another development" is predicated on the retreat of the state (the government, that is). In order for a process of development "from below" and "from within" to take root, the state must withdraw its responsibility for development with the concomitant "strengthening of civil society."

The scholarly and policy-making communities have identified a considerable range of alternative formulations of a new paradigm. The "new paradigm" (whether or not we can call it that it is a matter of ongoing debate) seems to have the following basic components:

- an emphasis on popular participation; that is, the incorporation of the identified beneficiaries of public policy and associated projects, particularly the poor and women;
- the decentralization of decision-making and the implementation and administration of public policy, sharing it with local (municipal and regional) governments and other partners (civil society, NGOs);
- prioritizing extreme poverty, alleviating its worst effects with projects financed by a special social investment fund set up for this purpose;
- specific health, education, and employment policies (in some versions, the promotion of micro-enterprise) and empowering women to actively participate in the development process; and
- structural reforms designed to create a favourable environment for a new social policy (NSP) and a social development process.

These characteristics not only define shared principles but constitute vital elements of a possible alternative economic model, a simplified theoretical representation of reality used to guide both policy and action. For government policy, the axis of this model is an NSP designed to give structural adjustment a human face, a social dimension that it did not have. This NSP seems to have its origins in Bolivia, in an experiment with neo-liberal policies beginning in 1985. But its paradigmatic case might well be the Fund for Solidarity and Social Investment (FOSIS) in Chile, and, to a certain point, Mexico's *Solidaridad* (the social policy implemented under the presidency of Carlos Salinas de Gortari, at the time the darling of the IFIs and the business press). In any case, the NSP substituted for the traditional social policy that had been part of a welfare state oriented towards universality (to benefit both the middle and working classes, the rich as well as the poor). In contrast, the NSP targeted the problem of extreme poverty found in marginal communities. At least this was the theory. In practice—in the exemplary case of Chile's FOSIS—it has been found that up to 25 per cent of benefits under the NSP go to the richest social stratum in the country. In any event, evaluations of programs based on this new social policy have demonstrated a mild positive impact in Chile, with some alleviation of extreme poverty. But outside of Chile, poverty has not been alleviated let alone reduced. Even in Chile, the NSP has not affected the underlying structure of poverty—a structure that continues to reproduce the conditions of this poverty (see chapter 3).

According to Michel Camdessus, managing director of the IMF at the time, the economic policy and the development model proposed by the IMF cannot be characterized as neo-liberal because IMF policies do not just depend on the invisible hand of the market. They also require the visible hand of the state and the third hand of "the solidarity between the rich and the poor"—the third pillar of IMF policy, according to Camdessus, and perhaps evidence of what we might term "social liberalism." The key institutions and agencies in the development process, the market and the state, are conceived in more balanced terms, granting more importance to the state than assigned it in the neo-liberal model. Here we find the ingredients of a theoretical (and thus political) convergence between neo-liberalism and neo-structuralism, the former representing the position of the World Bank; the latter of the United Nations Economic Commission for Latin America and the Caribbean (ECLAC).[1] But, despite the closing of the theoretical space between these two approaches and their associated models (neo-liberalism and neo-structuralism), enough distance remains to support a continuing debate on the respective roles and limits of the state and the market.

The critical point of this *social liberalism*, a term that could be used to designate this theoretical convergence and policy compromise between neoliberalism and neo-structuralism, is to recognize the need for a social consensus based on solidarity between the rich (the intended, if not specifically targeted, beneficiaries of the process due to their supposedly higher propensity to invest their savings) and the poor (the bearers of the social costs). To this end, both theorists and policy analysts have resorted to a strategy of administrative decentralization, popular participation, and social solidarity based on this new "social consensus" (or, as in the case of Mexico, a social pact between the entrepreneurs and the workers).

Participation and decentralization, two pillars of this model (social liberalism or structural adjustment with a human face), have been implemented in various contexts. Social liberalism is based on an expanded concept of development: Not only does it aim for an increase in per capita production, but also an advance in "human development," defined and measured as society's increased capacity to provide its members with choice, freedom, and opportunity to realize their potential. The strategies for decentralization, promoted by multilateral financial institutions (mainly the World Bank) and the operating agencies of the United Nations (UNDP, UNICEF, and others), have taken various forms, but they basically involve collaborating with local institutions, particularly municipal governments and the NGOs that operate as intermediaries between the central government and community-based grassroots organizations.

In Bolivia, for example, this concept of social liberalism was institutionalized via the Law of Administrative Decentralization (LAD), pioneered, as it happens, in Chile by the Pinochet regime in 1975, and the Law of Popular Participation (LPP), pioneered by the neo-liberal politician and twice president Gonzalo Sánchez de Lozada. These laws are in part a response to demands for territorial or regional autonomy and control over land and other productive resources by the country's indigenous peoples and diverse civic associations, as well calls on the left for popular participation.

In Bolivia and elsewhere, popular participation has been a central demand of the left in recent years at the municipal level, where it has had considerable success. The problem for the left, and in many cases for the communities involved, is that the policy of decentralization, of managing resources and decision-making at the municipal level, has had a dual purpose and impact. On one hand, this policy has opened some spaces at the local level for political action and for grassroots social organizations to participate in decisions about development projects and social development in the community. In this context, it is very difficult for the left to oppose this policy of decentralization and popular participation. On the other hand, the policy has not resulted in what the World Bank (Bebbington, et al., 2006) terms "empowerment" of the people. In Bolivia, the LPP has worked in practice to weaken community- or class-based organizations such as unions that previously had, and could have, some capacity to address issues that go beyond the community, to challenge the structure of economic and political power, and to effect change at the national level. The problem is that the decentralization of government responsibility and decision-making has generally been an initiative from above (the government) and the outside (primarily the World Bank). It has also been argued that NGOs, in their role as mediators between the central government and community-based social organizations, have tended to weaken the latter (see, for example, Petras and Arellano-Lopez, 1997).

THE WAR AGAINST POVERTY AND THE NEW SOCIAL POLICY

In the 1990s, after more than a decade of structural adjustment, some 200 million people in Latin America were forced to live in conditions of poverty (see chapter 3). Nearly everyone, other than those closest to the accumulated wealth of society, sees this poverty as the principal problem that needs to be addressed, either from a social justice perspective (a question of principle) or because of the conditions that poverty can bring about. But neo-liberals tend to see poverty as a pathology that has very little or nothing to do with their policies or with the system. In the words of erstwhile president of Mexico Ernesto Zedillo, poverty is "the legacy of many decades of statism and authoritarianism"[2]—and this after two decades of experience with the free market and neo-liberalism.

When poverty is analyzed in terms of its structural conditions, proponents of the new economic model blame the policies of yesteryear's interventionist regimes, in spite of the fact that these policies have not been seen for at least 10 to 15 years. However, neo-liberal thought on the matter is somewhat ambiguous or contradictory, given that poverty is also seen as a transitory condition that will disappear or be reduced in the process of structural adjustment and economic growth. Neo-liberal politicians and policy-makers do not see root causes in poverty, so their aim is not to eradicate poverty or even reduce its occurrence, but rather to alleviate or attenuate its effects.

Advocates of structural adjustment with a human face primarily approach poverty by dismantling traditional social programs and targeting extreme poverty more effectively with a "new social investment fund" created to this purpose. Within the framework of the Washington Consensus, this strategy, elaborated by the economists at the World Bank, the UNDP, and ECLAC, consists of three critical elements:

- an attack on extreme poverty, directing the social investment funds towards communities of greatest need and social marginality;
- privatization of the social welfare programs—of social security, health, and education (and reducing state expenditures in each area); and
- decentralization of those programs, with the participation of base organizations in the community, and of the local governments and local institutions (solidarity).

To clarify these points, we will briefly summarize how this policy was implemented in the paradigmatic case of Chile's FOSIS and the not atypical case of Mexico's *Solidaridad*, the social program initiated by Carlos Salinas de Gortari at the beginning of his presidency.

The New Social Policy in Chile

The Fund for Solidarity and Social Investment (FOSIS) was designed to significantly reduce the incidence of extreme poverty and alleviate its conditions in Chile. The Social Development Summit sponsored by the United Nations in 1995 presented it as the model of the NSP. It was initiated in 1990 by the government to combat poverty. However, despite the plaudits the international financial community has given the Chilean model, poverty still afflicts two of every five persons in the country (compared to 1970, when only 17 per cent of the population suffered from poverty).

In some respects, FOSIS differs from other Social Investment Funds (SFIS) in the region. First, it was institutionalized as part of the government's social policy division. Thus, it is subordinated to the Planning and Cooperation Ministry rather than controlled directly by the presidency, as it is in Mexico, Peru, and other places. At the same time, it was designed as a complement to other social programs instead of substituting for them, as it did in other places. It also stressed different priorities. Most programs based on the NSP emphasize short-term emergency projects to create employment and provide social assistance. FOSIS, on the other hand, is oriented towards long-term projects and uniquely directed towards the goal of attacking the root causes and not just the symptoms of extreme poverty. Thus, FOSIS has given priority to financing projects related to training and marketing, such as credit and technical support to small companies (33 per cent); capacity-building for community-based organizations (33 per cent); assistance to small producers and indigenous communities (16 per cent); and youth training programs (18 per cent).

FOSIS is widely perceived to be an efficient model of a social policy used to combat poverty. For example, it is an integral part of an amalgam of government anti-poverty directives to 71 communities identified by their high rates of marginality and extreme poverty. Almost 40 per cent of projects financed by FOSIS have been located in these communities.

FOSIS has not been free from criticism, however. In the first place, it is responsible to a significant degree for the demobilization of the base social organizations in many poor communities. This probably was—and is—an integral part of government policy, and NGOs for the most part have been converted into policy instruments of the government. They have become mediating agencies that in practice have not assisted capacity-building and empowerment of community-based organizations, many of which had emerged in the 1980s in the struggle against the military regime. On the contrary, NGOs have generally contributed to the demobilization of these organizations, a weakening and dispersal. In this perspective, perhaps, FOSIS might be seen as a success. Also questionable is FOSIS's claims to efficiency in the war against extreme poverty. An investigation and report to the senate in 1994 revealed the richest social stratum in the country received up to 25 per cent of program benefits (Vergara, 1996). So much for *focalización* (targeting the poor).

Mexico's NSP: A Matter of Solidarity

Several evaluations of *Solidaridad*, Carlos Salinas de Gortari's new social policy, concluded that it was more of a political instrument (a means of securing votes) than a social policy. (A similar policy was implemented in most countries in the region, notably in Bolivia, Chile, Honduras, and Peru.) The government had to pay dearly for these votes, although total expenses in the social sector were less than social expenditures in years prior to the inception of the SAP in 1983. *Solidaridad* lacked a productive orientation: the micro-projects it supported involved short-term investments and poverty alleviation rather than investments in infrastructure and new technology, and therefore contributed next to nothing to the technological reconversion of the productive apparatus (the modernization of industry) and was by no means able to replace the wages lost in the process.

To understand how *Solidaridad* operated, we need to view it from the perspective of the central government's social policy. A revealing example is the role *Solidaridad* played in the government's efforts to modernize the agricultural sector; that is, to transform production and its corresponding social relations by restructuring its inefficient and non-profitable small producer/peasant sector consisting of less than half of the agricultural area but including some four million *ejiditarios or comuneros* (producers with communal land tenure), *minifundistas* (workers or producers with access to mini-plots of land for basic subsistence), and labourers and their families—three-fourths of the rural population.

The development of agricultural restructuring has been traced out by Enrique Atorga Lira (*La Jornada*, "del campo," November 1, 1996: 10–11). He saw it as a conspiratorial process advanced in five phases. The first phase began with the dismantling of various forms of state support. Under the rubric of cutting expenditures, deregulating the economy, and correcting market distortions, credit was cut back, as was insurance support. The government program of technical assistance was also eliminated, as was the provision of seeds, subsidized credit for inputs, and support for coffee growers, the majority of whom are very small producers and 60 per cent indigenous. The price of electricity was allowed to rise, as were the costs of water for irrigation and other inputs. Support for marketing and price stabilization was terminated, and, finally, the banks were re-privatized, eliminating dozens of support programs. This restructuring forced the peasants to turn towards the commercial banks with credit at high interest rates and difficult terms, placing them in the hands of exploitative intermediaries, rapacious caciques, and usurers.

The second phase involved counter-agrarian reform, labelled by the government as "land for the peasants," a constitutional change designed to commodify communally owned productive land and incorporate it into the market, permitting peasants to freely sell or rent their property, which had been protected by the constitution in its collective form (as *ejidos*). This constitutional reform created better conditions of productivity and profitability by facilitating the formation of large-scale commercial enterprises with the capacity to compete on the world market and expelling marginal producers; that is, the peasant farmers and rural workers who make up an estimated 50 per cent of the "economically active population" in the countryside and who are viewed and treated as a surplus population by the NEM.

The third phase in the chain of events was a series of policies that, contrary to government rhetoric (and neo-liberal doctrine), had the overall effect of increasing indebtedness and poverty among small producers, and directly benefiting the powerful and rich landowners and capitalist producers. The limits of the process (and the depths of the government's duplicity) were reached when the government tried to secure the participation of the peasants in the process of their own destruction.

The fourth phase of the government's policy to modernize agriculture began with *Procampo*, a capital incentive program designed to speed up the construction of capitalism in the countryside. *Procampo*'s impact on agriculture has been to lower the price of corn and beans, the two basic staples of the peasant social and household economy—their basic means of subsistence. The underlying aim was to encourage if not force the peasants to sell or rent their land, or to shift production towards a more commercially viable or lucrative crop. *Procampo* gave a subsidy of $350 to the producer, some relief relative to their extreme poverty, but a lot less than the money they lost from the reduced price of their products, the increase in the cost of consumption, expenses incurred in the collection of this "subsidy," and the purchasing power of wages in the market (over half of all peasant producers are partially dependent on wages for household income).

The final phase of the restructuring process—not to mention the Alliance for the Countryside, a modernization program designed to benefit the medium and large growers in the sector—was delivered by the US government when it closed the border to the rural poor seeking their only remaining solution to the problem of their survival—migration.

THE SEARCH FOR ALTERNATIVE DEVELOPMENT: A NEW PARADIGM?

In the 1950s and 1960s, development was viewed as a matter of "economic growth" measured by the annual increase in the Gross National Product (GNP) and the income generated by the economic activity involved. However, in the 1970s, concerns emerged about the serious limitations of such a uni-dimensional concept of development, an approach that both failed to take into account the socio-cultural and other dimensions of the process and that over-relied on the agency of the state in bringing about the changes. In the wake of these concerns, an impetus to think about development in an entirely new way emerged—a movement to establish a new paradigm for development. One feature of this new approach—an essential element of a new paradigm—is an awareness of the multi-dimensional nature of development. Another is an emphasis on the need for an integrated or holistic approach; in particular, to combine the *economic* and the *social* in any development strategy.

Until the 1970s, analyses of the development process had always been advanced within the framework of one of two paradigms. The first is defined by a spectrum ranging from orthodox liberalism (*laissez-faire* capitalism) to a heterodox structuralism (a regulated form of capitalism and planned development). The second paradigm, political economy, is defined by theoretical and political positions and proposals (Marxism, Dependency theory)[3] predicated on the belief in the need for more radical systemic change—social transformation rather than reform of the operative capitalist system.

In this context, a movement was founded to construct a new paradigm that would escape the identified limits and assumptions of existing approaches, one that would conceive of development differently. This search for "another development" (AD) can be traced back to 1974, when the Dag Hammarskjold Foundation for Alternative Development and its publication *Development Dialogue* were established.

Since its beginnings, this search for an alternative development has crystallized in a movement of global scope and impact. Proposals consonant with the idea of "another development" that is more socially inclusive, human in scale, environmentally sustainable, and participatory in form, initiated from within and below, have been propagated from multiple organizations.

In the 1980s, this search for AD became an international movement dedicated to the advancement of the process. It has assumed multitudinous forms that include the need for development that is on a "human scale" (Max-Neef, Elizalde, and Hopenhayen); that is "participatory" (Rahman; UNRISD), "equitable and sustainable" (Wolfgang Sachs), "human" in form (UNDP), "liberating" (Goulet), autonomous and "self-reliant" (Schuldt; Amin), "from within" (Sunkel), from below and "people-centred" (Korten, 1990), community-based (UNICEF), socially inclusive, and empowering of the poor (World Bank).

The postulates, theoretical and political propositions, and models of these and other forms of alternative development are wide-ranging. However, it is possible to identify some guiding principles—the heart, we might say—of "another development," the domain assumptions of a new paradigm, and the pillars of the various models constructed within its framework. These can be summarized as follows:

- grassroots organization as the basis of development,
- popular participation as both means and end,
- the community as a locus for development, and
- development as an integrated process—economic, socio-cultural, environmental, and political.

Grassroots Organization as the Basis of Development

Alternative development is not based on the protagonistic forces or dynamism of either the state or the market, the two central institutions of the liberal-structuralist (orthodox-heterodox) approaches and models. Forms of "another development" (AD) are distinguished by their alternative ideas and propositions with respect to these two institutions; namely, the role and weight accorded to each. For the exponents of AD, the process of development is established in community-based organizations; it is defined at the level of the community, an entity characterized by an awareness of collective identity (what sociologists call "community spirit," something that tends to be lost in the processes of development—modernization, industrialization, urbanization, and so on). The community is the social base and the beneficiary of development, both object and subject of the process.

Popular Participation as Both Means and End

It is essential that the beneficiaries, the objects of the process, are also the self-constituted social subjects or agents of the development process, the principal protagonists in the development of the community in all its dimensions—economic, social, political, cultural, and ecological. Both neo-liberalism (modified as social liberalism) and neo-structuralism (as constituted by ECLAC) identify participation as an essential condition of the process of development, the missing link between the process of productive transformation and the achievement of equity or social justice in the distribution of productive resources. However, under these models, participation has involved incorporating the intended beneficiary into a process initiated at the centre of the system (from above and outside). Without participation of the targeted beneficiaries at the inception of the process, development as a general rule does not work and associated projects or programs fail to achieve their strategic objectives.

Incorporating women, the poor, and indigenous people, and respecting the environment have become basic principles and essential components of both neo-liberal and neo-structuralist proposals for development. This has been the corollary of the neo-liberal policy to decentralize decision-making and government administration—to delegate responsibility and transfer it to regional and local governments, and to implement public policy, deliver programs, and execute projects with the support of NGOs. But, in these models, participation means incorporating the intended beneficiaries into the development process, not recognizing them as a collective social subject with the objective of empowering people directly. This is the goal of an alternative development.

The problem is to identify and create the necessary conditions for this form of participation—of an alternative process. This is also the biggest challenge for exponents and agents of "another development."

The Community as a Locus for Development

The question of popular participation is related to the idea of local action, privileging forms of development that are rooted in the community. The models for national development advanced by neo-liberals and neo-structuralists share a global context. These models look to conditions created by international relations and the global economy, and aim to adjust to developments in this economy (by inserting national economies and their enterprises into the globalization process) in order to generate better opportunities and conditions for national development.

AD, on the other hand, presupposes the need for selective delinking from this world economy to pursue a path of national self-reliance, or, at least, an alternative focus on conditions that directly affect the local community. Proposals for AD focus on the need for

- using locally available resources, both natural and human;
- designing technologies appropriate to the human scale of small enterprises and using local resources (versus more capital-intensive imports that are monopolized by the multinationals, expensive and not locally available);

- encouraging the formation of local and regional centres of technological research and development, with respect to both appropriate technology and enterprise development and management;
- creating industry in, or close to, rural communities in the countryside;
- strengthening local and regional markets, and reorienting production facilities (preferably in co-operative form) to them;
- looking to these markets as a way to capitalize and encourage the formation of small and co-operative enterprises, with a high capacity for generating employment and income growth, thereby raising mass consumption level and promoting community development; and
- developing local financial institutions with the capacity to capitalize local companies and provide credit to them and to the producers of the locality.

Development as an Integrated Process—Economic, Socio-cultural, Environmental, and Political

Aside from the three principles of community focus, popular participation, and local action, the proposals (it is difficult to speak of models) for AD are characterized by their emphasis on the multi-dimensional and integral, or holistic, form of development. The critical elements of multi-dimensionality are as follows.

- *Economic*: increasing productive capacity and output of goods and services, which has traditionally implied or required industrialization.
- *Social*: improving the quality of life for the population and providing a more equitable or just distribution of society's productive resources and the benefits.
- *Political:* releasing and freeing individuals (and oppressed peoples) from structures and conditions that inhibit or limit their capacity to develop their human potential.
- *Cultural and ethnic*: assuring the respect for autonomy, human rights, cultural identity, and indigenous forms of organization,

particularly of the indigenous peoples that for centuries have been marginalized and oppressed—lost in the interstices of the dominant society and culture.
- *Ecological*: protecting the environment and not exceeding the limits of the ecological systems on which human life and the development process depend.

If we were to establish a hierarchy among the several dimensions of the development process, then, according to Ignacy Sachs, the emphasis must be on the social aspect, accepting the ecology as a finite and definite limit, and the economic as a means of achieving an integrated form of social and human development (Ignacy Sachs, 1995). In any event, what has to be underlined is the integrity of the process; namely, the fundamental connection between the social and the economic dimension and the environment (striving for a symbiotic relation of communion rather than one of dominance, respecting nature's limits and integrity), equity or social justice in the distribution of productive resources, and the human scale of the forms of organization and development.

To conclude, the weak point in the search for an alternative development has to do with its limited scale and connection with the national development process. A motto of alternative development is to think in global terms but to act locally. The problem is to connect the many community development projects with processes that reach well beyond these communities and that generate structural conditions of local development at national and global levels. The challenge is to take these structural conditions into account in that they create an inevitable context that community development practitioners too often are ignorant of or ignore. The problem, in short, is to connect the processes of national development with those that operate at the community level—the global and the local. The AD movement provides very few ideas to deal with this problem, aside from

- proposals to form connections and links between public policy and the actions of social organizations and citizens;
- democratizing the structures and the institutions of the state, creating political spaces for the actions of these organizations at the national level—and at the global level; and
- forming organizations and types of mediation (and networking) that can assure the effective participation of civil society in national institutions such as education, health, banking, and other indispensable state services.

These proposals have not been advanced without criticism. In fact, they have generated substantial debate. Many issues need to be settled in, one of them being that these proposals tend to avoid any discussion of the financial and other economic institutions that surround the global and national market, or of the relationships of class power that sustain these institutions and those of the state. In this failure, we can locate the theoretical and political limits of the movement in the search for an alternative development.

THE NEO-STRUCTURALIST PIVOT OF ALTERNATIVE DEVELOPMENT

The United Nations Economic Commission for Latin America and the Caribbean (ECLAC, or CEPAL, its better known Spanish acronym), with its headquarters in Santiago, Chile, is one of the few political and intellectual fortresses formed to contain the wave of neo-liberalism that swept over so much of Latin America in the 1980s. At the turn of the 1990s, the limits and contradictions of neo-liberalism had been clearly exposed, leading its exponents and apologists towards a search for reforms that would give it a human face and salvage it from the forces that threatened it.

Although the resulting facade could have softened the system's worst effects, it could not obviate its negative impacts or contain the forces of resistance and opposition. Even the defenders of the system and the ideologues of neo-liberalism had to search for an alternative model, one that would at the very least control and channel the protests. In this context, ECLAC designed a model that raised the possibility of putting Latin America on a new and viable road, one that would leave intact the basic pillars of the capitalist system. At least, this is how ECLAC viewed the challenge it confronted.

The debate about possible alternatives to neo-liberalism has travelled the extremes of the political spectrum: from technocratic proposals to make it more efficient and viable (reducing its social costs), to calls for a new utopia and rejection of the doctrine, to the construction of an alternative, more popular model. ECLAC occupies the centre of the discussion. In the 1960s, ECLAC had been the principal promoter of the import substitution industrialization (ISI) policy, in which nations unable to export in order to pay for their imports turn to producing their own manufactured goods. But with the apparent exhaustion or failure of this policy and the seeming success of the alternative policy of industrialization by export promotion (EPI) (advocated by neo-liberal economists on the basis of neo-classical theory and in light of the high growth rates of the East Asian economies), ECLAC lost much of its considerable influence. At the end of the 1980s, ECLAC sought to escape its intellectual and political isolation and recover its influence and pioneering role in development by constructing an alternative model based on neo-structuralist assumptions.

Although it is aligned to several assumptions that are antithetical to neo-liberalism, the neo-structuralist model constructed by ECLAC exhibits a curious amalgam of neo-liberal and alternative propositions. First, ECLAC theoreticians today are more or less in agreement with their neo-liberal counterparts about the need for a structural adjustment to reflect changes in the world economy. They agree that this adjustment must be pursued in a context of macroeconomic equilibrium; that is, fiscal discipline, balanced accounts, and control of inflationary tendencies, whether attributed to monetary causes (excess money supply), as the monetarists aligned with neo-liberalism maintain, or to the structure of the economy, as long argued by ECLAC economists. Thus, ECLAC now accepts the conservative argument against Keynesian deficit spending and fiscal imbalances, and endorses the need to avoid a substantial current account deficit. Nevertheless, areas of disagreement remain.

Redefining the goal of the development process is the essence of neo-structuralism. Instead of pursuing economic reactivation, the growth of production, at any social cost (under conditions of macroeconomic stability and a more efficient restructuring of the production apparatus), ECLAC argues the need to combine "productive transformation," the engine of growth, with "equity," a more just distribution of society's productive resources. In this regard, ECLAC essentially returned to the "growth with equity" approach advocated by the proponents of liberal and social reform within the dominant paradigm on the 1970s. Like the growth with equity approach of these liberal and social reformers in the 1970s, the ECLAC model of productive transformation with equity (ECLAC, 1990) is predicated on a series of economic and political reforms of the dominant capitalist system—to give it a human face.

The neo-liberal model derives from the idea that the benefits of growth, which of necessity are initially concentrated, sooner or later trickle down to other social sectors, including the poor. This absolves politicians and technocrats of the responsibility for assuring equitable distribution of those benefits of growth. ECLAC economists, however, do not subscribe to this theory; which is to say, they do not believe that it will happen. Nor do they believe it to be economically necessary. Instead, they postulate equity as both a necessary precondition for and a requirement of a process of development that is sustainable. This form of development requires specific measures that go beyond mitigating the conditions of poverty: improved access to productive resources of a broader range of economic resources, radical reform in the tax regime, and the redistribution of income and other resources. Such reforms imply a much more active role for the state than that proposed by neo-liberals.

In effect, ECLAC proposes an efficient developmental and regulatory state on the East Asia model, one with relative autonomy (vis-à-vis diverse social classes, including the dominant capitalist class) and that assigns the private sector primary responsibility for production. In alliance with the private sector, the state assumes responsibility for the regulation of capital, and will intervene in the economy as required to assure productive investment in infrastructure and social capital, technological reconversion of the productive apparatus, and a minimum if not optimum level of social welfare.

In practice, the policy of the current *Concertación* (socialist-Christian democrat) regime in Chile is perceived by many to be an exemplar of the ECLAC model. Others, however, see in this regime nothing but neo-liberalism with a human face (Leiva and Petras, 1994; Collins and Lear, 1995; Cypher, 2005). In any event, in its theoretical formulation of public policy, ECLAC appears to have advanced further than Chile's social democrats in regard to proposals designed to improve access to society's productive resources and provide a more equitable income distribution, agrarian reform, and a progressive tax regime.

The ECLAC model constitutes a set of postulates and proposals that are grounded to some extent in lessons drawn from the experiences of the rapidly growing countries in East Asia and Southeast Asia, and that discard key elements of neo-liberal dogma. As with so many models, its problem and weakness lie in putting it into practice. The issue is political. At the global level, the UN operational agencies have strongly endorsed the ECLAC model, but financial institutions such as the World Bank and the IMF are much less enthusiastic, even politely hostile. This is undoubtedly because they are tied to and committed to defending policies that play a role in the continued reproduction of global poverty. As for the World Bank, the established connection between these policies and poverty poses a serious problem not only of credibility, but also for its declared mission to "fight poverty with passion... and lasting results" (World Bank, 2004b).

Problems of implementation can be even greater at the domestic level. How to convert an ineffectual state, servile to the interests of the dominant class, into an efficient regulatory state that is relatively autonomous and capable of strategic planning, controlling capital and promoting development? How to impose a redistribution of market-generated incomes without provoking capital flight and an economic crisis? How to attract the foreign investment on which the model remains dependent (in its *rapprochement* with neo-liberalism, ECLAC [4] has rejected its earlier position on foreign capital), or to prevent its decamping once it is subjected to some restriction? With the resumption of some degree of protection to strategic industries, how can the government prevent or respond to the retaliatory moves of the US state and the World Bank?

Is the state in a condition to negotiate reduction or cancellation of an external debt of over 500 billion dollars, a debt that continues to severely constrain or strangle many economies in the region and that has in any case been paid many times over and is widely regarded as illegitimate? How to assure the state's relative autonomy from the operative social forces—of the pressures and demands of civil society? In the Asian NICs, this autonomy (and its political cost) was achieved by repressing the working class as well as using strong-arm tactics against recalcitrant sections or groups within the capitalist class. But ECLAC proposes democratic mechanisms—a policy of participation and decentralization of public policy decision-making and administration, the missing link between productive transformation and equity, the institutional means of popular participation. And how to reconcile immediate demands to pay back the large social debt contracted by neo-liberal regimes with the medium or long-term technocratic plans for development? These questions embody not only the challenge faced by ECLAC, but also its theoretical and political limits.

INTERNATIONAL CO-OPERATION FOR DEVELOPMENT AND THE NGO: CIVIL SOCIETY TO THE RESCUE?

In the 1960s, in the wake of the Cuban Revolution, the United States Agency for International Development (USAID) contracted a number of private voluntary organizations (PVOs) to deliver its program of development assistance (integrated rural development) to the rural poor in the Latin American countryside. Delivered within the policy framework of the Alliance for Progress (a US aid program designed to create economic co-operation between North and South America), the implicit aim of the program was two-fold. It was designed, on the one hand, to offset growing pressures for revolutionary change in the countryside by providing some tangible albeit very limited technical and financial assistance; and, on the other, to spread the good word and civic virtues of reform and democracy. In this partnered effort, the non-governmental organizations or PVOs contracted for the frontline operation were relatively successful, particularly compared to the Vatican's Catholic missionaries brought into the region more or less to the same purpose: to fight communism in the form of revolutionary social movements or guerrilla armies of national (and social) liberation—that is, to prevent another Cuba. The problem for the Vatican was that Liberation Theology and its subversive "vocation of the poor" turned many frontline Catholic aid workers, mostly priests but also bishops and others elevated in the church hierarchy, into quasi- and even effective revolutionaries (like Camilo Torres in Colombia).

This development with *Acción Católica* (Catholic Action)[5] was significant not only politically but also theoretically. For one thing, it meant that perhaps more often than not, development might be understood not by reference to the aims or strategies of the sponsoring organizations, but as the unintended result of pre-existing structures, conditions "beyond the will" of any individuals involved. Thus, organizations engaged in the project of international co-operation for development, such as the World Bank or USAID, might contract PVOs or NGOs to one purpose (as missionaries of political development or bearers of the gospel), but the frontline workers might think and act at cross-purposes, more concerned with changing the situation of the rural poor.

This point has a particular relevance for the armies of NGO workers sent into the field by a host of bilateral and multilateral organizations. In the 1980s, organizations such as the World Bank, the Organization for Economic Cooperation and Development (OECD), and the host of international development associations (IDAS) such as USAID and the Canadian International Development Agency (CIDA) increasingly turned to NGOs in the "third" sector (non-profit, non-public) to mediate relations with the targeted beneficiaries in the many poor and marginal communities in rural and urban society—to deliver "foreign aid."

By the end of the decade, this "self-development" approach of the IDAS—to use NGOs to indirectly engage the rural and urban poor as active participants in their own development—had resulted in a proliferation of NGOs. It is estimated that by the mid-1990s, these civil society or non-governmental organizations, from both the south and the north, numbered in the tens of thousands in Latin America. Not all of these NGOs were engaged in the development enterprise, in the project of economic, social, or political development. Many of them were concerned with women's issues, human rights, protection of the environment, and other causes. A large number of them, perhaps the largest category, were engaged in what we might term "development" education or "political" education for change—consciousness raising (Paulo Freire's "conscientization"[6]) or self-capacitation.

CONCLUSION

The failure and exceedingly high social costs of neo-liberalism have led to a widespread search for "another development," a more participatory and human form that is initiated from below and is socially inclusive and empowering, sustainable in terms of livelihoods and the environment.

Development in this alternative form reaches beyond the state and the market, the two institutions given priority in the mainstreams of development thought and practice, and into the urban neighbourhoods and rural communities where the majority of the world's poor live and work.

The major agency for this new form of development appears to be the non-governmental organization, acting in conjunction with and working for the IFIs and IDAs that dominate the world of development.

The emergence and rapid growth of these non-governmental organizations in the 1980s and 1990s is in part a response to a shift by IDAs away from a strategy of nation-building, infrastructural development, and large-scale development programs towards one of decentralized and local self-development in partnership with civil society—both "operational grassroots organizations," to use the World Bank's terminology, and intermediary NGOs. However, another perhaps more critical factor in the emergence and explosive growth of the NGO phenomenon is the retreat of the state from the economy and the development process. In this context, it would appear that civil society stepped in to respond to the challenge.

The issue here is complex and by no means settled. For one thing, it requires a closer look at the actual role NGOs have played in the development process, examined in subsequent chapters. It would appear that their role is ambiguous. On the one hand, some, perhaps most, NGOs operate as and can be viewed as functionaries or agents of the development enterprise. Thus, to the degree that this enterprise can be viewed as a disguised form of imperialism—the human face of a socially exclusive and economically destructive process—NGOs can be viewed as unwitting agents of that imperialism. But we should not be too hasty in this conclusion. For one thing, we should take care not to over-generalize. Not only is it invalid to generalize from a few cases to the entire universe of NGOs, but a perfunctory examination of the issue points to the existence of different types of NGOs and the need to differentiate among them. The case of *Acción Católica*, for example, suggests that NGOs can in fact play a progressive role in the development process, more concerned to make a difference in the lives of the poor and help conscientizise them than to support the agenda of the donor organizations. Subsequent chapters in the book will explore further dimensions of this issue.

NOTES

1   On the neo-structuralist model (theoretical propositions and policy prescriptions) see Sunkel (1993).

2   Zedillo is quoted from the summit of the heads of state of Spain and Latin America in Viña de Mar, Chile, October 10, 1996 (*La Jornada*, November 11, 1996: 54).

3   Dependency theory is a school of thought that emerged in Latin America in the 1960s to argue that underdevelopment is the result of a country's peripheral status within the world capitalist system. Proponents of this theory include and André Gunder Frank and Fernando Henrique Cardoso, later president of Brazil (see Kay, 1989).

4   ECLAC, founded in the 1960s, is responsible for a school of development thought ("Latin American structuralism") that has for many years provided an alternative perspective on development from the dominant liberal/neo-liberal school of development thought. On Latin American Structuralism see in particular Kay (1989).

5   Catholic Action was the Vatican's version of the US government's Alliance for Progress: a program designed to deliver the gospel (the good word) and rescue the rural poor from the lure of revolutionary change (communism and atheism). However, this agenda was to some extent subverted when many priests, and even some of the church hierarchy, turned towards liberation theology, which recognized that the source of the widespread poverty and immiseration of the rural population in Latin America was not communism but class exploitation, racial oppression, capitalism, and imperialism.

6   In his famous *Pedagogy of the Oppressed*, Paulo Freire, a Brazilian popular educator and activist, introduced the notion of "conscientization" to refer to the process by which the poor become aware that the roots of their poverty lie in the structure of their society and the power of the dominant class, and the elites' need to maintain this structure.

THREE

Social Capital and Local Development

The search for a new paradigm arose from the need for a participatory form of development. This new form of development should be not only more socially inclusive, equitable, and sustainable, initiated from below and within civil society, but should also empower those engaged in the process. However, a social capital focus on local development, a critical feature of the new paradigm (Atria et al., 2004), has little to do with the popular movement for social change. It is about sustaining the dominant model of capitalist development and globalization—a concern in some policy-making circles and international organizations. The viability of this dominant model, indeed its survival, is very much at issue. It is widely being challenged, not only in Latin America but all over the world, by growing and sometimes powerful forces of resistance within global civil society. The impetus behind the search for a new paradigm is to find a solution to the problems of neo-liberal globalization—which are threatening to reach crisis proportions—*within* the system. The implied aim of the proponents of "another development" is to turn the poor and grassroots organizations away from a confrontational approach to systemic social change; that is, to change not the structure of the system but people themselves; to seek change and promote development within the local spaces of this structure.

THE LOCAL AND THE SOCIAL IN THE NEW PARADIGM

The search for a new paradigm can be traced back to the 1970s, but it acquired a particular vigour in the 1980s, during a turn in mainstream development thinking and practice towards a new economic model (NEM) that prioritized the free market (Bulmer-Thomas, 1996). The proponents of this paradigm visualize development as community-based, reaching beyond both the state and the market into the local communities, particularly those marginalized by the globalization process.

In the 1980s, the need for a new paradigm was given a major impetus by a widely perceived theoretical impasse about diverse forms of structuralism and associated meta-theories of capitalist development, industrialization, and modernization. The paradigm shift is also about the long-standing need to give development a social dimension. Ever since the field of development emerged, it had been dominated by economics. In this conceptualization by development economists, the social and the political largely are abstracted from analysis, treated as externalities in a process of economic growth. But in the 1970s, this approach gave way to a new focus on the social dimensions of this process—to diverse efforts to conceptualize the role and weight of the social in the development process. One of these efforts examined the concept of capital, which was central to an economic analysis of the dynamics of economic growth. The economic analysis theorized that economic growth and its associated development process hinged on capital accumulation, which in turn is dependent on the rate of national savings and productive investment. Capital was conceived of as financial (monetary) and physical (technological), as assets or productive resources.

It was in this context that the concept of "another development" emerged. First, development was viewed more broadly in terms of its social conditions, such as health and education. Second, development as the accumulation of society's productive resources was analyzed in terms of the diverse forms—natural, physical, and financial, and, by extension, social and political—assumed by capital. The notion of social capital, defined as the norms, institutions, and organizations that promote trust and co-operation among persons in communities and the wider society, was initially advanced by several sociologists (Coleman and Bourdeau). It was then elaborated on by some leading development economists such as Chambers (1983) and Putnam (1993, 2000, 2002).

That (the 1980s) was then, and this is now, a new millennium on the verge of a new paradigm. Its framework allows for and supports the claim that stable relationships based on trust and co-operation, and norms of reciprocal (as opposed to money) exchange can reduce "transaction costs" (IFAD); produce public goods (North, 1990); facilitate the "constitution of sound civil societies" (Putnam, 1993, 2000); empower people as social actors; and, above all, promote development at the community level. It thereby reduces and ameliorates the socio-economic (and psychological) conditions of poverty. This emergent social capital paradigm aims at a unified theory that incorporates ideas from different fields: reciprocity, social networks, and participatory development and governance; as well as strengthening civil society and participatory development based on resources that the poor have in abundance.

Robert Putnam's *Making Democracy Work* (1993) generated widespread interest in social capital as a research and policy tool. But the rapid spread and ubiquity of this notion of social capital in academe, and its wide-ranging applications in research, policy-formulation, and practice, has given rise to serious questioning and several concerns. First, "what is striking about social capital," Ben Fine (2001: 11) notes, "is not only the extent of its influence and the speed with which this has been achieved, but also the fact that scholars and policy-makers alike are so drawn to it" Fine adds that "these features are aptly captured by the World Bank's notion of social capital as "the glue that holds society together" and, as such, as the missing link in an analysis of the development process. See also Bebbington et al., 2006; De la Rocha, 1994; Harris and de Renzio, 1997; Solow, 2000.

Second, "despite the plethora of survey articles that litters the intellectual landscape, the concept of social capital is notoriously difficult to define. Most of the recent contributions to the literature acknowledge this before adding a definition of their own to suit their own purpose" (Fine, 2001: 11). The elusive and ambiguous nature of social capital is reflected in the not infrequent suggestion that it is merely a metaphor or a heuristic device. This is even more apparent in the inverted logic used in World Bank projects to define social capital. Here, as Fine (2001: 11–15) notes, the World Bank confuses what social capital *is* with what it *does*, exposing the concept "to perverse, dark, negative, and down-sides." As Portes (1998) points out in this connection, the World Bank's logic is anything but clear, caught up as it is in a vicious circle of tautological reasoning without any basis in empirical fact.

Third, as Fine (2001: 12) notes, the concept of social capital is used to describe and "explain virtually anything and everything from the networks formed by the poor, the sick, the criminal, and the corrupt to the social dynamics of the (dys)functional family, schooling, community development, work and organization, democracy and governance, collective action, the intangible assets" of the social economy, "the analysis and promotion of peasant-level development" or, indeed, "any aspect of social, cultural and economic activity across time and place" (Fine, 2001: 12). Everything, it would seem, except the norms, institutions, and social networks formed by those that constitute the "brain trust of the world," the class that runs the global economy and makes up its rules.

The final concern about social capital is its ideological uses and political implications. First, what is missing in the analysis of social capital is any concern with economic and political power. Social capital appears to serve analysts and policy-makers in the same way that postmodern social theory serves social analysis: as a means of avoiding what is all too real for most people—the dynamic economic and political workings of the capitalist system and its global extension. In this process, the power relations that define and determine life for most people are inverted. What is essentially a class struggle over state and economic power appears under the guise of "empowerment"—a sense of participation in decisions that affect one's life and livelihood without the need to change *in reality* the operating structures of the system. To invert the maxim established by Marx, the point here is not to *change* the world but to *reinterpret* it: to think and feel differently, more positively, about oneself and the world—to change oneself rather than the system.

Another point about its political implications is that the concept of social capital as a research and policy tool is ideologically too convenient as well as politically demobilizing. Harris (2001) and others make several points about this. First, making people responsible for their own development falsely implies that they are responsible for their problems, such as poverty, and draws attention away from the operating structures of the economic and social system. In its broad focus on the workings of civil society, social capital ignores the dynamics associated with the formal structures and institutions of society's political economy, particularly that of state power.

Second, the way the concept of social capital has been applied has demobilized the project of social transformation or radical change. Development initiatives seek to make improvements within the local spaces of the power structure, and do so on the basis of very limited resources, rather than challenging this structure or demanding improved access to more critical productive resources, such as land and natural resources, capital in the form of credit, and technology. Ownership and control of these resources remains concentrated in the hands of the rich and powerful, while the poor and powerless are encouraged to exploit their own rather limited resources and to do so without challenging the holders of economic and political power. Some critics talk of participatory development and social capital as illusory, implying not so much that social capital is based on false assumptions or unrealistic expectations—the most common criticism—but that it takes away from people their intellectual and political tools for bringing about change.

We will elaborate on this point before proceeding to deconstruct the concept of social capital from a critical perspective. The objective is to explain why so many policy-makers and analysts are fascinated with the concept of social capital and also to deconstruct its political effects (essentially, community networks of solidarity). The concern is not so much to seek the putative motivation behind this fascination as it is to identify its deleterious effects.

MAKING DEMOCRACY WORK: PUTNAM ON SOCIAL CAPITAL

The concept of social capital predates R.D. Putnam's 1993 book *Making Democracy Work*. As Campbell (2001: 1) notes, "the work of J. Coleman, P. Bourdieu, and other foundational authors of the social capital paradigm (see Baron, Field and Schuller, 2000, for a review) preceded it by years." However, as Campbell (2001: 1) notes, "Putnam's book catapulted the concept of social capital to centre stage for an extraordinary range of research and policy agendas in community development." In this context, social capital is defined as the community cohesion associated with co-operative and accessible community networks and organizations; high levels of participation in these networks; a strong sense of local identity; and the trust, reciprocal exchange, and solidarity amongst members of the community (Campbell, 2001: 1). The World Bank and the IDB (see their websites and also ECLAC) appear to have stayed close to this definition, viewing social capital through the lens of social networks as a resource that can be mobilized to reduce poverty and promote good governance (Rao, 2002; Solow, 2000).

As a resource for self-help (development from below and within, as adopted by the World Bank and most other development agencies), social capital can be used to predict and explain a wide range of outcomes, including household incomes in Tanzania and the Philippines; the effectiveness of local governments in Italy, the US (Campbell, 2001: 1). It is often used to explain the complex dynamics of community-based, peasant, or indigenous development; and, of course, how to best reduce poverty and bring about relief—the World Bank's mandate. The IDB, ECLAC, the World Bank, and the UNDP have each set up a division within their organization dedicated to the advancement of social capital and have sponsored all sorts of workshops and publications, as well produced practitioner and policy-making guides.

Upon its publication in 1993, Campbell (2001) notes, "a leading international journal cited Putnam's *Making Democracy Work* as the greatest work of social science since Marx and Pareto"—an overstatement to be sure, but a clear reflection of the enormous interest that the concept of social capital would attract. It is difficult to determine why the concept generated such excitement and interest, but the attention it received among academics, policy-makers, and practitioners definitely coincided with an emerging interest in local development and the resurgence of the community development movement, which had been on the wane since the mid to late 1960s (when it withered on the vine of the popular state-led model of economic development). This rising use of social capital also coincided with a neo-conservative impulse to downsize the state and take it out of the economy, and a concomitant concern with constituting and strengthening civil society.

The ubiquitous search for "another development" provided the intellectual context for this interest in democratizing the relationship between the state and civil society. The World Bank added a twist on this search—one that placed people at the centre of the development enterprise—by designing a program of structural reforms in government policy to provide the poor and powerless (as well as the rich and powerful) "freedom of choice" and "the ability to shape their own lives" (Narayan, 2002).

To engage civil society in constructing a decentralized good governance regime, civil society organizations (CSOs) were formed in what was initially termed "the third sector." They were assigned the lead role in political (democratic) and economic (alternative) development—actively implementing, if not designing, economic, social, and political projects, and participated in constructing public policy (at least ensuring the transparency and accountability of public decision-makers).

World Bank studies by Rondinelli, Nellis, and Cheema (1983) on government decentralization helped establish this shift in development and political thinking within the global network of development agencies and governments responsible for constructing a new world order. They were concerned with the "politics of adjustment"—to ensure the stability of regimes committed to accepting the new economic model as the only way to pave the road for future prosperity, and, as the World Bank sees it, the best way to fight poverty. In this context, institutional reforms such as decentralization and strengthening civil society in relation to government were viewed as necessary adjuncts to a policy shift towards the free market (liberating it from government interference). The aim was to bring about a strategically important and politically convenient marriage between capitalism and democracy—economic and political liberalization. And the key to this marriage was good governance, which required democratizing relations between the state and civil society, reforming the former and securing the participation of the latter in constructing public policy and government decision-making.

Whatever the merits of Putnam's book, it hit a nerve. And, as Campbell (2001: 1-2) notes, "context is everything." Ben Fine (2001) among many others has pointed out that the concept of social capital was grasped so enthusiastically in part because, in the absence of any theoretical grounding within a broader theory of power relations, it served as a blank cipher that could be moulded to diverse political agendas. Above all, it allowed for a form of development that did not challenge the power structure. Social capital was useful in that it was easily accumulated (as an asset that the poor were deemed to have "in abundance")[1] and effectively mobilized without radical social change. Development (improved socio-economic conditions to reduce or ameliorate poverty and sustain livelihoods) was limited to the local spaces available within the existing structure of economic and political power. Social change in turn (and development is predicated on change) affected the individual more than the system. It could be implemented without attacking this structure or changing the distribution of capital (that is, it would not improve access to society's most critical productive resources). Theoretical models of development to that point were all predicated on accumulating and mobilizing capital, a political process fraught with social and political conflict, and difficult to implement.

After the sweeping, epoch-defining reforms instituted in the name of progress and economic freedom, as Campbell notes, "the concept of social capital came as something of a gift to the ideologues of the free market, who argued that grassroots voluntary organizations and neighbourhood networks should take over many functions (that is, welfare) previously assigned to governments." The building of social capital was used to justify cuts in welfare spending in more affluent countries and to reduce development aid to less affluent or poor countries—to make them more self-reliant, an interesting ideological twist on the structuralist ideology of national self-determination. Development, it was widely argued, should be owned by the poor themselves and based on their own agency (self-help), rather than relying on outside agents and resources.

These ideas, as Campbell (2001: 2) adds, coincided with the rising of "third way" (centre-right social liberal) politics and the turning towards an alternative, more participatory model by governments and development agencies, which explains the exploding interest in the concept of social capital among academics and development practitioners. Social capital has unfolded on the centre-right of the ideological political spectrum, but it has also appealed to many on the left, a phenomenon not so easily explained. The "new left," defined in social rather than political terms, argues that it is only through building social capital that the "hitherto excluded" will ever gain the confidence or power to lobby governments to meet their needs and to revert their social exclusion. Thus, Campbell (2001: 2) notes, "the need to build relations of trust, local identity, and neighbourhood networks." This means an economy of solidarity (Razeto, 1988, 1993); a new way of doing politics. This leads more or less directly towards the "anti power" or "no power" form of leftist politics that has made important inroads in Latin America (Holloway, 2002). This point of view avoids class struggle for state power and its associated confrontational politics.

SOCIAL CAPITAL AND ITS CRITICS: UNREALISTIC EXPECTATIONS OR POLITICAL DEMOBILIZATION?

A group of researchers affiliated with the London School of Economics (LSE) Gender Institute compared Putnam's social capital to local community life in southeast England (Campbell, Wood, and Kelly, 1999). They found that the concept would need to be quite dramatically reworked to reflect these small local communities. They also found that Putnam's idea of a "cohesive community," characterized by a sense of common identity and generalized trust between neighbourhood residents, bore little resemblance to the rapidly changing, dynamic, and divided nature of contemporary community life (Campbell, 2001: 3). First, membership in formal organizations of the type Putnam emphasized, such as residents' associations or church groups, was extremely low. People's social networks mainly consisted of informal face-to-face groups of friends and relatives. In fact, in a summary of these results, Campbell (2001: 3) notes that "the notion of generalized trust or a common identity with others in the same neighbourhood seemed rather bizarre to those interviewed"—the presumed actors in this type of social capital formation.

More generally, researchers found that once members of the "community" had paid the mortgage and cooked for the children, they had little or no time for—or interest in—community life, in either its informal or formal institutions. Little evidence was found for an actual or latent culture of community participation, presupposed in the concept of social capital.

Not surprisingly, Campbell and her fellow researchers also found that those community networks and resources that did exist were not created equally or accessed by everyone in the community (Campbell et al.: 1999). In terms of trust and common identity, the local community was fractured based on generation, gender, and housing tenure—not to mention class (although the interviewees themselves, as it happens, did not). The authors concluded that these divisions rendered impossible a sense of common identity or a belief in the value of co-operation and solidarity with other community members. In other words, they raised the question begged by virtually all community development scholars and practitioners: is there a community at all? Does community, as presumed or defined by the architects of social capital, even exist?

This question raises others. Can one meaningfully talk about social capital as the property of spatially located communities without taking account of intra-community differences in how social capital is created, sustained, and accessed? Community social capital is a particular form of social capital that comprises the informal content of institutions presumably aimed at the common good. But what is the common good when civil society is fragmented and members of a particular community do not participate equally, if at all, in its institutions? Large-scale survey studies that measure aggregate levels of social capital across states, towns, suburbs, or communities of one sort or another generally ignore such divisions, taking a community of interest and identity for granted. Diverse studies suggest that more often than not, there is no "community" (or *gemeinschaft* in Ferdinand Tonnies's formulation), only a class- or otherwise socially divided society (Tonnies's *gesellschaft*), characterised by unequal social and economic conditions.

Furthermore, the LSE Gender Institute found that in the small towns and suburbs where they conducted their research, the subjects not only did not constitute themselves as a community, but they identified themselves primarily in ethnic terms (e.g., Pakistani, Kashmiri, African-Caribbean, white English) and secondarily in class terms (socio-economic status). They also discovered dramatic differences in how groups create and access social capital. In effect, the study found that its subjects occupied a definable location in a social structure but did not in any way constitute a community; nor for that matter did many of the "residents" (defined in spatial rather than social terms) participate equally in the same informal institutions. When they did participate—in the family, for example—the institutions involved did not constitute residents as a social network or as members of a particular community with a commonality of interest.

John Durston, a social affairs officer in ECLAC's social development division, made a similar discovery in a review of the social dynamics associated with various World Bank- and IDB-funded anti-poverty projects, particularly in the "empty institutional landscape" of eastern Guatemala. For example, in the anti-poverty Support Project for Small-scale Producers of Zacapa and Chiquimula (PROZACHI), he found that despite the presence of a "dynamic repertoire of norms" that could support "solidarity and reciprocal practices," members of peasant communities displayed a relatively individualistic culture of dependence and domination (1999: 103). Significantly, community spirit (and thus social capital) is presumed to be more easily constructed in rural settings, such as in Guatemala, Ecuador, Bolivia, Peru, and other countries endowed with considerable indigenous populations (and that are thus the objects of "ethno-development") (World Bank, 1996, 2004b).

Despite his reservations, Durston is committed to social capital as a research and policy tool and argues that with "the recovery of institutional practices of the past ... opportunities for developing new group strategies" and "external support and training," it is possible to create social capital in these communities. This would "turn an excluded sector into a social actor on the micro-regional scene" (Durston, 1999: 103). It would appear—from the voluminous literature—that there is no shortage of development scholars and practitioners taking this line, even though several authors, including Putnam (1993: 184), acknowledge that it is difficult, if not impossible, to construct social capital where none exists. The dominant view is that it is possible and necessary to build on existing reservoirs of social capital—or, as Eric Lesser (2000) has put it, to "leverage" the social capital available within existing organizations or communities. According to Durston (1999: 115), "reciprocity norms and practices [which usually lead to co-operation] exist in small local groups everywhere [in most modern human cultures]."

As for how to generate and leverage social capital for development purposes, the literature is inconclusive (Durston, 1999: 105ff.). The one area of agreement is that social capital is based on a commonality of interest. It is the most important characteristic that brings people together to take action. It is "the glue that binds people who may otherwise not have much in common in terms of geography, wealth, power, leadership, degree of organization, social cohesion, ethnicity, income, gender, or education" (Narayan, 2002). In the context of realizing shared interests and common goals, it is argued that social capital enables local people to play an active role in their own development (Chambers, 1997).

Campbell and her colleagues at the LSE Gender Institute, among others, have established that most community development researchers have unrealistic or false expectations for social capital because the presumed commonality of interest or co-operative culture does not exist. It is assumed and often argued that this is absent because relations of trust, norms of reciprocity, and a sense of community entail not only relatively equal social conditions but equal social relations, as well as the construction of horizontal networks.

Drawing on research into social capital construction among families and groups of peasants in Guatemala and also on the wisdom of the anthropologist Marcell Mauss, Durston (like Bourdieu) argues that social capital can indeed be constructed in the context of hierarchical social and political relations. Thus, the "relatively individualistic culture of dependence and domination" displayed by the peasants in Chiquimula and Zacapa (embodied in clientelistic and other "vertical" relations of reciprocity and exchange) coexist with relations of trust and norms of reciprocity, which Durston argues are "found in all peasant societies everywhere" (1999: 110).

At the same time, whether they constitute a community or not, peasants can build on their co-operative culture by what Durston calls "scaling up" their social capital from small communities at the local level to leadership at the regional and even national level. Thus Durston, unlike most researchers in this field, does not see the existence of structured social inequalities as an impediment to the construction of social capital. Likewise, unequal relations of political power. Durston (1999: 115) argues that local communities and organizations of peasants should not only "scale up" their social capital, but they should take advantage of the "windows of opportunity" available to them within the existing power structure. He hypothesizes (without presenting evidence) that the "changes in national elites produce *windows of opportunity* for the *emergence* of local social capital" and that "alliances with reformist sectors in government open the way to social capital *building*." Durston argues that if social capital is anything, it is both part of the solution (poverty relief requires the accumulation of social capital or collective self-help) and part of the problem (poverty reflects the absence or weakness of social capital).

Other researchers, more critical of the social capital concept, have drawn a much different conclusion. For example, Campbell and her colleagues at the LSE Gender Institute address the fact that most studies of social capital tend to counterpose social capital and socio-economic status as competing variables. They take this approach to be problematic in the extreme. In fact, as they see it, it makes no sense to conceive of social capital (and existing inequalities in its distribution) independently of property in the means of production, material wealth, or poverty.

At this point, Bourdieu's analysis of social capital as a means of reproducing social hierarchies, as opposed to constructing horizontal networks, could be more useful. Here, Campbell and her colleagues at the Gender Institute's Research Programme on Ethnicity, Social Capital, and Health Inequalities depart from what they regard as the realistic (and empirically proven) assumption that material deprivation, low socio-economic status and class, and minority ethnic status are important sources of existing social inequalities and the variable conditions of social exclusion. Within this context, it is clear enough that the fundamental determinants affecting people's "class situation," to quote Weber rather than Marx, are lack of access to the community's (or society's) economic resources, such as land, capital, and technology. Furthermore, whatever social capital there might be, it is distributed unequally and access to it is also determined structurally and politically.

As Bourdeau has argued, along with Campbell and her associates and others, social and cultural forms of capital are more likely to reproduce existing social inequalities than to reduce them. Thus, for development agencies, solving the problem of poverty would require much more than building social capital. Indeed, the only so-called solution provided by social capital is a sense of participation in project-level decision-making. Chotray (2004) notes that this solution is more illusory than real, only allowing the poor to participate in decisions about how to spend the meagre poverty alleviation funds that might come their way, with non-governmental organizations acting as mediators. In this sense, the empowerment of the poor (including women and ethnic communities) is more psychological than political. As for politics, it is a negation more than an affirmation of their capacity to participate.

Within the social capital paradigm, development practitioners define this negation of politics and self-capacitation as "empowerment." But empowerment changes nothing; or rather, the "transformative change" that social capital advocates write about relates to the individual, not the system. Individuals change the way they think and feel about themselves rather than the structure in which are enmeshed. In theory, such change is liberating in that it predisposes and enables individuals to rely on their own resources and act collectively to bring about change in their own lives, rather than to rely on outside agents or resources. However, the economic and political power of the rich, which is based on access to and control over financial, physical, and natural forms of capital (its non-social forms), remains intact, untouched by any pressures to share or surrender it. The institutions controlled by the rich and powerful remain in place, functioning in their interest. The policies that determine the overall social and economic structure also remain in place, free from pressures for social change exerted by social movements. In light of local development ("sustainable human development" in its latest formulation) and the new social capital paradigm, the social and political forces of resistance and social change accumulated by previous social movements are demobilized.

SOCIAL CAPITAL, POVERTY, AND DEVELOPMENT

According to ECLAC (2003) and the International Fund for Agricultural Development (IFAD) (2001), at least 44 per cent of the population in Latin America lives below the conservatively defined poverty line—those subsisting on less than $2 a day. That figure rises to over 60 per cent in the rural sector. Over the last two decades, the number of poor people, particularly in rural areas, has increased in both absolute and relative terms. IFAD (2001) attributes the increase to various structural problems, which have been exacerbated by the free market policies pursued over the past two decades and promoted by the World Bank with repeated, almost mantra-like references to the Washington Consensus.

There is no agreement here as to the source of the poverty problem, although most institutionally sponsored studies point to widespread forms of social exclusion linked to gender and ethnicity (rather than class, which is unaccountably absent). A clear, almost paradigmatic, example of this non-structural and non-political approach can be found in several studies commissioned by the IDB and published in *Who's In and Who's Out: Social Exclusion in Latin America* (Behrman et al., 2003). In these and other studies of poverty, social exclusion is largely defined as a lack of access to economic resources and public services, such as education, health, and housing, that address the population's basic needs. As for the difficulties the poor experience in gaining equitable access to political and economic resources (land, capital, technology, employment, and political participation) IFAD, like other development agencies and the authors of the IDB publication, turns towards "social values and poorly developed rural organizations" (IFAD, 2001). That is, the poor themselves are to blame, the culprits in the problem. In the process, the system long held responsible for the production and reproduction of poverty in its socio-economic, structural, and psychological conditions disappears from analysis—and from the poverty-fighting strategies of the development agencies.

Just as there is no consensus on the causes of the problem, the link between macroeconomic policy and poverty is also unresolved. Not only has the debate on this issue not been settled, it continues to rage. However, a virtual consensus has emerged about how to best confront the problem—how to wage the war on poverty that the World Bank declared as far back as 1973 (and periodically reaffirms as its *raison d'être* and mandate). Now, the World Bank is joined by a broad coalition of development agencies and governments committed to macroeconomic policies and reforms that promote globalization and self-help (community-based and participatory development), predicated on the accumulation and mobilization of social capital. The degree of consensus on this strategy for reducing poverty, particularly the focus on social capital, is quite extraordinary.

The studies commissioned by the World Bank and the other poverty-fighting institutions that comprise the coalition of the committed all seek to establish the dynamics of "good practice." They define good practice as a combination of two factors: building and mobilizing social capital as the critical factor in the development process; and a macroeconomic policy regime that provides a supportive institutional framework and facilitating environment.

CONCLUSION

The concept of social capital was advanced in the context of a paradigm shift from a state-led form of development towards a more participatory form of development and politics. In the 1990s, however, economists at the World Bank and elsewhere reformulated it as the central element of a new paradigm for development. The World Bank was the chief instigator, if not initiator, of this poverty-alleviation approach towards development, providing the institutional and policy framework for its structural adjustment program of macroeconomic policy reform (privatization, deregulation, decentralization, and financial and trade liberalization). These policy reforms were defined as and are still presented today as "pro-poor"—the best, if not the only, way out of poverty (World Bank, 2004a).

By the mid 1990s, the notion of social capital as an essential ingredient of development and a large part of the solution to poverty was systematically if ambiguously formulated and presented at conferences and workshops that brought together "social capital leaders." Social capital was presented as "a person's or group's concern, caring, regard, respect, or sense of obligation for the well-being of another person or group that may produce a potential benefit, advantage, and preferential treatment for another person or group beyond that which might be expected in an [economic] exchange relationship" (*www.soccap-msuinitiative.org.*). Within this concept, social capital is seen to reside in "sympathetic relationships of caring, trust, regard, and respect." So conceived, it was presented as "an essential resource because it contributes to our economic as well as our socio-emotional well-being."

To be precise, the directors of the Social Capital Initiative (SCI) view social capital as contributing to "our [sic] economic well-being" because it "alters the terms and levels of trade which in turn influence the distribution of incomes." According to SCI, social capital "alters the terms and levels of trade" because those who are the objects of another person's caring, trust, regard, and respect have the potential to receive preferential treatment. The co-directors of the SCI point to recent data on the farmland market in which land sold to friends and family was discounted by nearly 8 per cent. But is this a significant improvement and major transformative change? In addition, they argue, social capital "makes important contributions to our [sic] socio-emotional well-being because it supplies socio-emotional goods that meet some of our basic socio-emotional needs, including the need for validation, experiences of caring, and information."

This perspective of social capital reflects a broad consensus and is representative of the scholarly literature on its so-called contributions. However, these contributions to our well-being hardly warrant the wildly enthusiastic interest social capital has generated in the most diverse intellectual and policy-making circles on the left as well as the centre-right of the political spectrum. To understand how this has happened, we have to look at social capital's perceived contributions in the area of economic and political development. Some view social capital as a panacea, and others see it as a major repository of resources that can be effectively mobilized to improve socio-economic and political conditions. These improvements range from poverty and community development to ways of making democracy work. However, even these perceived contributions do not explain the enthusiasm for social capital that many scholars and practitioners exhibit. It certainly does not explain at all the dynamics of national and global development. What it does provide, in its negation of politics, is a reformist alternative to pressures for more radical social change and for substantive improvement in socio-economic conditions of widespread and growing poverty.

The emergent social capital paradigm, Durston (1999: 104), notes, "aims to be a kind of unified theory, incorporating diverse concepts such as reciprocity, social networks, democratic governance." It is also focused on the strengthening of civil society, and participatory development based on resources that the poor have in abundance. The importance of participation in development programming and project design has been well established as a fundamental principle in both reformist and radical politics, a matter not only of social "equity" but of technical "efficiency."[2] Social capital is widely seen as highly functional—a useful means of advancing participatory development beyond consulting with the intended beneficiaries to fully engaging them in the development process from the outset (in the words of Chambers and Cernea, "putting the last first" or "the people first"). However, the social capital concept raises the same questions that have surrounded popular participation: is it possible to achieve genuine participation and bring about required structural changes by emphasizing consensus and operational targets, while negating the politics of development and ignoring patterns of local and national power and domination?

In effect, social capital is a means of promoting development without social change—bringing about improvements in people's lives without affecting existing property relations in the means of social production or the distribution of assets and incomes based on the structure of these relations. It means empowering the poor, providing them with a sense of participation and the opportunity to own their own development efforts, without disempowering the rich. In fact, this is what explains both the widespread interest in social capital and the lack of progress in over three decades of fighting poverty by the World Bank and other development organizations and agencies.

NOTES

1 In this connection, Amartya Sen views the defining characteristic of the poor as their lack of access to any productive assets, a view that more easily leads to an examination of the politics of power, which the World Bank and other economists were anxious to avoid.

2 The call for popular participation originated in radical politics as a rallying cry for revolutionary change, but in the 1970s it became a tenet of liberal reform and soon thereafter a fundamental principle of "another development." Participation in this context was viewed as "the missing link in the process of productive transformation with equity" (Boisier, et al., 1992; ECLAC, 1990). In the context of development programming and the project cycle, participation is essentially treated as a matter of principle and as such a matter of equity. However, for the World Bank, it is now also seen as a matter of efficiency, a way of improving the productivity of development projects (Blaikie, 1985).

FOUR

Participatory Budgeting and Local Government

The new economic model and proposals for "another development" called for a number of policy reforms, one of the most universally accepted of which was the need for administrative, that is, governmental, decentralization (see, inter alia, Blair, 1995; Rondinelli, et al., 1983, 1989). Decentralization, in theory, would be an important way to democratize the relationship of the state to civil society, and in the process it would strengthen civil society and bring government closer to the people. Thus, decentralization was an important adjunct to the democratization process, leading to a more participatory form of governance. In a milestone study, the United Nations Commission for Latin America and the Caribbean (ECLAC) viewed decentralization as the institutional basis for participatory development, defined as the missing link between productive transformation and equity in the development process (Boisier, et al., 1992; ECLAC, 1990).

This notion of participatory development and good governance was connected to another idea: that participatory development of necessity is local and that local governments need to play a central role in the process. However, this concept of local development begs a number of questions. Do local governments have the institutional capacity to play this assigned role? How can the institutional capacity of local governments or municipalities be strengthened? Where do the financial resources needed to promote and advance local development come from?

In this chapter, we will explore these questions through one of the most notable experiments in local participatory politics and development in Latin America: the "participatory budgetary process" initiated by the Workers' Party (PT) in Rio Grande do Sul in the south of Brazil. The World Bank, among other international organizations, takes this experiment as a model of participatory local development.

On the Move: Four

SETTING THE STAGE FOR PARTICIPATORY DEVELOPMENT: FROM THE OLD TO THE NEW REPUBLIC

From the mid 1930s to 1964, the Brazilian economy went through a profound transformation based on the development of both light and heavy industry, rapid urbanization, and an extensive network of public educational and health institutions, along with the beginnings of important social and labour legislation. This industrialization model of national development was based on a powerful state sector, public ownership of strategic industries, and protective tariffs and subsidies for locally owned enterprises. This nationalist–populist model secured social cohesion through populist reforms that benefited urban workers and state repression of class-based trade unions.

In 1964, the democratic republic of Brazil suffered a military coup, initiating a widespread regional pattern of military regimes acting against state-led development based on the nationalization of industry in strategic sectors of the economy, the regulation of foreign investment, and a more equitable social distribution of society's productive resources and national income. Because these military regimes tended to act in the interests of foreign capital (multinational corporations) and local economic elites, they were usually instigated and supported by the US government. The United States paradoxically (or cynically) called this military overthrow of democratically elected populist regimes "the restoration of democracy."

The period of military rule between 1964 and 1985 witnessed the emergence of an elite developmental model based on what Peter Evans (1979) termed the "triple alliance"—a union of big state enterprises, Brazilian private monopolies, and foreign multinational corporations. The model entailed both a continuation of and a rupture with the previous nationalist–populist model. Under a succession of military regimes, the state continued to play a major role in the economy, but in support of and in conjunction with foreign investors and the multinational corporations. Government regulations were loosened to allow a greater influx of foreign capital. The military also continued the policy of protecting local strategic national institutions (banking, capital goods, petroleum) and subsidizing industrial projects. The big change in policy was the liberalization of regulations regarding foreign capital. Under the military governments, foreign capital was seen as a "partner" of national manufacturing, and regulations specified an increasing percentage of national components in assembly plants of overseas subsidiaries (Evans, 1979).

In the mid 1980s, both in Brazil and elsewhere in the region, the period of military rule ("bureaucratic authoritarianism" in the academic lingo of American political science) and state-led development gave way to a process of globalization, structural adjustment, and re-democratization in the dual sense of a return to the rule of law and the strengthening of civil society in relationship to the government.

In Brazil, this re-democratization process led to the 1988 promulgation of a new constitution that provided the legal and institutional framework for the new democratic republic. It also provided the framework for a politics of electoral contestation between the traditional parties of the political class on the centre-left, the centre-right, and the far right, and also between these traditional parties that represented the economic elite and a newly formed Workers' Party (PT) led by Luiz Inácio ("Lula") da Silva, who would eventually, after a succession of neo-liberal regimes, gain state power as the country's president.

From 1985 to 1994, under the presidencies of José Sarney, Fernando Collor, and Itamar Franco, attempts were made to liberalize the economy according to the Washington Consensus. But while partially successful, these piecemeal efforts were not able to overcome the opposition of the burgeoning popular movements and the Workers' Party. Under Collor's presidency, several important state enterprises were privatized and a full-scale liberalization agenda was launched, only to be derailed by his impeachment for private enrichment and corruption, a not unusual occurrence under different forms of capitalism.

By this time, Brazil's neighbours had already succumbed to the neo-liberal doctrine, and a large part of the Chilean, Argentine, Peruvian, and Bolivian economies had been handed over to the private sector. However, up to 1994, internal opposition led by the Workers' Party in Brazil withstood the combined pressures of the World Bank, the IMF, and Washington. It took an ex-Marxist turned social democrat, Henrique Fernando Cardoso, to do what traditional conventional capitalist politicians were unable to achieve: bring about a radical rupture with Brazil's nationalist–statist legacy and impose a far reaching neo-liberalism, which continues to this day, even under the Workers' Party government.

Cardoso came to power in October 1994 in the wake of a global wave of social democratic reforms designed to pave a path—a "third way"—between capitalism in its neo-liberal form and socialism in its now defunct form. Features of this social liberal form of national development, which bears resemblance to Bolivia's development model, include the active engagement of civil society in the political process and a decided emphasis on local development and popular participation. The Workers' Party, which gained national power in 2000 under Lula's leadership, has continued down this road of participatory development at the local level and neo-liberalism at the level of macroeconomic national policy (Petras and Veltmeyer, 2004).

In Brazil, as elsewhere in Latin America, politics and development in the 1990s were geared to the neo-liberal model of free market capitalism and took the form of an adjustment to the new world economic order. The first round of neo-liberal policies was implemented in the 1970s during a series of military dictatorships. In the 1980s, a second round of neo-liberal policies were implemented under conditions that compelled the "democratic" governments then in place to come to terms with the dictates of global capital. These dictates, enforced by the agents of this capital (the World Bank and the IMF) materialized as structural reforms of national policy. These reforms entailed abandoning a policy of nationalization in favour of privatization (turning the economy over to the private sector) and the liberalization of trade and foreign investment (eliminating protectionism and government control over foreign investment). Significantly, it also meant a policy of administrative decentralization, turning over government responsibility for health, education, and welfare, as well as economic and social development, to regional and local governments. The significance of this policy reform—and constitutional reform in the case of Brazil—was that it created conditions for a more participatory form of politics and development, directly engaging civil society in both.

DECENTRALIZATION AND LOCAL DEVELOPMENT

One of the key changes that Brazil's 1988 constitution called for was the decentralization of government responsibilities, a change in response to demands from below, within the popular movement, but also (in line with developments across the region) an initiative from above, within the state itself. By 1988, virtually every government in Latin America had placed decentralization on its agenda and embarked on a program to bring government closer to the people and reduce the fiscal crisis of the state. This agenda had a double impetus. From the perspective of organizations in the popular sector of civil society, decentralizing government responsibilities and decisions to the local municipalities would create conditions for a more democratic system based on popular participation. From the point of view of the state, decentralization would help the federal government reduce the scope and costs of its responsibility for economic and social development, and allow them to establish a more viable and legitimate form of governance. The 1988 constitution added impetus to the decentralization movement underway in Brazil and elsewhere in the region.

DECENTRALIZATION IN PRACTICE: MUNICIPALIZING DEVELOPMENT

In the context of rapid growth of the economy in the old republic and somewhat diminished growth in the transition to the new republic Brazil experienced considerable advances in the social conditions of development from 1988 to 1994. These improvements are reflected in the statistics on child mortality, which dramatically declined, and longevity, which steadily increased. For example, in Didema, a municipality of Sao Paulo's industrial belt, the rate of child mortality from 1980 to 1994 fell from 82.9 per 1000 to 20.6 per 1000. In Janduis, a municipality of Rio Grande do Sul, the mortality rate fell from 161/1000 to 41/1000 in just the 5 years from 1986 to 1991 (Abers, 2000). In other municipalities, similar developments have been recorded. These advances, for the most part, can be attributed to programs instituted not by the federal government but by local governments, municipalities that had responded to the challenge of decentralization.

Responding to the transition from a military to a civilian regime, some municipalities experimented with participatory projects in local community development. Social organizations of the poor or neighbourhood associations were the major agents for change and development in some of these municipalities. In others, the municipality itself assumed this role, for example in Lages in Santa Catarina, Boa Esperança in Espirito Santo, Piraçicaba, and Sao Paulo. These experiments in local development ranged from popular health councils (*conselhos populares de saúde*) in the eastern zone of Sao Paulo; the People's Assembly (*Asembléia do povo*) in Campesinas; the Popular Budget Councils (*Conselhos Populares do Orçamento*) in Osasco; and, most notably, the participatory budget process (*Orçamento Participativa*) in Porto Alegre and Belém Novo. These initiatives and experiments in health, housing, education, and municipal budget-making were modelled in part on similar earlier experiments organized, inter alia, by the Italian Communist

Party in 1976 and in Barcelona in 1979 (Borja, 1987), and, closer to home, by the popular assemblies in Bolivia.

In Porto Alegre, a metropolis of 1.3 million in southern Brazil where the Workers' Party (*Partido Trabaljadores*) gained power in 1989 and continues to this day, and Belém Novo, thousands of citizens, including the poorest, were mobilized by popular participation in the design of municipal budgets. By 1995, over 15,000 people had participated in the public assemblies set up to construct the budget for the municipality, and nearly 1000 worked year round as delegates or councilors (Abers, 2000: 2).

Collective action on such a large scale, involving thousands of people who are overwhelmingly poor—those who Stiefel and Wolfe (1994: 6) labelled "the hitherto excluded"—is an anomaly, both in Brazil and elsewhere. In the late 1970s and 1980s, such mobilizations were not uncommon, but were clearly directed against the military or authoritarian regimes that still dominated the political landscape (see Leiva and Petras, 1994, for Chile). They were part of an upsurge of social movements resisting against military dictatorship and trying to rebuild civil societies across the region. By 1989, however, the last of these regimes (in Chile) had been removed, leaving in place a series of civilian governments committed to liberal democratic principles throughout the region (see O'Donnell and Schmitter, 1986). The popular movement soon subsided, and the activism of thousands of NGOs and other civic associations gave way to a mediated retreat. In Brazil, the popular movement probably peaked in 1988, when a new constitution had been designed and an estimated 1288 NGOs formed (Landim, 1988). Despite widespread decentralization and other conditions favourable to community-based participatory development under local governments, many if not most NGOs returned to the old politics of clientelism. By the mid 1990s, the emerging social movements of the 1980s had largely disappeared, and the flame of local democracy had been virtually extinguished.

By contrast, the success of local and participatory community-based initiatives in Porto Alegre and elsewhere in Brazil needs to be explained. Luciano Fedozzi (1994) does not offer an explanation but rather the gratuitous observation that the activity of NGOs tends to wax under repressive military or authoritarian regimes and wane under reformist, civilian ones. Others have focused on the inherent incapacity of grassroots organizations, particularly NGOs, to bring about social transformation—rather, a radical overthrow of neo-liberal policies and institutions is needed. Indeed, a number of others (including the author of this book) have observed that despite their rhetoric of empowerment, popular participation, and social transformation, many

NGOs have effectively become extensions of the World Bank, other donor or bilateral aid agencies, or the government itself.

Although this explanation might seem extreme, it does explain quite well some salient facts. For example, although organizations in the popular movement and governments across the region had put decentralization on their agendas, it didn't happen until the World Bank exerted pressure. Decentralization, therefore, was initiated from above, partly in response to external forces and the state and partly in pursuit of the neo-liberal concern to create a minimalist state. So, far from being—as ECLAC would have it—the missing link in a process of productive transformation with equity, popular participation in decision-making is a trap designed by the World Bank and other agents of neo-liberal capitalist development. This trap has worked by incorporating grassroots organizations, via the NGOs, into the decision-making process at the local level, on the condition that such participation be restricted to issues that are local. Thus, neighbourhood and civic associations are invited to "participate" in decisions about how to spend available resources directed to alleviate poverty. In exchange for this participation, macroeconomic policies remain in the hands of the central government and all organizations such as unions or class-based social movements with an anti-systemic or anti-state agenda are either disarticulated or destroyed, often with the complicity of the intellectuals and consultants in the NGOs. These NGOs could well be labelled "agents of imperialism."

Popular organizations formed in the 1980s were also demobilized because NGOs were by various means accommodated to the agenda of the World Bank and such multilateral organizations, or rather manipulated by them with talk of "partnership" and offers of poverty alleviation funds. This mechanism's institutional form is the World Bank Partnership Program, now replicated by most governments and other international organizations. Under this program, financing is provided on the condition that the project has a participatory component. NGOs, as executing agents, are generally dependent on this financing. As a result, by the mid 1990s, government programming across Latin America regularly called for citizen councils or NGO forums, such as the much-publicized Belém Novo set up by Cardoso in Brazil. Like other such projects and programs, the CSP calls for small town councils to monitor the distribution of federal government funds. However, the result of these projects, variations of which can be found across Brazil and Latin America, has been mixed at best; at worst, meager. In a number of different situations, they have increased popular participation, but only on issues that are purely local and often with insufficient resources and a high level of institutional incapacity to accept and administer these resources. In addition, more often than not, local elites have shown themselves to be as capable of controlling and manipulating the funding and the decision-making process as has the elite and dominant class at the national level. New forms of clientelism have proliferated in these situations.

PORTO ALEGRE: A MODEL OF PARTICIPATORY DEVELOPMENT?

As noted above, in some places such as Porto Alegre, the community development story has unfolded in a different way from that discussed in the previous section. Here, there is clear and substantial evidence of a successful effort to mobilize and even empower the "hitherto excluded" segments of the population, including the poor. Rebecca Abers argues that for the first time in the history of Porto Alegre—and perhaps the country—government spending actually favours the impoverished neighbourhoods, rather than benefiting elite groups (Abers, 2000: 4). Abers concludes that contrary to the views and predictions of both liberal pluralists and Marxists, the decentralized state should not be viewed as merely a repository or captive of reactionary social forces. In fact, she sees the success in Porto Alegre with the participatory budget (*Orçamento Participativa*) as evidence that the state is relatively autonomous from the social forces in civil society, a theory formulated by the French Marxist structuralist Nicos Poulantzas (1978), among others. As Abers (2000: 13) sees it, the Brazilian state has shown itself capable of acting against the interests of the dominant social group; that is, class, in Brazilian society. Specifically, she argues that with the *Orçamento Participativa*, the decentralized Brazil held by the opposition PT "promoted the mobilization of poor people and their organizations into new networks of civic groups by creating ... an *enabling environment* for collective action" (2000, 15). She suggests that the PT administration's large-scale popular mobilizations created conditions for somewhat combative and horizontally organized groups of citizens that were able and willing to defend their position against the complex arguments thrown against them by the technical staff and to resist efforts to co-opt them. So, developments in Porto Alegre were somewhat different than in other government-initiated participatory forums in which governments normally seek to reduce the organizational capacity of participants lest they contest its broader priorities. In effect, she argues that the PT created something that it could not foresee or control if it wanted to—a politically conscious and combative force for participatory development.

Although Abers's argument is persuasive, perhaps the conclusion she draws from the case of Porto Alegre is too general. In fact, the decentralization agenda of the Cardoso government has resulted in a highly differentiated form of community-based development, with a few municipalities recording a successful level of development, but the vast majority showing no institutional capacity or political interest in an alternative form of development. In the first place, most community-based alternative forms of development exist more as utopian ideals than realities; in practice, even the most successful cases do not amount to a model for national development that could be extended across the country and break down the power structures of neo-liberal capitalist development. Second, in most cases of decentralization, the municipalities have been prey to all of the clientelistic behaviour and elite manipulation characteristic of national politics in Brazil. Even when this has not been the case, the resulting developments have usually been either short-lived or have had few and limited outcomes beyond the illusion of enhanced participation.

Thus, the question posed at the outset remains: is Porto Alegre a special case of community-based participatory development? If so, what are its defining conditions? Under what conditions could this or an even greater form of participatory development take place? Is it possible to generalize from this form of development—to extend it to a model for national development? What about the workings of the federal state, which is clearly controlled by a neo-liberal agenda for capitalist development and in service to the dominant, ruling capitalist class, a willing hostage to foreign capital?

TRANSFORMING LOCAL GOVERNANCE: THE CHALLENGE OF LOCAL POWER

Although the union movement was the original impetus behind the formation of the Workers' Party (PT) in the 1980s, several other popular movements and radical groups joined the party. The PT became a network of party nuclei, strongest within the industrial and urbanized southeast of the country, but spreading to the whole country. These centres included groups associated not only with the industrial union movement in the ABC region of Sao Paulo, but also base communities set up by the Catholic church, the urban neighbourhood movement, peasant unions, leftist revolutionary and reformist groups, and human rights activists. In effect, the PT served as an instrument for bringing together and uniting, to some extent, various oppositional social and political forces in the popular sector. These groups organized into a wide and ever-fluctuating amalgam of national and regional "tendencies" or factions that have intensely disputed the party ideology and programs ever since.

Given the heterogeneity of the groups that make up the party, it is not surprising that the official ideology of the PT was and is quite vague, combining the experiences of a variety of social movements, most of which, like the landless Rural Workers Movement (MST), have retained their relative autonomy, with the views of socialist intellectuals of various stripes. However, from the very beginning a sort of consensus emerged on certain issues. First, they shared a general commitment to democracy, an ideology opposed to elitism, dogmatism, and the revolutionary vanguardism of earlier socialist parties. Second, the PT as a body was concerned about an *inversão de prioridade* (inversion of priorities) vis-à-vis government policymaking. The party demanded an end to the clientelistic and authoritarian tradition of elite politics and called for government policy to directly address the needs of the poor with structural changes, and not just Band-Aid solutions. Third, the PT wanted both internal democracy and the decentralization of government decision-making, along with a redistribution of the resources available to the government. Fourth, there was general agreement that the party should not attempt to absorb and replace the autonomous social movements that make up its base (Silberschneider, 1993: 79). In short, the PT was founded on and perhaps unified by a participatory ideology, an egalitarian ethic, and an anti-capitalist (socialist) project. It could be argued that such an ideology predisposed the PT towards a participatory democracy in its approach to policy-making and development in its ascent to power in Porto Alegre and in the state of Rio Grande do Sul. This approach was embodied in the notions of popular councils and the *Orçamento Participativa*, both of which originated in a successful grassroots health movement (Alvarez, 1993).

The ideology and experience with popular councils in SP, elsewhere in Brazil and in Bolivia, provided a context for the PT experiments with the *Orçamento Participativa*. Other factors were the agenda to decentralize the government and the transition from a series of bureaucratic-authoritarian regimes to the new republic, in which the citizenry would participate in the making of public policy. The idea of a parallel power structure outside of the State, similar to the notion of the original institution of *soviets* in Russia, emerged. From this perspective, the central government should not be seen to take part in the formation of popular councils (*conselhos populares*). Rather, they should evolve out of autonomous civil society organizations. Others, however, argued that the *conselhos* should be initiated or formed by the government and so serve as a means of democratizing the decision-making and policy formation process. A variation of this view, that alone seemed to have prevailed, was that the government should participate in promoting *conselhos* but with the primary objective of "strengthening civil society," currently one of the mantras and development principles of the World Bank and multi- and bilateral international organizations. The rationale for this objective is that the strengthening of civil society would at some point create an effective agency for democratizing—and transforming—the state and its institutions (Silberschneider, 1993: 105–06).

As it turned out, this debate would be tested (if not resolved) not in theory, through further discussions within the PT on democracy and participation, but in practice, through practical experience in municipal governance. This experience unfolded within the framework of a new constitution and in the wake of the 1988 municipal elections, in which the PT candidates rose to the office of mayor in thirty-six municipalities, including Sao Paulo and Porto Alegre. Where the PT won office, their administrations introduced the notion of an *Orçamento Participativa*. However, in most places this policy turned out to be unsuccessful and was either aborted or undermined by a return to the clientelistic politics of old. In only a few cities, including Porto Alegre and later in Belo Horizonte (1993–1996) did a city-wide participatory council system flourish.

THE WORKERS' PARTY IN PORTO ALEGRE: THE PARTICIPATORY BUDGET PROCESS

It is not clear how the PT administration in Porto Alegre managed to avoid the pitfalls of participatory development, including internecine divisions among various factions. Notably, the PT in Porto Alegre even managed to incorporate the communist PRC (*Partido Revolucionario Comunista*), renamed after 1987 as *Nova Esquierda*. Whatever the reason, the capacity of the PT administration to unite with much smaller parties, such as the PCB (*Partido Comunista Brasileo*), seemed to have created conditions for a successful experiment in participatory democracy. Under these conditions, Porto Alegre seemed to have provided an opportune context for this ongoing experiment, which continues to attract wide attention as a possible model not only for a participatory form of democracy but a participatory form of community-based development—that is, as an alternative to the dominant neo-liberal model that underlay and guided policy at the level of the federal government under Cardoso.

In almost every other case, decentralization resulted in co-optation and elite manipulation, rather than the empowerment of "the hitherto excluded." Aside from the PT's apparent success in uniting a broad constellation of oppositional forces and political organizations, other factors were clearly involved. According to Abers (2000: 60ff.), one of these factors was broad public support for the PT's efforts to combat clientelistic and elite politics and to promote a participatory form of democracy, for example, Olivio Dutra's 1988 campaign for governor of the state. Dutra's campaign made a connection between winning at city hall and a broader "democratic socialist" strategy to gain control of the capitalist state by electoral means, with the ultimate goal of overthrowing it. In Dutra's own words, "The conquest of the municipal government of Porto Alegre should be understood as a moment in the accumulation of political, organizational, and programmatic forces in the process of constructing socialism" (Olivio Dutra cited in Fedozzi, 1994: 29).

Two explicitly political factors might explain why the experiment with participatory democracy and an alternative form of development has worked in Porto Alegre. In addition, Stiefel and Wolfe's argument (1994: 102–03) on the major obstacles to instituting a successful participatory and inclusive form of development might also be relevant. According to Stiefel and Wolfe, who make reference to a broad range of worldwide state-initiated experiments in participatory democracy and development, the most significant obstacle is the state itself, which creates six major barriers. According to Abers (2000: 67ff.), each of these six factors was absent in Porto Alegre.

We thus have a possible explanation for the continued success of the PT administration's experiment in popular democracy. However, this explanation does not fully take into account a number of conditions and political dynamics found in and perhaps specific to Porto Alegre. For example, as Abers herself notes, in its first year in office in Porto Alegre, the PT saw the question of popular participation in the budget-making process as a side issue (Abers, 2000: 71). At the time, few within the administration thought that the budget would or should become the centrepiece of its politics. A PT document at the time makes this point very clearly. In fact, after a year in office, the PT government was unable to respond even in a limited way to the grassroots option of participatory democracy. This failure to respond to the political forces that had been mobilized in favour of participatory democracy caused widespread disenchantment with the regime and a crisis from which the PT might well not have recovered.

However, the administration's response was more astute or fortuitous, leading to what it termed *a grande virade* (the great turnaround) and a highly popular government that has won each subsequent election with a comfortable and increasing margin.

According to Abers (2000: 75–76), several factors were responsible for this great turnaround, including actions taken by the *prefeitura* to increase revenues and a process of administrative restructuring that made the *Orçamento Participativo* the centrepiece of its strategic planning process—to promote popular participation as a "line of strategic action." Another factor was negotiations with public sector workers and employees—20,000 municipal employees, over 1500 teachers, and 1000 health service workers (Pozzobon, 1997). On this last point, municipal workers were organized by unions affiliated with the Unified Workers' Confederation (CUT), the labour confederation or union central with the closest ties to the PT. The ability of the PT administration to maintain the support of the municipal employee unions, even at the cost of a financial crisis (created by meeting union wage and salary demands), undoubtedly was critical in helping the regime weather the storms to come and stay on course.

By the end of the PT's first term in office, a process of administrative restructuring had paid off. The *Orçamento Participativo* was an incontrovertible success. By 1992, thousands of ordinary citizens were participating in this process and doing so in a meaningful way. By 1995, upwards of 15,000 people had been mobilized to participate in the budget-making process, and in many parts of the city, the *conselhos populares* drew more than 500 at a time. For whatever reasons, conditions in Porto Alegre allowed for the successful implementation of popular participation. Whether these conditions can be replicated elsewhere in Brazil, converting the Porto Alegre experiment into an alternative model for national development, remains to be seen. This question requires much closer study of developments across Brazil in diverse regional and local contexts. What can be said with some confidence is that the prognosis is not good. All of the weight of the Cardoso neo-liberal regime was ranged against it.

CONCLUSION

The quest for an alternative community-based form of participatory development has provoked the emergence of a number of interesting albeit insufficiently documented experiments. However, in very few cases have these experiments created any long-term and large-scale developments. The workings of the Cardoso government, with the full support of the nation-state apparatus and the social forces ranged behind it, ensured that any such experiments would not prosper. Macroeconomic policies and the various powers of the state remain very much under the control of the government. The neo-liberal model that underlies these policies, and the social forces behind them, creates the conditions under which the economy, for the most part, is developing. The only way that an alternative form of development might arise and prosper is if a large-scale mobilization of anti-systemic and oppositional forces takes place across the country. As we have shown over the course of the four chapters, the objective or structural conditions for such a political development are surely at hand. And there is certainly a social base for such a development in Brazil's heterogeneous working class, located in the remaining factories and production sites, a well as in the streets of the large and small urban centres and the countryside. The problem is political: how to organize and mobilize the fragmented mass of oppositional political forces into anti-systemic action—to bring about a different Brazil.

FIVE

The Development Dynamics of Social Exclusion

Over the past two decades in Latin America, successive regions have undergone structural adjustment and globalization, and have experienced far-reaching changes in the socio-economic conditions of their development. Although the profound social impacts of the new economic model responsible for these changes have been well documented and analyzed, some questions remain as to the strategic and political responses to them. This chapter explores some of these issues in Latin American rural development.

The chapter opens by exploring the offensive launched by capital against labour. This offensive, in the form of a neo-liberal program of structural adjustments to the economy and a campaign for legislated labour reforms is part of a protracted class war that can be traced back to the early 1970s both in Europe (Crouch and Pizzorno, 1978; Davis, 1984) and in Chile (Leiva and Petras, 1994). In this war, the working classes have borne the brunt of the structural adjustment process and its conditions of social exclusion.[1] We identify and briefly review these conditions before turning towards the search for "another development"—alternative ways of thinking about development and putting it into practice in the rural sector. Two of these models are discussed, one elaborated by economists at ECLAC and the other currently advocated by reformers within the international development community. The chapter ends with a brief assessment of this second model as a tool in the fight against global poverty. Based on a sustainable livelihoods approach (SLA), it is currently very much in fashion and highly favoured by the community of international development organizations such as the United Nations Development Programme (UNDP). Like the ECLAC model profiled in chapter 2, SLA is predicated on reforms to the structural adjustment process, giving it a social dimension and a human face. However, it appears that neither ECLAC's neo-structuralism nor SLA provides a model for combating effectively the problems of social exclusion and widespread poverty. Change of this kind would require an anti-systemic approach that moves beyond mere reform to a direct confrontation with the structure of economic and political power. This is, in fact, the approach of the new wave of indigenous or peasant-based sociopolitical movements in the region, as well as that of the ongoing struggle of landless rural workers in Brazil and the more recent unemployed urban street workers (*los piqueteros*) in Argentina. But do these and other such movements have the capacity to mobilize effectively the forces of resistance and opposition, and bring about substantive social change using politics of direct action, social mobilization, and confrontation? This issue is addressed in chapter 8.

NEO-LIBERALISM AND THE OFFENSIVE AGAINST LABOUR

The neo-liberal model is profoundly exclusionary.[2] However, analysts of capitalist development and the neo-liberal model have tended to focus on the exploitative nature of the system and on the social conditions of this exploitation, such as inadequate wages, inequalities in the distribution of income, and poverty. But the greatest social impact of the capitalist development in its neo-liberal form may not be its exploitative character, but rather its propensity to create social exclusion (Bessis, 1985; Pochmann, et al. 2004).[3] For example, the neo-liberal model is geared to benefit only a small segment of proprietors and business operators, those few private enterprises, estimated at around 15 per cent, able to compete in the world market. Another segment of private sector enterprises, estimated at around 35 per cent, are deemed to have productive capacity but are oriented towards local markets. In a neo-liberal environment, these enterprises are subjected to the "discipline" of market forces and given little support, protection, or benefits from government policies. This leads to a process of economic restructuring that in theory shakes out the most inefficient. Finally, at least 50 per cent of all economic enterprises are left to twist in the winds of change propelled by the neo-liberal model— primarily those activities based on the peasant economy in rural areas, and, in the urban environment, those owned by operators of micro-enterprises in the informal sector. The casualties of this model are everywhere: in the growing masses of producers and workers disposed from their means of production, marginalized in the process of capitalist development, and excluded from both the formal political and economic processes of this development. Under this system of social exclusion, an increasing part of Latin America's population is experiencing a social crisis of growing and devastating proportions.[4]

Mechanisms of social exclusion also operate in the broader context of structural adjustment and globalization: privatization, liberalization, deregulation, and labour market reform (Veltmeyer and Petras, 1997, 2000).

A New Labour Regulatory Regime

Latin America experienced considerable advances in the 1990s, with the introduction of new technologies, downsizing of the workforce in the industrial sector, and experimentation with a new post-Fordist production paradigm (Boom and Mercado, 1990; Camargo, et al., 1995; Gómez Solórzano, 1992; J. Katz, 1996; Olave, 1994; Ominami, 1986). The key to this new form of production is increased flexibility in the use of capital and labour. However, many unions resisted this post-Fordist form of flexible organization, and a web of labour laws enacted under the Fordist regime of the old economic model also inhibited its introduction. As a result, governments in the region, as part of a campaign orchestrated by the World Bank, introduced new legislation designed to increase the power of employers and plant managers to hire and fire workers, and to relocate them in the production process as needed. Parallel to these moves, governments compliant to the neo-liberal model also sought to remove the constitutional protection of job tenure in the public sector introduced under the old economic model of prior populist regimes. (Most notably, the government of Carlos Menem in Argentina, the *Concertación* regime in Chile from 1990 to 2002, Ernesto Zedillo in Mexico from 1994 to 2000, and Fernando Cardoso in Brazil later in the 1990s were most amenable to neo-liberal demands.) This move against public sector workers was mandated by the IMF, which, at the outset of the Cardoso regime in Brazil, demanded the reduction of 10,000 public sector employees as the condition of an agreed-to loan. In April 2002, a similar stipulation was placed on Argentina's government, which continues to be caught in a scissor-squeeze between the demands of the international financial community (and Washington) and a restive population pushed against the wall by a severe economic crisis generated by neo-liberal policies. However, as discovered by presidents Cardoso in Brazil and Menem in Argentina, the constitutional protection of public workers under the old regimes makes it difficult to obtain the required level of congressional approval to implement these changes mandated from outside.

Given the difficulty of removing these political obstacles to "free enterprise," a dualist industrial structure has been generally reinforced. On the one hand, in addition to the processes of structural adjustment and globalization, large-scale capitalist enterprises in the formal sector have undergone a process of technological conversion and productive transformation, resulting in a reduced workforce, increased management flexibility, and, it seems, only a marginal increase in total factor productivity (Camargo and Neri, 1999; J. Katz, 1996). On the other hand, most of the dynamic growth in production has occurred in the unstructured informal sector of small, largely family managed businesses and micro-enterprises, outpacing the formal sector of medium to large-scale enterprises by a considerable margin (Portes, 1989). In fact, the Regional Employment Program of Latin America and the Caribbean (PREALC) (1993) and the International Labour Organization (ILO, 2000) estimate that the unstructured informal sector accounted for up to 80 per cent of the net employment created in the regional economy over a period of a decade and a half. As Table 5.1 shows, there is a regional pattern to this.

The trend towards labour market de-structuring can be traced back to the early 1980s (J. Katz, 1996; Pochmann, 1999: 65ff.). However, in the 1990s, many governments introduced legislation that accelerated the trend and consolidated the reduction in the number of wage workers receiving full benefits, the expansion in the rate of unemployment, and the rapid growth of workers in the informal and unorganized sector of micro- and small enterprises (ECLAC, 1998). According to the ILO (see also Pochmann, et al., 2004), by the end of the 1990s and into this millennium, Latin America's unstructured informal sector was larger than the formal sector—encompassing up to 56 per cent of workers (from between 48 to 52 per cent in the late 1980s). As a result, micro-enterprises that are reliant almost entirely on unwaged

TABLE 5.1 STRUCTURE OF URBAN ECONOMIC ACTIVITY, LATIN AMERICA 1980, 1995

	Informal Sector						Formal Sector	
	Total	Own	Account[a]	Domestic	Micro	Total	SEs[b]	PEs[c]
1980	52.5	24.6	6.9 21.0	47.5 15.4	32.1		15.4	32.1
1995	56.1	26.5	7.1 22.5	43.9 13.2	30.8		13.2	30.8
Difference	3.6	1.9 0.2		1.5 -3.6	-2.2	-1	-2.2	-1

(a) Self-employed. (b) State Enterprises. (c) Private Enterprises.

family labour—or those who work on their own account (self-employed) and generally do not receive any social protection or other benefits (*encargos socáis*)—have proliferated. They are excluded from the labour market as well as from government programs, and they work and live under conditions of economic insecurity, low income, and poverty.

As for the formal sector, the dominant trend has been towards a degree of productive transformation along three dimensions (without the "equity" called for by ECLAC): the introduction of new labour-displacing information technologies, more flexible forms of labour regulation, and a downsizing of the workforce independent of new technologies.

The effects of this restructuring have been far-reaching and include the following:

- a marginal increase in overall productivity in the industrial sector;
- an increase in rates of over-employment and under-employment, as well as unemployment (up to 21 per cent among workers in the ABC region of Sao Paulo and Gran Buenos Aires);
- more jobs with non-standard contracts, without any social security protection or benefit coverage, and little to no union affiliation;
- a disproportionate number of de-skilled, low-wage jobs;
- an increase in sub-contracting, generating a complex system of interdependence between the informal and formal enterprises; and
- a steady decrease in the value or purchasing power of wages and in the government-set minimum wage.

In the 1950s and 1960s, the mean average wage rose 30 per cent, and in the 1970s another 15 per cent. In the 1980s, with a region-wide recession and debt crisis, it fell 11 per cent. In the 1990s, in an environment of neo-liberal reforms, wages managed to maintain most of their purchasing power; but even so, by the end of the decade, they had not yet recovered from the decline in the 1980s (Lesbaupin, 2000). As for the minimum wage legislated by governments in the region under the old economic model of state development, the statistics are startling. Taking 1945 as 100, the index of the real value of the minimum wage had fallen to 29 by 1990; by 1994, the index stood at only 22.7. By 1998, notwithstanding a dramatic decline in the rate of inflation and the World Bank's major region-wide campaign against "excessively high wages" and minimum wage legislation that was leading to "the withdrawal of capital from production" and "problems of informality, unemployment and poverty," the real-value index of the minimum wage had retained only 26.6 per cent of its 1945 value (Lesbaupin, 2000).

In the light of these developments, Pochmann (1999: 119) among others (see Leiva and Agacino, 1995, on Chile) writes of the "progressive destruction" of labour markets, a trend that is clearly facilitated by the neo-liberal policies and labour legislation of regimes in the region. Collectively, these policies and legislation constitute a major offensive in the undeclared war that has been unleashed against the working class.

The Social Impact of Structural Adjustment: Six Pillars of Social Exclusion

From 1995 to 1998, the Cardoso regime in Brazil achieved an accumulated growth rate of 16 per cent in the capital goods sector of industrial production and 11 per cent in the consumer goods sector. But this represented an annually averaged overall growth rate of only 1.4 per cent, versus. 1.7 per cent over the course of the 1980s, the decade "lost to development," and 2.6 per cent for the region in the 1990s overall.[5] These macroeconomic indicators suggest a stagnant development path, one taken by virtually every other country in the region and a far cry from the years of unprecedented rapid growth in the 1950s, 1960s, and 1970s. Other indicators, however, tell a different part of the story. They point towards a process of productive transformation and technological conversion, and a deep restructuring of the economy that has had a major impact on the lives of most people in the country, particularly workers (Boom and Mercado, 1990; Camargo and Neri, 1999; J. Katz, 1996; Leiva and Agacino, 1995). This process has incurred a high social debt, which, by all accounts, exceeds the dimensions of the external debt accumulated over the same period.

The social dimensions of this debt are reflected in a range of indicators of *social exclusion,* possibly the most critical condition of the economic restructuring process underway across Latin America.[6] Pochmann (1999) identifies six pillars of social exclusion, derived from the way production is organized on the basis of the capital-labour relation. These conditions primarily affect the working class in its diverse and changing forms. It is possible to elaborate these six major forms of social exclusion, based on Pochmann:

1. lack of access to labour markets, reflected in the rate of labour force participation;
2. inadequate access to the opportunity to work, reflected in the rate of unemployment;
3. lack of access to "good quality" or "decent" jobs, reflected most clearly in evidence of increased rates of over-employment (working too many hours) and under-employment, and in the growth and prevalence of jobs that are contingent in form (involuntary part time, short term, etc.) with a high degree of informality and low pay, as well as employment on "one's own account";
4. reduced access to social services and forms of social development such as education, health, and social security (see discussion below);
5. lack of access to means of social production and income; and
6. incapacity of household members to meet their basic needs, reflected in indicators of relative and absolute poverty.[7]

Some of these indicators point to the contraction of the industrial sector as a base for formal employment—fewer well-paid, full-time industrial workers. In Brazil, for example, at least 897,000 formal sector jobs were lost over the course of Cardoso's first term in office from 1994–1998. These labour-related indicators also stem from a gradual but persistent rise in the rate of unemployment, from 6 per cent to 8 per cent nationally over the course of Cardoso's two terms in office, and increasing up to 20.3 per cent in the ABC region of Sao Paulo (SEADE, 2000). In Argentina, this pattern was particularly dramatic—with unemployment rates rising from 6 to 8 per cent at the beginning of the 1990s, but increasing to 18.4 per cent at the end of the decade and 20 per cent by mid 2001. In addition, Latin America experienced a persistent increase in informal work relations and conditions during the 1990s. In Brazil, the region's largest economy, the informal sector rose from 36 per cent of the labour force in 1990 to 53 per cent in 2000, an increase of 34 per cent in just 10 years (*Folha do S. Paulo*, May 23, 2000: 9A; SEADE, 2000).[8] As Cibils, Weisbrot, and Kar (2000) have shown, the statistics on these "developments" have been even more striking in Argentina, with estimated rates of unemployment that have reached 60 per cent in some parts of Gran Buenos Aires and a dramatic spread and depth of income poverty.

As for social exclusion from lack of access to health, education, and social security programs, the statistics are staggering. ECLAC, the ILO, and a host of university-based researchers have documented a regional pattern of reduced coverage and deteriorating conditions (ECLAC, 1998; ILO, 2000).

Other income-based or related indicators of widespread social exclusion include a persistent decrease in labour's share of national income (as well as its reduced value to production); reduced real value of wages; and an increasingly unequal distribution of household incomes, as well as more poverty, both relative and absolute. Statistics show a rise in crime and other forms of social disorganization, reflecting this inequality and poverty.

The Condition of Labour: Forms of Social Exclusion

In Cardoso's first term in office, employment in the industrial sector fell by 22 per cent and 30 per cent in the capital goods and consumer or wage goods sectors respectively. As noted above, this contraction in industrial employment corresponded to a process of growth in the value of output. This simultaneous growth in output and decline in employment is a clear indicator of both technological conversion and a sloughing off of labour, a downsizing of the workforce without technological conversion. Notwithstanding reduced inputs of labour and capital under this double restructuring process, the GNP did increase. However, as in other countries that exhibited the same trend, such as Argentina, labour received no part of this productivity gain; virtually 100 per cent of it was appropriated by capital. In fact, while wages over the period in question (1994–1998) showed an accumulated increase of 11 per cent per worker, this increase constituted a decrease of 15 per cent in the mass of accumulated wages. Over the whole decade, this decline was in the order of 40 per cent, paralleling Argentina, Mexico, and elsewhere. In Brazil, despite a recovery and upsurge in the GDP, total national income in the form of wages fell by 7.7 per cent in 1997 (Lozano et al., 2006). In Argentina at the same time, economic production slumped and then entered a four-year period of sluggish growth and decline, reaching crisis proportions at the turn of the millennium and leading to an increase in unemployment and a decline in the share of wages in national income. These developments in the region reduced the share of labour in national income overall. Clearly, this is a long-term, region-wide trend, but it is particularly accentuated in Brazil, where after a decade of state-led "market-friendly" reforms, labour received only 34 per cent of national income—versus almost 70 per cent in the late 1950s (*Jornal Sem Terra*, XX, No. 117, January 2002: 15). The bulk of this income accrued to capital in one form or another.

The above data suggest that labour has borne the brunt of the adjustment and reform process in the 1980s and, in the case of both Menem's Argentina and Cardoso's Brazil, in the 1990s. Income data show the same thing. For example, during the period of rapid growth in overall and industrial output in the 1960s, social inequalities in the distribution of national income, already among the very worst in the world, significantly increased and the owners of capital and the top income earners appropriated the lion's share of income growth. In the 1970s, in a different context of sluggish growth, these inequalities further increased, as they did again in the 1980s during a region-wide debt crisis and recession. In the 1990s, under the regimes of Collor and Cardoso in Brazil, Zedillo in Mexico, and Menem in Argentina, neo-liberal destabilization measures and policies of structural adjustment exacerbated the social inequality and inequity in national income distribution to the point that UNDP named Brazil as one of only three countries (along with Sierra Leone and Guatemala) in which disparities in the distribution of wealth and income constitute a serious barrier to economic development. Income distribution is not much better in other countries in the region: Latin America exhibits a rate of income disparity that is at least twice the rate found in any other region in the world (Bulmer-Thomas, 1996). In the region as a whole, the richest tenth of the population receives or appropriates 40 per cent of overall income, while the poorest 30 per cent receives only 7.5 per cent (United Nations 2005). The income share of the richest 20 per cent of households compared to the poorest 20 per cent of income earners in Latin America is 22 to 1, twice that of the next regional ratio of 11 to 1 in sub-Saharan Africa and three times the rate of 7 to 1 in the industrial countries.

Recent studies (IDB, 1998) show that the top 10 per cent of income earners in Brazil appropriate close to 50 per cent of the national income, leaving but 7 per cent for the bottom 40 per cent of income earners, most of whom are income poor. In Mexico, according to the National Statistics Agency (*Instituto Nacional de Estadística, Geografía e Informática,* or INEGI) and the Bank of Mexico, the poorest decile of households in 1984 received only 1.7 per cent of national income, a share that was reduced to 1.6 per cent by 1989 and 1.5 per cent in 1992 (Saxe-Fernández, 1994: 333). At the same time, the share of the richest decile of families rose from 32.8 per cent in 1984 to 37.9 per cent in 1989 and 38.2 per cent in 1992.

The distribution of income in the 1990s was even worse than in the 1980s, after two decades of rapid growth under the old economic model. Brazil has the highest index of income concentration in the world, according to researchers at the *Instituto del Tercer Mundo* (Roque and Corrêa, 2001), an NGO watchdog system that monitors the commitments governments made at the World Summit for Social Development. This disparity, they add, "has increased systematically.... Today it is much higher than in the first half of the 1980s" (2001: 2).[9] The income of the richest 10 per cent is nearly 30 times that of the poorest 40 per cent (Roque and Corrêa, 2001). While official government statistics indicate that the overall incidence of poverty decreased marginally under Cardoso, the depressingly high degree of income disparity increased. And, of course, this disparity is not just the unequal distribution of productive resources and wealth; it reflects the highly concentrated incomes in the banks and corporations, the big economic groups of the bourgeoisie (Basualdo, 2001).

According to the World Bank (1998), only Sierra Leone has a higher Gini coefficient than Brazil, which points to a staggering degree of social inequality in the distribution of productive resources and income. The source of this disparity includes growing unemployment; fewer opportunities for formal sector employment and a burgeoning informal sector; a trend toward wage dispersal (deviation from the mean), a major contributing factor in the 1990s according to ECLAC; a dramatic fall in the value of the minimum wage and an increase in the number of workers remunerated at or below this rate; and a decline in the level of social wages: benefits channelled through government social programs.

Under these and other structural and policy conditions of social exclusion, only some of which predate the neo-liberal regimes in the 1990s, the number of poor in Latin America increased from 106 million in the early 1990s to 129 million a decade later—an increase of 18 per cent.[10] The poverty rate tends to be higher in the rural sector than in the urban centres despite the massive exodus of the rural poor to the cities and abroad In this connection it is estimated that up to 70 per cent of the rural population across Latin America is either landless or suffering from conditions of social exclusion, separated from any means of production and the labour market, and excluded from the income and other benefits associated with the national development process (ECLAC 1998; Jazairy, et al., 1992).[11]

Up to 70 million in Brazil alone can be defined as poor on the basis of the World Bank's new international poverty line, set arbitrarily at the ridiculously low income threshold of $2 a day or $60 a month (World Bank, 1998).[12]

In fact, one of every four (23.6 per cent) Latin Americans fall below even the World Bank's conservative measure of extreme poverty, set as $1 a day or $30 a month.[13] The Brazilian government's own economists calculate that over one half of the country's labour force barely earn the minimum wage of $77 a month or, for the millions working off the books, even less. Despite the efforts of the Cardoso regime to put a favourable gloss on its social policies, and the highly publicized and much-vaunted anti-poverty campaign initiated by Betinho de Souza and supported by the government, this situation represented a clear deterioration relative to earlier administrations. The January 2000 currency devaluation, combined with reduced social expenditures (a huge budget cut of $1 billion in May alone), made this situation even worse, pushing millions of workers and their households below the poverty line overnight, able to make ends meet only under the greatest duress. Today, some five years later, the situation has changed very little, notwithstanding the governing Workers' Party (PT) announcement of a major new offensive in the war against poverty. In Argentina, once the richest and most highly developed country in Latin America, the situation is even more desperate: a large and growing part of the working class now finds itself in dire straits, while a substantial part of the once large and powerful middle class has joined the ranks of the poor.

CAPITALIST DEVELOPMENT AND THE SEARCH FOR ALTERNATIVES

Neo-liberal capitalist development is profoundly exclusionary, but it has also tended to generate powerful forces of opposition and resistance. In fact, it is difficult today to find strong advocates of the neo-liberal model. Even Michel Camdessus, former executive director of the IMF, a key institution in the design and implementation of this model, has backed away from neo-liberalism. According to Camdessus, despite the barrage of criticism levelled against the IMF—even by George Soros, Salinas de Gortieri, Jeffrey Sachs, Joseph Stiglitz and other architects of capitalist development and self-appointed guardians of the new world order—it is not (or is no longer) neo-liberal in its orientation and policy advice. Its policies, he argues, have three main pillars: 1) the *invisible hand of the market*, the most efficient mechanism for allocating resources to factors of production according to neo-classical theory; 2) the *visible hand of the state*, the basic agency for economic development according to the proponents of structuralism and neo-structuralism; and, more enigmatical and highly problematic, 3) *the solidarity between the rich and the poor*. In fact, it could be argued that the neo-liberal model is staked out in the front lines of the class war between capital and labour (and the contentious arena of politics and ideology) as a false target, one that *no one* is prepared to defend but that allows the guardians of the capitalist world order to reposition themselves—to find a more defensible and sustainable form of capitalist development.

In light of current proposals for redesigning the model of capitalist development, three major variations on the theme of alternative development can be identified. First, there is the neo-structuralist model advanced by ECLAC (see Sunkel, 1993), outlined in chapter 2 and reviewed below. Secondly, there are models for another development initiated "from below and inside," rather than "from above and outside," that is equitable and socially inclusive, human in form and scale, people-led or centred, empowering, and sustainable for the environment and livelihoods. Many models are based on a broad commitment to these principles and the agency of non-governmental and grassroots organizations—the strengthening of civil society.[14] Thirdly, a number of proposals or projects for change and development move in the direction of social inclusion and cohesion based on the agency of anti-systemic social movements and direct action.

A Critical Look at ECLAC

The ECLAC model, *Productive Transformation with Equity* (1990), was advanced as an alternative to neo-liberalism. Accordingly, it was designed to broaden the social base of the production process, to incorporate rather than exclude diverse sectors and units of economic activity, including informal sector enterprises and activities within what Luis Razeto (1988, 1993), a Chilean economist connected to the ILO, defined as the "economy of solidarity." The primary mechanism for broadening the base of productive economic activity was to create a more participatory and socially inclusive form of development by decentralizing government decision-making (Boisier, 1987; Borja, 1989, 1987; Calderón, 1989; Garcia Delgado, et al., 1989; Laurelli and Rofman, 1989; Veltmeyer, 1997a). According to ECLAC (Boisier, et al., 1992), popular participation is the missing link in the productive transformation-equity chain within the development process: the means of ensuring "productive transformation with equity."

As ECLAC sees it, the issue is not just to secure a more equitable distribution of income and improve health, education, and welfare (matters of social justice and government action), but to ensure greater access to society's productive resources such as land, capital, and technology. In the neo-liberal model, the allocation of these productive resources and the distribution of income are left to the free market. However, armed with a neo-structuralist perspective and analytical framework, the ECLAC economists made the following arguments:

1. The market needs to be regulated for an optimum and equitable resource allocation.
2. Improved access to society's productive resources requires a measure of structural change and policy reform on the part of the government (land reform, rural credit schemes, etc.).
3. Poverty reduction if not eradication requires a new social policy, one that both targets the poor and involves them in decision-making.
4. A policy of social inclusion dictates a strengthening and extension, not a weakening and dismantling, of established government programs of health, education, and welfare.

The new social policy was designed in collaboration with the economists at the World Bank and broadly implemented in the 1990s. Whereas the old social policy was universal in its orientation and coverage, the new social policy took an investment rather than an expenditure approach. Rather than being universal, it was targeted (*focalizado*) at the poor, and focused on health and education, the pillars of social inclusion. It was based on a partnership approach to reducing and alleviating poverty, as well as decentralizing decision-making.

The new social policy was widely implemented by governments across the region, most particularly Bolivia, Chile, and Mexico. This is reflected in the large volume of evaluative and assessment literature on both the conditions of social exclusion and the policy itself (Veltmeyer and O'Malley, 2001). There is some evidence that the numbers of poor have been reduced in Chile and their conditions of poverty somewhat alleviated, but their social exclusion remains unchanged. Other than this possible exception, the ECLAC model in practice has not yielded any substantial change or benefits to the poor. There are a number of apparent reasons for this, all of them studiously evaded in the assessments and evaluations commissioned by international development or UN organizations such as UNDP and ECLAC itself.

One reason for the general failure of the ECLAC model is that it endeavours to create a more humane form of the structural adjustment and stabilization policies mandated by the IMF and the World Bank. But despite its attempt to put a social dimension and a human face to the whole process, the model is still predicated on policy measures that have been shown to generate and exacerbate the problems of poverty and social exclusion.[15] A second reason the ECLAC model failed to bring about any substantive improvements in the lives of the poor is that its implementation has been based on a nefarious deal with the World Bank and other IFIs, such as the IDB, to limit or avoid any significant structural change. It is clear enough to most people that development is predicated on such change. For example, any significant improvement in the lives of the poor requires more than expenditures on social programs or investments in resources made available by the poor themselves: their social capital.[16] What is required, first of all, is a significant change in the ownership and distribution of natural productive resources, such as land; and secondly, improved access to capital and technology and other such productive resources that are social but have been privately appropriated.

Both these and other changes, however, require a confrontation with the power structure—the political and economic power of the local or national elite. The effective deal between national governments and the World Bank (along with other agents of global capital and international development) was to increase the participation of the poor in decision-making, but to limit this participation to decisions that are local. For example, they could share in decisions about how to spend the poverty alleviation funds or to design local development projects. The deal also stipulated a non-confrontational approach to change, based not on direct action but on dialogue, negotiation, and use of the market and electoral mechanisms (UNRISD, 2000). Of course, the non-governmental organizations that litter the landscape of Latin America's increasingly active and mobilized civil society have been the often-unwitting partners in this form of participatory development—its executing agents (Petras and Veltmeyer, 2001).

The Search for Another Development

In the 1990s, the search for "another development" (AD) became a major social movement, involving NGOs that can now be numbered in the tens of thousands on a global scale. Today, in every region of the world and in many countries, it is possible to identify nodal points in the search for AD in the form of research groups, programs of activities, or journals that provide an outlet for collaborative research, programmatic statements, and news.

THE DEVELOPMENT DYNAMICS OF SOCIAL EXCLUSION

A Latin American example is *Instituto Intercultural para la Autogestión y la Acción Cultural* (INAUCO) and its journal, *Revista Iberoamericana de Autogestión y Acción Comunal* (RIDAA), at the *Universidad Autónoma de Madrid*. Other examples include the Stockholm-based Dag Hammarskjold Foundation for Alternative Development and the journal *Development Dialogue* (both of which can be traced back to 1974 and constitute, in effect, a foundation stone in the movement); *Confederación Latinamericana de Cooperación y Mutuales de Trabajadores* (COLACOT) in Sante Fé de Bogota, Columbia; *Equipo Pueblo* in Mexico City; the International Foundation for Development Alternatives (IFDA) and its IFDA *Dossier*; and several operational agencies of the United Nations, in particular the United Nations Research Institute for Social Development (UNRISD), whose conferences and publications over the years have been instrumental in propagating the idea of a community-based, socially inclusive, and participatory form of sustainable development.

AD takes diverse forms. One of the earliest is associated with the ideas of Manfred Max-Neef, a Chilean economist whose reflections on human-scale development (*La economia descalza*, 1986) are an important reference-point in the search for a more socially inclusive form of development. A different form of AD is associated with another Chilean economist, Luis Razeto (1988, 1993), connected to the ILO's Regional Program on Employment (PREALC). Roberto Guimarães is a Latin American scholar and Brazilian economist who has also made a significant contribution towards AD. A series of studies commissioned by UNRISD, coordinated by the Colombian theorist of social action Fals Borda and published in 1974, presented a critical departure point for Guimarães and others on the Latin American experience with co-operativism. On the basis of extensive field research and case studies, these reports concluded that co-operatives generally were an ineffective form of organization to meet the basic needs of the poor and were unsuccessful as agencies for social transformation. The general conclusion reached by the UNRISD team, and supported by Guimarães, who now works with ECLAC, can be summed up in four statements:

1. Co-operatives are not agents for change, producing few benefits for the poorest sectors of the population; indeed, the strengthening of co-operatives in most places led to an unexplained increase in income gaps.
2. Co-operatives tend to reproduce the structure of community relations and conditions, rather than transform it.

3. They tend to reinforce, as well as extend and deepen, pre-existing social inequalities, partly because groups and individuals who are accommodated to the power structure are more likely to control the key committees and the administration of co-ops.
4. In the few cases where co-ops actually were composed of poor peasants and represented their interests, they were manifestly incapable of promoting those interests (Guimarães, 1989, 285–86).

A central notion in AD is that participation is a source of empowerment and social inclusion (Goulet, 1989; Oakley, 1991; UNICEF, 1989). The term *participation* first appeared in development discourse in the late 1950s. At the time, development practitioners began to notice that common people were almost completely excluded from the formulation and implementation of development projects. They thought that the inclusion of local people would increase efficiency and lead to improved development. This attitude towards participation is now widely accepted by most NGOs, development workers, and even governments. In fact, these days it is taken as a matter of principle in the design and execution of development projects, as well as the process as a whole. Thus, participation serves as a primary tool for project evaluation by the World Bank and other donors and aid agencies. Blaikie (1985) adds the following gloss on this point: "When joined with the processes of political democratization, it is not surprising that the international community is looking to 'participation' as a means of making their development projects function better, helping people cope ... [and] as an indispensable dimension of ... policies ... that can no longer be evaded or postponed."

However, the notion of participation has turned out to be contentious. In one view associated with the World Bank, participation is not so much an alternative form of development that is socially inclusive, empowering, and transformative as it is a means of ensuring greater efficiency and cost effectiveness in project design and implementation (Blaikie, 1985). With this view, the development agenda is predetermined, objectives are defined, and solutions are envisaged before local people come into the picture. In a second view, participation means that people are brought into the development process from the outset and are actively engaged in every phase. This perspective was initially aired by UNRISD and then widely disseminated at a number of their conferences in the 1970s and 1980s. However, it did not come into its own until the late 1980s, when for many practitioners and scholars, it displaced the old paradigm of the World Bank, ECLAC, and other such mainstream development organizations.

The mainstream views governments, in partnership with NGOs, as the major executing agency for development. Therefore, they are primarily responsible for ensuring increased participation in the development process. From the perspective of AD, however, participatory development is not seen as a strategy to be implemented from above and the outside, but instead from below and within, with the agency of community-based or grassroots social organizations. In this view, people need to be incorporated into the development process front and centre, from the outset, to define the problem, identify possible solutions, and finally, take action. Participatory development (PD) is viewed not as a *project* but as a *process*, designed to bring about a decentralized, non-authoritarian, and democratic form of development that is not only socially inclusive, but sustainable and based on a sense of real community.

The Sustainable Livelihoods Approach (SLA)

The international development community has set out to reduce by half the number of people living in extreme poverty, many of them in rural societies, by 2015. Over half way into the first decade of the new millennium, the world is far from achieving that target. In fact, the number of poor people has increased in recent decades, as has the global divide in incomes and living standards. As early as 1973, the World Bank recognized that alleviating, if not the eradicating, extreme poverty is the major challenge confronting the world community of development agencies and practitioners. Later, this goal was placed front and centre of the new development agenda set by these agencies in the 1990s (see World Bank, 1990). However, despite almost two decades of work using diverse strategies to reduce it, the problem of extreme poverty persists. Nor has there been an improvement in the problem of relative poverty: the growing numbers of those unable to meet their basic needs. Whether absolute or relative, poverty is the most critical factor of social exclusion.

Social exclusion is viewed by all proponents of AD as the basic problem. However, none of its proponents could design any specific strategies for addressing poverty at its roots, reducing its incidence, or eradicating rather than merely alleviating its worst conditions. In Latin America, it is difficult to find any "best practice" cases of AD that have successfully translated theory into practice, despite many diverse experiments with community-based forms of development from below and views to the contrary. Each of these experiments has failed to address the problem of social exclusion and poverty in a systematic way, to formulate an effective strategy for overcoming the problem—a strategy that takes into account relations of economic and political power, and the local impact of outside forces (e.g., globalization). This is where the sustainable livelihoods approach (SLA) comes in.

Using ideas advanced by Robert Chambers (1997) among others and adapted by CUT, the UK Department for International Development (DFID), the UNDP, and the Society for International Development (SID) have responded to this situation by advocating a new sustainable livelihoods approach to achieving a more socially inclusive form of development. The essence of SLA is to place local and community-based development within the context of conditions created by "external" structures, agencies, and processes. The focus is to analyze and act on how these structures and processes have affected the "livelihood assets" of the community—their capacity to generate financial, social, human, natural, and physical capital (Amalric, 1998).

SLA also aims to identify the forms of action that can minimize the negative effects of the external processes and transform them. It has focused attention on associations—producer groups, co-operatives, and community-based organizations of various sorts. In the course of examining experiments with local development all over the world, these organizations have been identified as having the greatest potential for achieving *social empowerment*—a process in which individuals and groups within a community learn to interact with one another in a constructive manner, co-operate towards a common objective (identifying and addressing their problems), and undertake the collective action needed for social transformation and economic development.[17]

Recently, this empowering process has been viewed as a strategic way to build on the assets of the poor, their capacity to organize and network and for collective action (see chapter 3). In the discourse of recent development theorists and practitioners, at issue is "social capital," which in theory can be constructed without the accumulation and expenditure of financial capital—hitherto always regarded as *the* driving force of the development process. Even better, from various points of view, is that social capital in theory can be built without any major structural change and without confronting those who occupy positions of power in the society.

The SLA model is structured around the five "productive resources" or livelihood assets: natural, physical, financial, social, and political (Almaric,

1998). The first three of these assets, however, are central to all development theories and models to date, and the proponents of SLA do not advance any new ideas about how to distribute them more efficiently and equitably, or improve access to them. Incorporating these three factors of production into the development process has defeated all theorists and practitioners to date, largely because it requires radical structural change, which is difficult to come by. Within mainstream development thought and practice, in both the old paradigm and the new, the approach has always been reform; this is, change that does not confront or challenge the power structure or allow for any substantive shifts in the situation of the poor, who are excluded from economic and political power. So, SLA focuses on assets that, it is argued, the poor have in abundance and that are not predicated on major structural change or government policy.

An increasing number of development projects, especially in rural areas, are designed on the basis of SLA. Above all, these projects are concerned with building social capital, without any specific strategies for securing the redistribution of, or improving access to, the other productive resources that are recognized as essential to the development process and the securing of sustainable livelihoods. In effect, development agents operate within the community, using support (poverty alleviation or social investment funds) from outside agencies, in participation with grassroots organizations in the community or the broader civil society.

CONCLUSION

SLA represents a cutting edge of change in alternative thinking and practice within mainstream development theory. The ECLAC model still has considerable weight in government and policy-making circles, but in Latin America, there is a growing anti-globalization movement based on a global civil society and oriented towards a more radical alternative to neo-liberalism, a more ethical, human, and equitable form of capitalist development. In this context, SLA has a number of attractions and advantages for mainstream development over ECLAC. For one thing, it is based on initiatives taken from below, at the grassroots level, as well as from within. For another, SLA provides a better counterweight to growing pressures for more radical or revolutionary change. In addition, SLA does not break with the system; nor does it entail a direct or violent confrontation with the power structure. This is an attractive option for both liberals and the social left, oriented towards a new way of doing politics—bringing about social change.

On the other hand, SLA can be criticized from a number of standpoints. For one, the social capital built in the process of the development project cycle has no solid foundation because it is isolated from structural change and government action. Another is that building social capital does not empower the groups and individuals involved. As the UNDP has finally acknowledged in its 2001 *Human Development Report*, the building of social capital does not in and of itself lead to social transformation, a prerequisite for a more socially inclusive form of alternative development. Not only does social transformation require a fundamental redistribution of natural, physical, and financial forms of capital along with an accumulation of social capital, it also requires political capital—people's accumulated capacity to make decisions about conditions that shape their livelihoods. As political economists in the radical tradition have argued for decades—and as even noted by the UNDP (2003: v), an advocate of reform in the direction of greater equity and human development—social change requires political power.

Since the conditions of political power originate in forces and structures outside the local community, and since decision-making power tends to be highly concentrated and centralized in elites, social empowerment of the poor dictates a relative disempowerment of the rich and the powerful few. Power-sharing ("solidarity between the rich and the poor") cannot be achieved unless the rich and powerful surrender their disproportionate portion of economic and political control. The solution currently offered to the poor by all modalities of the development project (World Bank, ECLAC, AD, and SLA) is to participate in decision-making regarding local development: how and where to spend the poverty alleviation funds. It will not work. It is both inadequate and unacceptable. It is clear that the rich and powerful are not likely to surrender or negotiate any effective sharing of their real power.

Thus, states, or at least governments, will have to instigate the structural changes required for a more equitable[18] redistribution of society's natural, physical, and financial resources. Indeed, this is the implication of the UNDP's conclusion that what the poor need, above all else, is *political power*—the capacity to make, participate in, and influence those decisions that determine their lives and affect their livelihoods. Given that this power is highly concentrated, and given also the dominant position of a country's economic elite in the institutions of the state—and the corresponding exclusion of the direct producers and working class—this is not likely to happen without a protracted political struggle of opposing forces.

The conclusion is inescapable, even though neither ECLAC, the UNDP, nor other exponents of the new paradigm is willing to accept it. If governments refuse to act towards substantive change in the structure of economic activity and political power, the only alternative is for people to take direct collective action themselves. This is the road currently taken by the social movements of oppositional and anti-systemic forces that dominate the political landscape in Latin America today. This is a topic for chapter 8.

NOTES

1 The term *social exclusion* (Stiefel and Wolfe, 1994) carries with it some of the connotations of the term *marginality* in former years. In the 1960s and 1970s, the concept of marginality denoted the existence of a mass of labour-power that was surplus to the requirements of capitalist development and that in Marxist terms constituted an industrial reserve army. In the 1990s, a number of analysts have turned towards the term *social exclusion* to essentially describe the same and other associated social conditions (Escoral, 1996; Freund in the preface to Xiberras, 1996: 12). In their use of the concept, they reached back to the earlier studies such as Castel (1995), Paugam (1994; 1996), and Nascimento (1994), possibly the first to use the term in the sense of marginality. More recently, the ECLAC and ILO scholars Stiefel and Wolfe (1994) and Xiberras (1996), among others, have expanded on the notion of social exclusion in terms of more general sociological processes and conditions of exclusion from participation in the economic, social, and political institutions of the broader society, i.e., lack of participation in the benefits of the development and modernization process. In this context, Stiefel and Wolfe (1994) treat social exclusion as "a process that involves the trajectory of vulnerability, fragility, and precariousness, a breaking of ties along [diverse] dimensions of human existence—work, socio-familiar, cultural, and human."

2 On this model see, inter alia, Bulmer-Thomas (1996); Veltmeyer and Petras (1997, 2000); Petras and Veltmeyer (2001).

3 At the colloquium organized at Roskilde University as part of the UN World Social Summit in Copenhagen (1995), a number of panelists highlighted the centrality of the notion of social exclusion for understanding the poverty and other conditions lived by a large and growing part of the world population in the new global context of deepening income disparities, liberalization and globalization of economic activity, the increased reliance on market forces, and the retreat of the nation-state from responsibilities for economic development and social welfare (see Benner, 1995, for a synthesis of these considerations and conclusions). In an analysis of the social crisis created by these conditions, panelists argued that the conditions of social exclusion and poverty, attributed to "the mutations of the 1980s" and

analyzed generally by sociologists, have displaced those of exploitation, a concept favoured by economists.

4   Given the large array of international organizations and research institutions, both within the UN system and the international development community involved in the war against poverty and the broader conditions of social exclusion, it is clear that the problem has not only reached critical proportions but that it is global in scope. One of many organizations set up in the search for solutions to the problem of social exclusion is the Research Centre for Analysis of Social Exclusion (CASE), established in October 1997 at the London School of Economics (LSE) with funding from the UK Economic and Social Research Council.

5   While Brazil led Latin America in annualized rates of growth throughout the 1950s, 1960s and 1970s (from 6.8 to 8.7 per cent versus 4.8 to 4.9 per cent) and even in the 1980s, Brazil's annual growth rate was barely two-thirds of the Latin American growth rate in the 1990s.

6   According to Rodgers, Gore, and Figueiredo (1995), the concept of social exclusion captures the form and content of the interaction between economic restructuring and a society's social institutions; thus, they can be identified in both the worlds of work and family life.

7   A poverty-oriented basic needs approach dominated the study of international development in the 1970s. It originated in the 1973 discovery by the World Bank that upwards of two-fifths of the world's population was in a state of relative deprivation, unable to meet its basic needs. According to Amartya Sen (1989), a household without sufficient income to meet the basic needs of its members is poor, a condition that can be measured in terms of a head count; that is, the number and percentage of the population that falls below a defined income poverty line. Another measure of the gap in income distribution is to multiply the income gap ratio by the number of the poor, which provides a coefficient of specific poverty.

8   Official statistics compiled by IGBE show considerably lower rates of unemployment, but most observers take as more reliable the statistics compiled by the Departamento Intersindical de estadístico e Estudos Sócio-económicos of SEADE (*Fundação Sistema Estadual de Análise de Dados*).

9   As for the incidence of poverty, at the bottom end of this income distribution, the relevant index peaked in 1994–95 during the initial implementation of the *Plano Real*, but even though the poverty index in subsequent years (1996–97) for which data are available is somewhat lower than the indices for 1994, it is still higher than the indices for 1993 (Roque and Corrêa, 2001: 1). And, the authors note, a similar pattern exists for wealth distribution indicators.

10 In this connection, Mexico's experience shows that it is possible to reduce the incidence of poverty while social inequality in asset and income distribution increases. In Mexico, between 2000 and mid 2005, the poverty rate fell 6 per cent in regard to income and 6.1 per cent for the non-income dimension of poverty (education, health, housing, clothing, transportation). In 2000, 53.8 per cent of Mexicans were unable meet their basis needs in these areas; in 2005 the rate of poverty so defined fell 6.1 per cent, affecting 47.7 per cent of the population. However, the World Bank notes, at the same time as this "significant reduction" in the rate of poverty, particularly in the rural area (a pattern noted for all of Latin America), social inequalities in the distribution of assets and income generally increased, a problem that Isabel Guerrero, director of the World Bank for Mexico and Colombia, attributes to an over-concentration of market power (Gonzalez and Vargas, 2005).

11 According to IFAD (Jazairy, et al., 1992), there are at least 10 distinct processes responsible for the production of rural poverty, all of them clearly in evidence in rural Brazil.

12 In the first month of 2000, still in the throes or wake of a severe financial crisis, the Brazilian government under Cardoso engaged in a public squabble with the IMF over the government's announced plan to spend US$22 billion on poverty-oriented social programs over the next decade (Rohter, 2000). The IMF insisted that the government should use these funds, on part dependent on the $41.5 billion rescue package provided by the IMF in November 1998, to reduce the country's external debt rather than fight poverty.

13 The government of Argentina, until recently (before the latest drawn out economic crisis) the wealthiest country in the region with the highest per capita incomes, has formally recognized that 51.4 per cent of the population, 18.2 million people, now fall below the poverty line (*Clarin*, June 10, 2002). This includes from one-third to one-half of what was once Latin America's largest and most powerful middle class. This class now constitutes a significant part of what the National Statistics Institute terms "the new poor."

14 On these models, see Veltmeyer and O'Malley (2001).

15 Osvaldo Sunkel, an ECLAC economist at the time and a major architect of Latin American neo-structuralism (2003), back in 1989 commented to the author on the intended theoretical (and policy) convergence between the two schools of development thinking, one represented best by the World Bank, the other by ECLAC, which for over thirty years had led the opposition to liberalism and neo-liberalism within the development community.

16 On this notion of social capital and its application to the development process, see Coleman (1988); Knack (1999); Portes and Landolt (1996); Rubio (1997); Woolcock and Narayan (2000); Woolcock (1988).

17 On the various dimensions of SLA, the most recent formulation of AD, see Chambers (1997) and Liamzon, et al. (1996).

18 Not "equitable" in the sense given the term by the World Bank, namely, "equality of opportunity," but in the sense of social justice.

SIX

Rural Struggles and the Land Question

Rural movements for social change in Latin America have always revolved around landlessness or near-landlessness, a central problem that began when direct producers were separated from their means of social production. In more historically specific terms, this means that peasant farmers were driven from their land, and others expropriated it. The problem of landlessness has also been posed as a matter of land hunger and cultural identity: peasants and other rural producers and workers need to be reconnected to the land as a source not only of productive activity, but of everything that gives meaning to their lives. For governments, the question of land is one of land reform; for the rural producers, indigenous communities, and peasant farmers, it is often a question of land invasion or occupation; and for rural development practitioners armed with a model of sustainable rural livelihoods, it is a question of how the rural poor can overcome their social exclusion and improve their access to means of production.

The dynamics of land reform are very complex and can best be understood in political terms; that is, a protracted struggle of peasant farmers and other rural groups for land and land reform, the reaction of the landholders to this struggle, and the workings of the state. This chapter will place the dynamics of rural struggle over land in Latin America in historical and political perspective. For example, the strategy of land occupations pursued by organizations such as Brazil's rural Landless Workers Movement (*Movimento dos Trabalhadores Rurais Sem Terra*, or MST) includes a tactic of class struggle and direct collective action, a fundamental strategy for gaining access to land.

Guided by this perspective of the dynamics of land occupations, the chapter is divided into two parts. First, the class struggle involved in land occupations is reviewed in historical terms. Then, we turn to three basic, more recent, paths towards reform; that is, since the Cuban Revolution in

1959. The Cuban Revolution created an entirely new context for a new wave of revolutionary movements in the countryside of Latin America (urban land invasions and the occupation of unused land on the peripheries of the cities) and a new cycle of state-led land reforms. These "developments," along with the widely implemented new economic model and process of democratization, set the stage for another wave of peasant-led grassroots revolutionary movements, as well as a new twist in the land reform program—a transition from a state-led to a new market-assisted plan.

Some analysts view this transition as the death of land reforms. We see it differently as a new take on the political option presented by the bilateral and multi-lateral institutions that provide overseas development assistance to a new generation of peasant producers. The tactic of land occupations adopted by social movements of landless workers today acquires its political significance in the context of this approach by the World Bank.

LANDLESSNESS AND RURAL POVERTY: THE PEASANTRY AND THE STATE

The capitalist mode of production, as Marx analyzed so well in Europe, is predicated on a process of "primitive accumulation" designed to create a group for hire, a wage-labouring class. Historically, this process of primitive accumulation meant separating the direct producers from their means of production, usually in the form of the violent seizure of native communal landholdings. As Marx saw it, this process allowed money accumulated through mercantile trade, pillage, theft, enslavement of Amerindians, and other ways, to be converted into capital, and allowed various modes of pre-capitalist production to be transformed into capitalism. In what would emerge as the New World of the Americas, this process can be traced back some 500 years to the beginning of an extended period of colonial rule, when pre-capitalist and pre-colonial indigenous societies were rather abruptly destroyed and transformed into proto-capitalist, class-divided, and dominated versions of transplanted European societies.

The period of colonial rule—from the so-called discovery of the new world in the fifteenth century and the "conquest" of the indigenous population, until the movement toward national independence in the nineteenth century—is a history of land expropriation and primitive accumulation. However, there is another side to this history. From the outset, this process met with widespread resistance. The peasantry, who were the major social and political force in the largely rural society, instigated numerous outbreaks of rebellion, including land occupation. The state responded with agrarian reform laws that consolidated the gains achieved by the peasantry during their land occupation. A major case was the rebellion of Túpac Amaru II in the late-eighteenth century and the subsequent land reform laws of the 1820s (Jacobsen, 1993).

In the aftermath of the national independence movements, various forms of class struggle developed in the newly independent or self-proclaimed nation-states. Throughout eighteenth- and early nineteenth-century Peru, Haiti, and Mexico, the enslaved, indentured, and semi-proletarianized rural workers (most of whom self-identified as peasant farmers) challenged the power of the colonial state. In the late colonial or post-colonial liberal reform period in El Salvador, Honduras, Nicaragua, and Guatemala, the rebellious peasants, indigenous peoples, and landless rural workers protested state actions that favoured the semi-feudal landed oligarchy. The state responded by instituting repressive legislative and policy and measures to squash their labour unrest and keep them under the control of the big landowners (*latifundists*) (Wheelock Román, 1975; Gould, 1983; Amador, 1990: Mahoney, 2001).

For the small landed oligarchy, land—the basic productive resource—was the source of their personal fortune, privilege, and power. But for the vast majority of workers, producers, and indigenous communities, land was their primary source of *livelihood*. This struggle pitted the semi-feudal landed propertied class, with their preponderant political influence over the state, against a rural population largely composed of peasants and serfs, a vast proletariat of landless or near-landless rural workers, and indigenous communities of peasant producers. The semi-feudal or mercantile propertied class (the landed oligarchy) were in a position to control not only the government of the day, but other parts of the state as well, such as the judiciary and the security apparatus (the police and the military), all of which came into play in the land dispute (Harris, et al., 1978; Lindqvist, 1979; Orlove and Custred, 1980; Vilas, 1995). On the other side of this struggle, organized groups of peasants and a large semi-proletariat used all the weapons and tactics at their disposal, notably land occupations and direct actions against the holders of political and economic power or their agents (Fogel, 1986; Foley, 1991; Heath, 1969; F. Katz, 1988; LeGrand, 1983; Loveman, 1976; Horton, 1998). Those engaged in this resistance were involved in diverse relations of production. They ranged from enslaved plantation workers to producers enserfed under the production relations of the *encomienda* system (land tenancy, debt peonage, indentured servitude, labour rents); from sharecroppers to a semi-proletariat of seasonal rural workers and subsistence farmers; and from a rural proletariat of landless workers to indigenous communities of peasant farmers.

The land struggle took different forms in different places, and engaged various groups of "peasants" whose struggles were generally sporadic and localized. As yet, there has not been any systematic study into the class dynamics of these struggles (e.g., which groups participated, how, and under what conditions), but it is clear enough that diverse types and groups of peasants and landless rural workers joined the rebellion at various times and in different circumstances. The tendency was encapsulated by the Mexican Revolution in the second decade of the twentieth century, in which peasants and indigenous communities won rights to large tracts of land that had been expropriated from them. The Mexican Revolution was also a watershed in peasant–state relations throughout Latin America.

In the wake of the Mexican Revolution (and the October Revolution in Russia) and under pressure for more revolutionary change, the state in Latin America reoriented itself towards programs of land reform, designed to not only improve access to land for various categories of landless or near-landless peasants, but also to keep the social peace.

In the 1930s, significant peasant-based mass movements emerged in Mexico, El Salvador, Nicaragua, Colombia, Brazil, and Peru. At the same time, rural workers, particularly sugar workers in modern plantations in Cuba, the Dominican Republic, and Puerto Rico, as well as in Guyana and elsewhere in the Caribbean, engaged in class warfare. In each instance, the state took extremely violent and repressive measures either to suppress or to destroy these rural rebellions. (However, in the exceptional case of Mexico under Lázaro Cárdenas, agrarian reform was extended to include hundreds of thousands of poor rural families.) In El Salvador, the peasant uprising was crushed and some 30,000 were killed; a similar event occurred in Ecuador, under almost identical circumstances and with the same devastating effects on the incipient class struggle. In Nicaragua, the Dominican Republic, and Cuba, the US occupation army and its newly anointed tyrant-presidents—Anastasio Somoza, Rafael Leónidas Trujillo, and Fulgencio Batista slaughtered thousands, decimating the burgeoning peasant and rural workers' movements. In Brazil, the Getulio Vargas regime defeated Luís Carlos Prestes's rural-based guerrilla army, while pursuing a strategy of national industrialization; in Chile, the popular front of radicals, socialists, and communists aroused—and then abandoned—the peasant struggle, together with demanding agrarian reform in an implicit gentlemen's pact with the traditional landed oligarchy.

In the best of cases, peasant-based revolutions were able to secure institutional reforms in the agrarian sector; that is, land redistribution. These reforms often followed a period of de facto land occupation. The government, in effect, was compelled to legalize the status quo as well as dampen pressures for a more radical land redistribution. In Mexico, this process began in the early 1900s and reached its high point in the 1930s.

In the subsequent 50 years, particularly in the 1960s and 1970s, virtually all of the national governments in Latin America used the power of the state to alter the distribution of land for different categories of producers and households, and to redefine the right to land for those given access in the process. This happened regardless of the complexion of the regime in power. In 1952 in Bolivia, a revolution of miners and peasants led to sweeping agrarian reforms—the expropriation of most of the large estates (Beltrán and Fernández, 1960; Dandler, 1969; Dunkerley, 1984; Lora, 1964; Malloy and Thorn, 1971). In Cuba, the victory of Fidel Castro's 26th of July Movement in 1959 led to the confiscation of most of the US- and Cuban-owned plantations. The land was either collectivised or distributed to smallholders (MacEwan, 1981). Substantive land reforms also took place in Peru (from 1958 to 1974), Brazil (from 1962 to 1964), Chile (from 1966 to 1973), Ecuador (from 1964 to 1967), El Salvador (from 1980 to 1985), Guatemala (from 1952 to 1954, and again after the civil war following the peace accords), Honduras (in 1973), and Nicaragua (from 1979 to 1986). These reforms were state-led; but regardless of whether the state was authoritarian, military, liberal reformist, or proto-revolutionary, they were responding to mass peasant mobilizations and a general threat of social revolution (Blanco, 1972; Cotler, 1978; De Janvry, 1981; Kay, 1981, 1982; Midlarsky and Roberts, 1995; Vilas, 1995).

Rural and Urban Dynamics of Land Occupations

In spite of these efforts at land reform, many types of rural households remained—and still remain—landless or near-landless. As late as 1998, 90 per cent of all arable land in Latin America is concentrated in large holdings, in the hands of only 26 per cent of all farmers and representing the lion's share of total land and farm production. Since 1988, Brazil has undergone land reform programs from below and from above, as well as a rural exodus of staggering proportions: 30 million over the past 25 years. Still, 3 per cent of the population owns two-thirds of the country's arable land, and there are still upwards of 4.8 million families in rural areas without any access to land.

In addition, in Brazil and virtually every other country in the region, the majority of those who do have access to some land are barely able to eke out a subsistence-level existence, let alone make a commercial living. The smallest 50 per cent of all production units or "farms" in the region, with barely 2 per cent of the land, entail economically marginal operations, only allowing for the subsistence of the families that remain on the land.

In response to this highly unequal and unfair distribution of land, vast numbers of a dispossessed rural proletariat have been forced to migrate to the urban centres, causing one of the major upheavals and social transformations in modern times: capitalist development of urban-based economic activity and the transformation of a rural peasantry into an urban proletariat. Today, all countries in the region are at least 50 per cent urban in terms of residence and economic activity. Argentina and a number of places are over 80 per cent urban. One of the many consequences of this great transformation (industrialization, modernization, urbanization, and capitalist development) is that the land struggle has been transferred from the rural sector to the periphery of the new urban metropolises. This process was particularly pronounced in the 1960s and 1970s, when up to one-quarter of the rural population migrated to the urban centres in search of wage employment and housing. Most of this housing was constructed on a self-help basis by communities of rural migrants who invaded and settled (illegally occupied and squatted) unused urban land areas, creating in the process the *pueblos jóvenes* (young towns) of Lima, the *favelas* (shanty towns) of Rio de Janeiro, the *rancherias* of Caracas, and the *poblaciones* of Santiago, Chile. Up to 60 per cent of the urban population lives in precarious housing conditions as a result of urbanization (Guimarães, 1997: 191).

Now, land occupations occurred in a new urban context. They replicated some of the dynamics of the rural struggle, but took different forms: land invasions, squatting, negotiations with municipal governments for services and legal title to "property," and grassroots efforts to upgrade these neighbourhoods into the working-class barrios that surround so many Latin American cities today.

From 1986 to 1999, up to 9 million landless workers in Brazil were forced to leave the countryside to escape rural poverty and engage in this urban struggle for inclusion in the economic development process. The social dynamics of this process are complex and varied. Many families are forced to break-up, with some of the women staying behind to tend subsistence plots of land, while many of the men seasonally migrate from these plots or work within the unstructured informal sector of the urban labour market (Portes, 1989;

PREALC, 1993). Even without access to land or other means of social production, many landless workers are unable or unwilling to break their connection to rural society. Nevertheless, the structure of landholding continues to reproduce conditions of rural poverty and fuel migration by large numbers of dispossessed peasants or landless rural workers.

As recently as 1997, over 60 per cent of all rural households in Latin America (and 40 per cent overall) were mired in poverty. For 60 per cent of these households, this poverty was extreme (ECLAC, 1998). Some of this poverty was new in the sense that it derived from a structure put into place by a neo-liberal program of policy reforms—*privatization* of the means of production and public enterprises; *liberalization* of trade and the flow of investment capital; *deregulation* of capital, product, and labour markets; and a retrenchment of the state from social programs (Veltmeyer and Petras, 1997, 2000). However, some forms and conditions of this poverty preceded these new developments and are entrenched in the structure of landownership in the rural areas. Not even the relatively radical or extensive land reform programs in some countries had managed to substantially change the structure of land ownership. In Chile and Nicaragua, these programs were reversed. Land concentration and landlessness in the Brazilian countryside has continued to accelerate, despite years of land reform. In 1970, estates of over 1,000 hectares, representing 0.7 per cent of the total farms, accounted for 40 per cent of the land; in 1996, 1 per cent of the landowners with farms of over 1,000 hectares owned 45 per cent of the land. At the same time, over 4 million farm workers were without any land at all, while large numbers were near-landless. In Honduras, where 409,000 hectares were redistributed (120,000 hectares from 1973 to 1977 alone, the heyday of agrarian reform), only 13 per cent of the rural population were the beneficiaries. Over 200,000 families (44 per cent of the rural population) still have no access to or very little land. These families, as elsewhere in Latin America, continue to live in very poor conditions and constitute the nucleus of extreme poverty.

Rural poverty has also persisted because when significant gains *were* made in the course of state-led land reform, these gains eroded in the medium and long-term, and the peasants and rural landless workers suffered a series of setbacks. This does not even take into account "the new poor," those pushed into poverty as a direct result of the neo-liberal model. For example, the substantive gains made by peasant producers in Chile in the 1960s and early 1970s were arrested and reversed by the Pinochet regime, which initiated what amounted to a counter-revolution for Latin America in 1975. A few years later, an astute analyst of agrarian development David Lehmann (1978) could write of the death of land reform (in Brazil in particular), a view echoed by others such as Cristóbal Kay (2000) and Billie De Walt and Martha Ress (1994). With neo-liberal adjustment—and the counter-revolution—state-led land reforms were over. The state was generally in retreat. Where not in retreat, it had an entirely different agenda. When Ché Guevara was captured and executed in Bolivia, and most of the guerrilla armies for national liberation in the region were contained or destroyed, if not defeated (with the exception of the FARC), the threat of social revolution had evaporated—and a major wave of peasant rebellion disappeared with it.

The Disappearance of the Peasantry?

The central protagonist in Latin America's class struggle over land has been the peasantry. However, the nature of the peasantry as a socio-economic and political category and its role in contemporary land struggles have been subject to considerable reconceptualization and ongoing debate. First of all, the precise meaning of the terms *peasant* and *peasantry* is at issue (Kearney, 1996). A second set of debates surrounds the role of the peasants in the political struggle. Recent research and analysis on this issue has tended to oscillate between two competing political conceptualizations. On the one hand, the peasantry is regarded more or less as a passive entity, the disempowered object of various kinds of state agency (legislation, taxation, agricultural production regimes, systems of regulation, macroeconomic planning, etc.). Most sociological studies in the structuralist tradition of modernization theory take this view, a view reflected in the writings of historians such as Eric Hobsbawm. They see the peasantry as a category that is declining in number and political significance, defeated by the process of modernization and change (Bryceson, Kay, and Mooi, 2000). On the other hand, an alternative perception of the peasantry views it as an active and empowered force that continues to contest the class struggle over the land (see in particular Petras 1997).

This difference in perception reflects the epistemological debate between proponents of structuralism as a mode of analysis (Marxism, etc.) and those who reject all forms of structuralism in favour of grassroots postmodernism (Esteva and Prakash, 1998) and "discourse analysis" (Escobar, 1992). For structuralists generally, including Marxists, the peasantry is an economic and political category that corresponds to a transitional organizational form, destined to disappear into the dustbin of history and whose presence on the world stage is now disguised—as a rural proletariat, an urban lumpen proletariat trapped in a proliferating informal sector (Bryceson, Kay, and Mooi, 2000; Kay, 2000). This process of transformation is viewed as involving many steps: land expropriation and concentration, rural exodus and land invasions on the periphery of the large urban centres, settlement on these lands, and gradual incorporation of the rural migrants into the structure and life of the city. The end result, in theory, is fewer peasants to act as an economic agent and a political force for change. For structuralists, the peasantry as a traditional social category has been decimated by modernization, urbanization, and capitalist development of urban-centred industry (Bartra, 1976; Cancian, 1987; Kay, 2000).

This is by no means the only view on the peasantry. For one thing, some structural analysts have detected a trend in the reverse direction in certain contexts, namely a peasantization (Bakx, 1988). James Petras, among others, also articulated a different perspective on agrarian transformation. In his perspective, the peasantry cannot be understood purely in numerical terms as a percentage of the labour force or by the size of the peasant sector of the economy. The peasantry remains a force whose weight and significance is greater than its number. Indeed, the peasantry constitutes the most dynamic force for anti-systemic change in Latin America, where they are on the crest of a new wave of class struggle: the struggle for land for indigenous people, land reform, autonomy, social justice, and democracy. The political irruption of the Zapatista Army of National Liberation (*Ejército Zapatista de Liberación Nacional*, or EZLN) in 1994 can best be understood in this way, rather than as, according to Burbach (1994), the "first postmodern movement in history."

THREE PATHS TO REFORM

International development in the 1950s and 1960s was presented as a means of reforming the capitalist system so as to allow for a more equitable distribution of society's wealth. This project, however, was challenged from both the left and the right, leading to various calls for an alternative project: social revolution from the former, and a neo-liberal counter-revolution from the latter. The agency for revolutionary change generally took the form of social movements rooted in either the working class or the peasantry, while the agents of counter-revolution turned towards the state to implement the neo-liberal model of free market capitalist development and globalization—to create what George W.H. Bush termed "the new world order" and to release thereby what George W. Bush termed 10 years later "the forces of freedom, democracy, and free enterprise" (in his 2002 National Security Report).

Implementation of this new model of neo-liberal capitalist development has created an entirely new dynamic for the land struggle in different parts of the world. While a number of analysts have invoked the "death of land reform," some, such as Gwynne and Kay (1999) and Kay (2000), write of a process of "agrarian transformation." As to the nature of this transformation, Alain De Janvry et al. write of the movement from state-led to grassroots-led land reform, while others highlight the change to a "market-assisted" approach to land reform. James Petras (1997) and I (Veltmeyer, 1997b) point to the emergence of a new wave of peasant-based and peasant-led movements that push beyond land reforms towards more revolutionary or radical changes in government policy, as well changes to the neo-liberal model behind it and the system created by its implementation. In effect, it is possible to identify three divergent paths towards land reform, each characterized by a distinct overall objective and a mixed bag of tactics:

- state-led land reform (expropriation with compensation, land redistribution, rural development);
- market-assisted land reform (titling; commodification, which encouraged peasants to buy land; and land banks); and
- grassroots land reform (occupations, negotiation, and struggle).

State-led Land Reform

It is a given that in Latin America, as elsewhere, the state has been essential in maintaining and defending the dominant social relations of production. In each specific form of agricultural production over the years, the state has been instrumental in forming, extending, reproducing, and transforming the system involved, benefiting some classes—most often the large landowners—and disadvantaging mainly workers and peasants (Feder, 1971; Huizer, 1973). The theoretical point here is that the growth of the market is inexorably linked to an activist state, as is the process of agrarian reform. The state has been central to the process of changing the dominant relations of economic production and the class systems based on this process. The repressive apparatus of the state has been brought into play on numerous occasions, in different historical contexts, to maintain the existing regime of property in the means of production. The judiciary also has been called upon to play its part in this regard. Thus, for example, in the Landless Workers' Movement (MST) in Brazil, the state actively tried and imprisoned activists, but when the propertied class acted in defence of their property rights, they were granted legal impunity, even when murder and massacre were involved. Clearly, powerful links exist between the large proprietors and the judiciary, and Brazil is no exception to the rule: of the 1,158 rural activists assassinated in land disputes between 1985 and 1999, only 56 gunmen were brought to trial and just 10 were convicted. Since Cardoso rose to state power in 1995, 163 MST activists have been assassinated, and not one of those responsible for the deaths has been brought to legal accounts (Figueiras, 1999: 40; MST, 2002). Sixteen MST activists were assassinated with virtual impunity in 2001. In 2003, Luiz Inácio "Lula" da Silva's Workers' Party has continued this policy of repressing the MST where and when it has refused to toe the government line (that is, to be patient and show support for the government's land reform program). In addition to the continued imprisonment and assassination of MST activists, the government has also sent the military police to surround the MST headquarters and intimidate the leadership.

In state-led land reform, particularly in the twentieth century, governments of the day have acted on legislation in which the propertied groups in the dominant class generally have had the predominant influence. Over the years, it has entailed a protracted struggle; first, to have the reforms implemented; and then, to consolidate the gains made. In most cases, the advances made by peasants and rural workers in this struggle were preserved, if not consolidated. In some cases, however, as when Pinochet ascended to power in Chile, the gains made in a process of land reform were halted and reversed.

The essential factor determining the outcome of the struggle was the relation of the peasant movement to the state. Thus, in Mexico, Bolivia, and Peru, a prolonged process of state disinvestment in the reform sector culminated in legislation that provided incentives to agro-export monopolies, alienating community lands (the *ejido* in Mexico) and stimulating cheap (subsidized) imported foodstuffs. A politics of alliances with other progressive social sectors (workers, etc.) was critical in how land reforms played out. The peasantry, generally subordinate to the urban petit bourgeoisie and bourgeoisie, would often secure an initial round of redistributive reforms and state assistance. But subsequently peasant movements tended to fragment and divide along "official" and "oppositional" lines, the former of which became a transmission belt for state policy.

On the Move: Six

When the state initiated land reform programs in the 1960s, they were essentially defensive responses to the lessons of the 1959 Cuban Revolution, and thus were designed to prevent the emergence of more radical demands for change. The government in almost every country initiated a broad program of agrarian reform. The political objective was to incorporate the peasantry into a dual agenda: not only to divert existing and future dissent into constitutional channels, where it might more easily be co-opted by the state, but also to bring smallholders into the orbit of capitalist development, thereby offering them an alternative to systemic transformation or socialism.

Under the rubric of agrarian reform legislation designed to modernize agriculture, the ownership of productive tracts of land has been further concentrated, and redistribution occurs only within the peasant sector itself. This has led to a process of internal differentiation with three distinct strata: a small group of rich peasants, some of whom are converted into rural capitalists; a somewhat larger middle layer of self-sufficient peasant farmers with productive capacity within the domestic market; and a rural proletariat, composed of a huge mass of semi-proletarianized—that is, landless or near landless—migrant workers. In most contexts, however, attempts to accommodate and co-opt the peasantry, including unionization from above and setting up parallel or government-controlled peasant organizations, either failed or were only partially successful. Usually, they tended to unleash class conflicts that continued into another more radical phase of land reform. For this reason, once Latin American governments had instituted a land reform program they devoted their energies to preventing its radicalization, using a combination of strategies ranging from corporativism, controlling peasant organisations, and co-opting their leadership, to outright repression (Thorpe, et al., 1995: 131–43).

In each phase of capitalist modernization, the state has played a crucial role in promoting, financing, and protecting the dominant modernizing classes from the threat of peasant and rural worker movements, forcing the rural proletariat and peasantry to bear the costs of transition. This pattern reappeared in the 1980s, in the transition towards a neo-liberal new world order facilitated by a process of structural adjustment and globalization (Gwynne and Kay, 1999; Kay, 1999; Thiesenhusen, 1989, 1995). Among those disadvantaged by the application of neo-liberal measures in Latin America, the peasantry and rural workers figure prominently. The virulence of their opposition and periodic outbreaks of rural violence attest to this (Barry, 1987; Veltmeyer and Petras, 2000).

Market-assisted Land Reform

To recap, the state (including the government, legislature, judiciary, and the forces of internal order: the militarized police) was the dominant agency for agrarian and rural development and land reforms in the 1960s and 1970s. These reforms were instituted to quell revolutionary change exerted from the grassroots. In the 1980s, an alternative path towards agrarian development developed in response to the requirements of the new world order, based on the workings of the free market and private enterprise (Deininger, 1998). We can identify two responses to the institution of the new economic model: (1) the emergence of a new wave of peasant-based and peasant-led anti-systemic socio-political movements oriented towards direct action; and (2) the evolution of a market-assisted approach to land and agrarian reform. This second approach, advocated by the World Bank and other Official Development Aid (ODA) organizations, dominated government policy throughout the 1990s.

In response, policy-making and academic circles all across the region initiated a debate on alternative forms of agrarian and land reform. At the centre of these discussions was the idea of promoting land markets as a way to improve the access of poor households to society's productive resources—to expand "use of the market mechanism in the process of agrarian development" (Ghimire, 2001). The dominant model of rural development, one still very much in use today, is predicated on the accumulation of social capital rather than the natural capital embedded in the land (Coleman, 1988; Chambers and Conway, 1998; Helmore and Singh, 2001; Woolcock and Narayan, 2000). This focus on social capital, which, in theory, is abundantly given to the poor in the form of their capacity to network and act co-operatively, reduced if not eliminated the pressure on governments to expropriate and redistribute land. Similarly, class or state power, always a central issue in the land struggle, was depoliticized—transmuted into a question of social empowerment. Nevertheless, landlessness and lack of access to productive land remained an issue, leading the ODAs, particularly the World Bank, to advocate policies to modernize agriculture and stimulate the growth of a land market. These policies included land titling (giving legal title and security of tenure to those with access to land), commodification (eliminating landholdings that prevented individuals from buying and selling land), and instituting land banks (Bromley, 1989; World Bank, 1996).

The World Bank has instituted pilot land bank projects in Brazil, Colombia, and the Philippines. The aim of these projects was not only to promote a market for land and to create a "new rural world," but also, in Brazil at least, to counteract the tactic of land occupations used by grassroots organizations and social movements. The aim, in other words, was to stimulate the use of the market mechanism (UNRISD, 2000) in lieu of what the leaders of these movements take to be the broader class struggle (Stedile, 2000).

Hardly a country in Latin America with a significant agricultural sector has escaped this impulse to create a land market. In the early 1990s, country after country instituted agrarian modernization or reform law in one form or another, invariably designed to promote a land market. In Mexico and Ecuador, this meant abolishing constitutional protection for indigenous communal lands. This policy was successfully instituted in Mexico in 1992, where the dominant peasant federation was in the pockets and under control of the government. However, it hit a political snag in Ecuador in the form of an indigenous uprising. More generally, countries in the region shifted their focus from redistributing land to providing the legal security of land tenure. They managed to institute a program of land titling, which provided the infrastructure for a market-assisted approach to land reform. This approach was further advanced when land banks were introduced in order to provide credit to rural poor landholders so they could purchase land or access other productive resources, such as new technology.

The neo-liberal policy program of structural adjustments to the economy, widely implemented in the 1980s, provided the context for this path to land reform (Veltmeyer and Petras, 1997, 2000). By the end of the decade, there were only four holdouts in this "reform process": Brazil, Peru, Argentina, and Venezuela. In relatively short order, these countries also came on board with some of the most radical forms of SAP instituted anywhere in the world (Petras and Veltmeyer, 2002, 2003).

Between 1991 and 1994, at the behest of the World Bank and within the framework of the neo-liberal policy reform agenda, the governments of Mexico, Ecuador, Bolivia, Peru, and a number of other countries in South and Central America turned towards a market-assisted approach to agrarian reform. This approach, established in one country after the other, was based on legislation that abolished constitutional or legal protection of communal property and granted legal entitlement to land worked by smallholders. The aim was that by increasing their capacity to sell their land, a land market would be created and the efficiency of production would be increased. However, rather than resolving the agricultural crisis, these measures (land titling, commodification, and land banks), combined with the elimination of subsidies to local producers, the reduction of protective tariffs, and in many cases an overvalued currency, created what analysts have termed a "difficult environment" for various categories of producers of tradable products. Particularly in Peru, small-scale peasant producers were extremely vulnerable to the inflow of cheap agricultural products (Crabtree, 2003: 144). But the pattern holds for other countries in the region. This increase in agricultural inputs has not only undermined or destroyed local economies, forcing large numbers of local producers into bankruptcy or poverty, but it has also caused or accelerated a fundamental change in production and consumption patterns away from traditional crops, especially grains like quinoa, kiwicha, coca, alluco, beans, and potatoes. The impact of this change, and its implications, has yet to be evaluated.

In many cases, such as in Mexico and Peru, the recourse to the market mechanism has caused a drastic deterioration in the market for small producers, who have been forced to sell their goods at prices below their production costs and have accrued enormous debts. In many cases, they have been pushed into bankruptcy. In Mexico, this situation has generated one of the largest mass movements in a long history of land struggle—a million-strong organization of highly indebted "independent" family farmers (*El Barzón*). As for the peasant economy in Peru, Ecuador, and Mexico, and in Central America and elsewhere in the region, it was devastated. Large numbers of peasants were forced to flee the countryside in search of wage employment in the cities and urban centres. The only alternative was—and is—rural poverty.

Studies in this area point to a pattern of increased social inequality and rural poverty. In the not atypical case of Peru, poverty rose from 41.6 per cent of rural households in 1985 to 54.1 per cent in 2000—this after a decade of agricultural modernization and capitalist free market development (Crabtree, 2003: 148). The same study shows a pattern of decline in extreme poverty, down from 18.4 per cent to 14.8 per cent for the same period. The study provides no analysis or explanation for this reduction, but the answer probably lies in the World Bank's methodological approach, which is to reduce poverty by statistical fiat (defining it in terms of earnings of less than $1 a day).

Peasants in Action: Land Reform and the Social Movements

From the 1960s to the 1970s, the struggle for land and land reform was at the very epicentre of the class struggle in Central and South America. This struggle had taken shape and assumed diverse forms in previous decades, but the Cuban Revolution gave it a new impetus. The protagonists in this struggle were the state (generally acting on behalf of those with landed property in the means of production and access to the capital needed to expand it) and communities of peasant producers, along with a rural landless or near-landless proletariat (organized in the form of social movements that for the most part were oriented towards land reform). The social movements were engaged in a multi-faceted struggle with the state, responding to government strategies to accommodate them, incorporate them, co-opt their leadership, and repress them outright. The state was fundamentally concerned with avoiding another Cuba. However, some of the peasant-based social movements took a radical stance and, like those in Cuba, were drawn to revolutionary struggle based on direct action in land invasions and the use of armed force in relation to the state.

The 1980s provided a very different context: one of debt, neo-liberal reform in the guise of the SAP, a return to democracy and civilian rule, decentralized government decision-making, and an emergent active civil society. In this context, the land struggle, in both its reformist and revolutionary forms, subsided and gave way to a new wave of struggle and social movements. In these new social movements, the major protagonists were no longer peasants or workers, but rather the urban poor and diverse issue-oriented social organizations (Ballón, 1986; Brass, 1991, 2000; Calderón and Jelin, 1987; Escobar and Alvarez, 1992; Slater, 1985, 1994).

In the 1990s, these new social movements in their turn gave way to a third wave of socio-political movements that were both peasant-based and peasant-led and, in some contexts, were rooted in the struggle of indigenous communities for land, territorial autonomy, and freedom and democracy, if not social justice. By most accounts, the most dynamic of these movements is the Landless Workers' Movement (MST), a national organization of Brazilian peasants (rural landless workers) formed in union with the broad civil struggle to establish "the new republic" and the newly founded Workers' Party (PT), whose leader, Lula da Silva, has just won the presidency of the country for a second term. Similar movements were formed elsewhere, most notably in Mexico (the EZLN) and in Ecuador [Confederation of Indigenous Nationalities of Ecuador (*El Confederación de Nacionalidades Indígenas del Ecuador*, or CONAIE)]. Collectively, these and other such movements changed the political landscape of rural society. In Paraguay, for example, the *Federación Nacional Campesina* used direct action land redistribution tactics combined with confronting the state with the demand to legalise and finance agricultural credits and inputs (*Informativo Campesino*, No. 91, April 1996; Fogel, 1986). In Bolivia, Colombia, and Peru, peasant movements have been at the forefront of the struggle to develop or maintain alternative crops as a source of livelihood in the face of neo free market policies that have inundated local markets with cheap imports. All of these movements are peasant-based and peasant-led, which differs from the wave of peasant movements that hit Latin America in the 1950s and 1960 (largely demobilized and destroyed in the 1970s).

In this context, direct action by grassroots movements in the 1990s took diverse forms that were part of what Pedro Stedile (2000), leader of the most dynamic social movement in Latin America (the MST), terms "the broader class struggle." However, like in Túpac Amaru's class struggle in the late eighteenth century in what is now Peru, land occupations are at the centre of the strategy for direct action and radical reform, figuring predominantly in MST's arsenal of tactics. The MST's strategy has been one of occupation, negotiation, and production.

This tactic of land occupation is based on the agrarian reform legislation established in the 1960s. The gist of this legislation, like the legislation established in the state-led land reform programs of the 1960s and 1970s, was to expropriate large land holdings that were deemed to be unproductive; that is, to have no social use. In Brazil and elsewhere (El Salvador and Honduras, for example) this law allowed for a program of state-led legal expropriation and land redistribution. However [as noted by William C. Thiesenhusen (1995) among others], little land had actually been transferred by the 1990s, leading the way for reorganised peasant movements to take action in diverse political and legal forms. In El Salvador, they pressured the government to act upon its own legalisation. However, as previously noted, other movements (particularly the MST in Brazil) adopted the direct action tactic of land occupations in the context of a broader class struggle (Stedile, 2000). The MST mobilized its membership to take direct action in large-scale land occupations that typically involved from 1,000 to 3,000 families. Once the land is occupied, the leadership of the movement immediately enter into negotiations for legal title to the land, making use of the government's own legislation to expropriate landed properties that do not have social use.

In Brazil, this strategy has been so successful that it forced the government to revive and step up its own land reform program, distributing land using the market mechanism, *cedulas da terra* (legal titling), and instituting *bancos da terra* (land banks). This market-supported land reform aimed to redistribute land not necessarily to the tiller, but rather to the most "productive." Consequently, the actual acreage of land transferred by this mechanism is relatively modest, if not quite small. Today, after 15 years of struggle and a revamped state-led land reform program, 3 per cent of the population still owns two-thirds of the country's arable land, much of which continues to lie idle.

The rhythm of MST occupations and *assentamentos* (settlements) has been maintained over 15 years of struggle, averaging 345 a year—settling over half a million families (569,733) on 25,598 hectares of land (Dataluta, 2002). In just four months in 1999 and at the height of its conflict with the government, the MST along with the National Confederation of Agricultural Workers (*Confederación Nacional de Trabalhadores na Agricultura*, or CONTAG) mobilized 22,000 families to occupy over 155 large estates. By mid 1999, over 72,000 families—over 350,000 farm people—were encamped on land, waiting for the government to legalize the de facto expropriation. However, some families continued to live in the temporary settlements or camps for up to four years, some for even longer. By withholding federal funds and launching a program to offer loans so small farmers could purchase the land, the Cardoso regime hoped to discourage the land occupiers and undermine public support for the MST.

The government's strategy, however, did not work. In 2001, it launched a triple-pronged attack on the MST by implementing the World Bank's alternative land bank program, by organizing an extensive media publicity campaign, and through outright repression. Nevertheless, the MST undertook 294 separate occupations, settling 26,120 families on 344,513 hectares of land in 2001 alone (MST, *Setor de Documentação*, 2002). This contrasts with the fewer than 140,000 hectares settled under the government's alternative market-assisted land reform program over the course of four years, from 1995 to 1999.

Over the course of two decades of struggle, the MST has mobilized up to half a million families of rural landless workers to occupy land, negotiate its legal expropriation, and put it into production. During its 20 years of existence, the National Institute of Colonization and Agrarian Reform (INCRA), the institution established by the government under the agrarian reform law, has expropriated very few landholdings and settled fewer than 7 per cent of the landless rural families—some 330,000 out of 4 million. In fact, most of these land settlements were initiated by MST-organized occupations that were later legalised by INCRA.

SOCIAL MOVEMENTS IN LATIN AMERICA—OLD AND NEW

The struggle for social change in Latin America and elsewhere has taken various forms, the most important of which has been the emergence of social movements. In Latin American, these were formed on the crest of three distinct waves. The first of these waves hit in the 1960s, in the wake of the Cuban Revolution. Organized workers in the urban centres and revolutionary peasant organizations (guerrilla armies of national liberation) generally led by urban middle-class intellectuals formed the most important and dynamic of these early movements. Both the urban-centred labour movement and the peasant-based struggles for land and social change made substantial gains, improving the general situation of their members and advancing the class struggle. However, by the end of the 1970s, most had been either defeated or destroyed in a complex process that involved state-led projects of community-based development, the accommodation or corruption of the movements' leaders, and, when and where required, outright repression (Petras and Veltmeyer, 2000).

In the 1980s, in a very different urban context (debt crisis, a new economic model, a state in retreat, a process of democratic renewal) Latin America was hit by a second wave of social movements that emerged from within civil society—both in its popular sector (the urban poor) and the middle class. Well into the decade, sociologists and other analysts, armed with a post-structuralist form of analysis (Laclau, 1989) and a postmodernist perspective (Slater, 1985, 1994; Calderón, 1995; Calderón and Jelín, 1987; Escobar and Alvarez, 1992), dubbed these movements "new" because of the subjective and heterogeneous conditions that gave rise to them, their broad social base, and their fundamental concerns. These movements were seen as a new social actor on the political stage, rather than in class terms. However, no sooner had these new social movements been so constructed by theorists than they disappeared into the spaces within the structure of political and economic power—spaces created by the process of democratization and alternative development.

In the ebb and flow of changing political tides towards the end of the 1980s, there emerged a third wave of social movements that included Brazil's MST, a dynamic and successful movement that has turned the tactic of land occupation into an art. Unlike the "new" movements of the 1980s, these movements were formed in the rural sector and were both peasant-based and peasant-led. A number of them also had an ethnic character and social base in the indigenous communities of peasant farmers. This was the case, for example, in Mexico with the EZLN, in Ecuador with the CONAIE, and in Bolivia with the *cocaleros*, an organization of 30,000 coca-producing peasants.

Although the dynamics of these movements and their future in the twenty-first century remain uncertain and require further study, it is clear that they can be viewed as new in a number of respects; that is, different from their predecessors. What is not new is the struggle for land and land reform. What is somewhat new in these movements can be summed up in the following terms. Unlike the peasant-based movements of the 1960s and 1970s (with the exception of FARC in Colombia), these movements are peasant-led. Secondly, not only is the leadership composed of peasants, but these leaders also maintain close links to their rural social base and the membership of the movement. In this regard, the austere conditions that they share with the membership are striking. There is no question here of the formation of a well-paid bureaucratic organizational elite, which has been a major factor in the declining power of organized labour and the virtual demise of the labour movement. Unlike in the labour movement, critical decisions about strategy and the general direction of the movement are always made in close consultation with the members, usually in the form of popular or community-based assemblies.

The movement also reflects changes in the political context in which it operates. For the MST, these changes include an internal transition towards gender parity at all levels and a firm position to maintain autonomy as a social movement vis-à-vis the Workers' Party (PT). (Until the PT's Lula da Silva was elected president of Brazil in 2002, the MST had maintained cordial relations and tactical—even strategic—alliances with the party.) The other peasant-based and peasant-led social movements in the region have generally followed the MST, linking up with social and political organizations in the urban sector as well as intra-regional and international advocacy organizations. However, the other peasant social movements have not followed the MST's lead regarding gender parity, possibly a reflection of the greater willingness of the MST to accept the support of the NGOs that prioritize the issue of gender equity (incorporating women into the development process) over the land question. As of the mid 1990s, the MST and other new peasant socio-political movements in the region are beginning to see a need to form strategic alliances with civil society and class organizations in the urban centres, to build public support for the movement, and to reach out to intra-regional organizations of peasant producers and international advocacy groups. In this connection, the MST has become a critical component of the World Social Summit and the worldwide anti-systemic and anti-globalization movement.

CONCLUSION

Land invasions and occupations have been a major political development in the 1990s in Latin America. The Latin American experience, reviewed and analyzed in this chapter, suggests that land occupations can best be understood as part of a protracted class struggle. The dynamics and forms of this struggle are variable and contingent, but in the context of a worldwide struggle against capitalism and neo-liberalism, land occupations are part of a broader popular anti-globalization movement for another (better) world.

The driving force behind this movement in Latin America is the peasantry, a socio-economic and political category that has been dismissed by many as a serious political actor and a force for revolutionary change. This chapter suggests that this view is mistaken—that in the era of neo-liberal capitalist development and globalisation, the peasantry remains a significant factor of social change.

SEVEN

From the Barricades to the Ballot Box

Two decades of protests, spontaneous and organized, against neo-liberal policies in Latin America have had mixed results. Waves of spontaneous protests in some countries against IMF-mandated austerity measures have had little to no effect. Likewise, two decades of structural adjustments, such as the privatization of public assets and enterprises, have brought about only marginal changes in government policy, despite widespread, albeit sporadic, mobilizations against these measures. Only in Ecuador, and more recently in Bolivia, has the popular movement of resistance against neo-liberal policies resulted in a halting, and to some extent reversion, of neo-liberal policies of privatization and associated structural reforms. In Argentina, five years of severe economic and political crisis did result in the fall of the government and a temporary suspension of payments on the debt owed to and managed by the IMF. However, mobilizations in that country were directed against the government's management of the crisis rather than against the specific policies, such as privatization, implicated in the crisis. In Ecuador in 1987, a popular movement did lead to the shelving of announced neo-liberal measures, and they brought down the country's president, Abdala Bucaram, but in the end, subsequent regimes extended and deepened neo-liberal policies, and even instituted the dollarization of the currency. Also, in Brazil, Nicaragua, Venezuela, and Uruguay, organized forms of protests against various privatization or other neo-liberal measures have had some impact in blocking proposed new measures. But in countries like Mexico and Argentina, the power of the state is so centralized in the office of the president that the protests have had little possibility of diverting the country from its neo-liberal road to development and globalization. In Venezuela, President Hugo Chavez has pulled or pushed the country in another direction based on an agenda (the Bolivarian Revolution) that combines anti-neo-liberalism and anti-imperialism with socialism (in rhetoric if not in practice). Of all the major countries in the region, Venezuela is the only one that did not wholeheartedly embrace the neo-liberal agenda (like Mexico, Chile, and Bolivia did in the 1980s and Argentina, Peru, and Brazil did in the 1990s).

Only in Bolivia was a serious dent put into the wholly adopted neo-liberal policy program, implemented almost everywhere on the basis of presidential decree rather than congressional approval, for example, in the privatization of firms in the hydrocarbon sector. In Bolivia, mobilizations against the government's attempt to extend this privatization to the commercialization of water created conditions that not only led to the overthrow of two governments but to the installation of the first president with solid roots in both the indigenous communities and the popular movement. One of the first actions taken by President Evo Morales, who had led the *cocaleros* (coca-producing peasants of Chaparé) and the Movement toward Socialism (*Movimiento al Socialismo*, or MAS), in his first 100 days in office was to declare hydrocarbon resources (primarily gas) the property of the state, thus nationalizing (albeit in limited form) the industry. This move to reverse a well-entrenched policy of privatization is a major challenge for the left (given the forces of support for privatization in the congress), but in the Bolivian context the government had little to no choice. The popular movement was not only solidly behind the policy of nationalizing the country's oil and gas reserves, but it was actively mobilized to demand it. However, a more serious problem for the forces of opposition to neo-liberalism is that neither the political parties in opposition nor any other organization in the popular movement has been able to present a coherent alternative nationalization program. Thus, in spite of a history of resistance (see chapter 8), the popular movement in its actions (protests, roadblocks, and marches on public buildings, as well as mass demonstrations) has produced little more than a political vacuum in most places and a lack of confidence in the possibility of change.

The fact that protests do not transform into electoral victories is an indication of their political limits. During the last years of protests, national elections have characterized what has been called an "apparent schizophrenia": a trend towards electing rightist regimes given to neo-liberal policies at the central government level and leftist regimes oriented towards opposition at the local and municipal level. In the 1988 elections in Brazil, for example, the PT experienced a notable success in the municipalities of Sao Paulo and Porto Alegre (see chapter 5), among others. In 1992, the PT extended its control to 55 communities and became the number-two political force at the municipal level (although it lost Sao Paulo to a right-wing populist). In the 1996 elections, the PT maintained its position at this level, while losing ground at the central government level (after having previously lost the presidency to Fernando Henrique Cardoso, a social democrat turned neo-liberal). This trend towards leftist municipal governments is also apparent in Montevideo, which has been in the hands of the Frente Amplio, a broad front of leftist parties, since 1988. (This finally translated into control over the central government in the 2005 elections). The same occurred in Asunción, Caracas and Buenos Aires, a city of 10 million that in 1994 fell into the hands of a coalition of parties on the centre-left. However, in the latter case, a popular uprising in December 2001 would break this centre-left coalition and bring down the government.

In the 1990s, where the left acquired a modicum of power it was normally at the local level without the capacity to control resources or to derail the national policy of neo-liberalism. Of course, in the twenty-first century, this would change with the emergence of left-of-centre regimes in Venezuela and Bolivia, quasi-left regimes in Brazil and Argentina with Lula da Silva and Néstor Kirchner—and most recently (January 2007) in Ecuador. In the 1990s, however, the dominant pattern was for the electorate to give power to neo-liberal regimes at the national level and a more populist or a left-of-centre regime at the local level. Thus the scope for changing neo-liberal policies was limited. Nevertheless, within these limits, the left was able to sow the seeds of a new participatory form of politics that contributed to an explosion of more promising social movements. And in the process, it gained a reputation for efficiency and honesty that contradicts widespread distrust of the "political class" overall. If the left can capitalize on this political resource, as it has managed to do in Bolivia and Ecuador and as Hugo Chavez managed to do by himself almost single-handedly (without a well-organized left) in Venezuela, it might have a future. But recent developments, even in light of an apparent shift to the left (or rather centre-left, since leftist parties have had to turn to the centre if not the right in order to position themselves for state-power), are not too promising.

In spite of the alternative visions and proposals given at the municipal level, the opposition has not been able to translate widespread protests against neo-liberalism into national power. Only a few parties have been able to do so on the basis of rhetoric about the social market and the role of the state in providing a social democratic reform program in education and social welfare. Examples include Ernesto Samper in Colombia and Rafael Caldera in Venezuela, a survivor (or fossil, to be more exact) of the old populist policy whose last expositor was Alan Garcia, who has managed to reinvent himself as a neo-liberal populist in Peru by defeating the nationalist–populist political leader Antauro Humala in the 2006 presidential elections. As for Caldera, he won the 1993 election with the support of the MAS. However, like the Socialist Party of Chile, the MAS was converted into a party of the government, transformed by the process of seeking access to national power. It also lost any pretence about representing the popular forces. This was left to Hugo Chavez's current program of a socialist and nationalist Bolivarian Revolution.

What carried Caldera to power in Venezuela was a mix of nostalgia for the by-gone prosperous days of the oil era and his contradictory promises to control inflation and the fiscal deficit, increase government expenditures, and eliminate the value-added sales tax. But once he had the instrument of national power in his hands, Caldera, like other populists in and out of power, made a sharp turn to the right—to neo-liberal policy.

The examples set by Samper, Caldera, and the *Concertación* (socialist/Christian democrat) regime in Chile, which is cut from the same social democratic cloth (with an appeal to the left but an inevitable swing to the right in power), have made it clear that such regimes are not able to represent the forces of opposition and resistance to neo-liberal policies. Not one of them has been able to construct or implement an alternative program. Just as with the regimes of Albert Fujimori in Peru and Carlos Menem in Argentina, once in power they without exception submitted for one reason or another to the pressures of the international financial community and the national middle class in favour of neo-liberalism. From mid 1996, for example, Caldera has actively flirted with Agenda Venezuela, a right-wing adjustment program manufactured in Washington and thus bearing a striking resemblance to those in place in Argentina and Mexico.[1] Just as the program currently in place everywhere across the region except in Cuba, Agenda Venezuela was based on a policy of privatization, the elimination of state subsidies, and reforms intended to increase the flexibility of labour and create a more competitive industry.[2]

For a variety of reasons, the dynamics of which have not been systematically studied, the political class of the left has not been able to realize an opposition program to neo-liberalism. In some contexts, such as in Brazil and Mexico, a party with a social democratic or populist tinge and with a rhetoric of opposition towards neo-liberalism has presented itself, and others have perceived it as such—a political instrument of opposition, even a force of resistance against neo-liberalism. But without exception, these parties have either lost their electoral opportunity or have made an opportunistic swing to the right, with negative or disastrous consequences. Despite Mexico's generalized cynicism and disillusionment with government policy and all politicians, in 1994 the citizens chose as their president a technocrat in the neo-liberal mould, the candidate of the long-governing Institutional Revolutionary Party (*Partido Revolucionario Institucional*, or PRI). Cuauhtémoc Cárdenas, the presidential candidate for the opposition Party of the Democratic Revolution (*Partido de la Revolución Democrática*, or PRD), presented himself as a champion of nationalism and the popular forces, as well as an opponent of neo-liberalism. Then, during the campaign, he wrote an article for The Wall Street Journal praising the neo-liberal North American Free Trade Treaty to which he had been so opposed in the past. Thus did the PRD betray and dissipate the opposition forces ranged behind it, and failed once again to meet its electoral promise by placing a distant third behind the right-wing National Action Party (*Partido Acción Nacional*, or PAN), an even more avid supporter of neo-liberal policies than the governing party. In the current conjuncture of another presidential election, the PRD candidate, who had been well ahead in the polls, is now running neck and neck with the PAN candidate. By a number of accounts, and with some evidence of announced policy intentions, López Obredor (ALMO), made a number of deals to smooth his way to possible state power (he missed out by a difference of less than 1 per cent of the vote in the 2006 presidential elections). The fact that Carlos Slim, the third richest man in the world according to Forbes and certainly a major beneficiary of the neo-liberal policies of previous and incumbent regimes, is very much in his corner and on his side speaks volumes in this regard.

The path of Lula da Silva and the PT in Brazil has been somewhat similar to Cardenas and the PRD, although in 1997, the latter scored an important political success by winning the mayoralty of Mexico City, a city of over 20 million and, as it has turned out, an excellent vantage point for the 2006 presidential elections. By mid 1994, Lula, the PT candidate for president, was way ahead in the polls, with 40 per cent declaring support for him versus 20 per cent for Fernando Henrique Cardoso. In the end, Cardoso, an erstwhile Marxist turned social democrat, won the elections because he had successfully implemented the Plano Real, a new currency stabilization program, during his term a minister of finance. Evidently, it was a mistake for Lula and the PT to ignore or oppose the popular Plano Real, which did manage to control the galloping inflation that had been eating away at the purchasing power of the masses. But in the end, the PT's principal problem was the same as that of the PRD in Mexico: they lacked a coherent alternative program that appealed to the common sense of electors. The PT succumbed to the same dynamic that has made it impossible for the political left to take power. People everywhere have lost confidence in this class and its politics, with its double discourse, swings to the right, and opportunist double-dealings with the enemy.

This has continued to be the problem of the left, notwithstanding an apparent tilt to the centre-left in recent years with the current presidency of Lula in Brazil (although in practice, Lula has turned to be a convinced neo-liberal); the election of the socialist Michelle Bachalet in Chile; the presidency of Hugo Chavez in Venezuela and the popular movement that has kept him there; the election of Evo Morales to state power in Bolivia; the election of a socialist coalition in Uruguay in 2005; the response of Néstor Kirchner, President of Argentina, to the demands of the popular movement; and the growing electoral support for the centre-left presidential candidates in the 2006 elections in Peru and Mexico. In his reflections on this point in the mid 1990s, Ruben Zamora, leader of the Salvadoran left, argued that "never before were so many parties on the left so close to taking power." What prevented this from happening, according to Zamora (1995: 11), were "external forces opposed to the interests of the majority." At the time of his writing, he argued that those forces had never before been so determinant in the outcome of Latin American power struggles. Zamora could be right: we should look beyond internal conditions to explain why the left failed to take national power in so many instances. On the other hand, recent political developments that include an apparent swing to the centre-left and to anti-imperialist and anti-neo-liberal policies (ALCA, the regional free trade agreement sponsored by the US is "dead" in the currents of political change) suggest that internal forces are beginning to override external ones.

SOCIAL MOVEMENTS ON THE RISE

The significance of the 1980s in Latin America could be described in two ways: a stagnation and economic setback on the one hand, and an advance of civilian constitutional regimes over military dictatorships on the other. Perhaps what is most striking in this context is the working class movement's failure to act as strong protagonist and its own structural weakness, given that they were the principal base of the struggle for social change in the 1960 and 1970s. Another striking feature of the changed political landscape in the 1980s was the explosion of social protests and collective actions that forced the generals back to the barracks. These protests took centre-stage in the popular movement against the neo-liberal agenda of globalization and structural reform in the 1990s.

As for the weakness of the working class, some explanations point to objective and structural changes: a dramatic involution in the internal structure of the class (the disappearance of the traditional full-time worker in heavy basic industry and the public sector); repression; and reduced manoeuvring space left to the unions. An additional change has been the drastic fall of employment in the formal sector, another devastating consequence of the adjustment process. Another line of explanation focuses on more subjective factors, such as a failure of leadership, an inadequate political response to the neo-conservative offensive launched against the working class, and the intellectual and ideological crisis of the left.

Surprisingly, the urban poor and an amalgam of social movements moved into the vacuum left by the political parties and unions in the political and social struggles in the 1980s. The social base and leadership of these movements were inhabitants of marginal urban areas; women denouncing government policy and the lack of democracy, as well as sexual discrimination; indigenous communities demanding autonomy and respect for their organizations and culture; many youth excluded from school or work; and family members of those who had been incarcerated, tortured, or made to "disappear" (that is, murdered) for political reasons by the military regimes in place (De la Garza, 1994).

The emergence of these new social movements (NSMs) created a torment of theoretical explanations, including the idea that the heterogeneity of these movements, in terms of their social base and their demands, discredited them from a strict class analysis. It has been argued that something other than class analysis is needed: a new form of analysis that can encompass their complexity and diversity, and the dynamics of their struggles to establish their identity in local spaces and in very specific contexts (Escobar and Alvarez, 1992).

However, the attempt to banish class from the analysis and theory of these social movements, and to substitute a postmodernist, non-structural form of identity analysis, has manifestly failed.[3] To confront this failure, and to seek a reconstituted form of class analysis, we follow Jose Michael Candia (1996) in locating Latin America's NSMs within an analytical framework that classifies social movements in terms of their social base (the sectors of population that constitute their base of support and action, and the type of demands that serve to mobilize this social base). With an eye to the tradition of class analysis, we could examine the movement's ideological direction or scope towards either reform or revolution.

Although a systematic analysis of these movements does not exist (and we will not attempt to create one), their principal demands fall under the following basic categories:

- class struggle (in most cases)
- regional problems that sometimes have a class dimension
- ethnic or gender claims for equality and struggles against oppression, the relations and conditions of which also appear, more often than not, to have a class dimension
- demands for the respect of fundamental human rights that tend to have either a class or an ethnic/gender dimension
- demands related to environmental protection or inter-generational issues raised by youth organizations that have an ethnic and/or class dimension.

The dominant approach to examining these movements has been to describe in detail one movement in one country, without any attempt at comparative structural analysis. But, in anticipation of such studies, we can say that given the clear class character of so many social movements in the region, it would be at best premature to abandon class theory and analysis and at worst an idealist escape from reality—realities that most people in the region cannot escape.

Certainly, it is not possible or desirable to reduce an analysis of these movements, their social base and their dynamics, to the issue of class alone. But who would do so? In fact, what is missing in the analysis of these NSMs is precisely the question of class. We will address this question in the following section, providing some elements of a reconstituted class analysis.

NGOs AND PARTICIPATORY DEVELOPMENT: SOLIDARITY FROM BELOW

The basic elements of a model for "another development" (AD) were elaborated in the 1970s. One of their sources is the Dag Hammarskjold Foundation for Alternative Development, which provided the initial impulse to form a movement devoted to the search for an alternative development, a movement that now can be found all over the world. Ironically, the AD movement originated in the same year (1974) that gave rise to:

- the World Bank's discovery of poverty as a global problem and its elaboration of a basic needs strategy designed to alleviate the conditions of extreme poverty
- the counteroffensive launched by capital against the working class (in different contexts and forms, but as evident more in the south than the north)
- the height of the liberal reform movement and its growth-with-equity model, its politics of state-led structural reform (land reform, income redistribution, progressive taxation, etc.), and its proposals for development and social welfare, designed to prevent more radical solutions such as social revolution.

These liberal reform policies and programs reached their limits at the end of the decade. The liberal-social reformers who dominated the theory and practice of development succumbed to blows by the neo-liberals on their right and the Marxists and Dependency theorists on their left. Unable to explain the failures of so many developing countries or the successes of the newly industrializing countries (NICs) in East Asia, the reformers lost confidence in their postulates and political and theoretical recipes, and they abandoned the scene. This opened up a huge space that was in little time occupied by the neo-classical economists and neo-liberals. In theory and practice, the counter-revolution had begun. And so had the era of structural adjustment, with its devastating attempt to restructure economies around the world in search of conditions to re-establish the process of capital accumulation.

At the end of the 1980s, neo-liberalism had clearly reached its political limit and faced a crisis in the form of resistance and opposition to its policies and their high social costs. The context for this decline, as we have seen, included a social and economic crisis with a significant political dimension, and the democratic conversion of existing military regimes. In addition, civil society had been reconstructed in the emerging popular sector of organizations and social movements predicated on resistance and oriented towards construction of an alternative to neo-liberalism. This civil society formed the social base for various proposals for alternative development.

Various forms of alternative development were advanced. As we have seen, one set of such proposals (constituting a "new paradigm") were actually authored by the World Bank itself, in conjunction with the UNDP and other operating UN agencies such as UNICEF, in an effort to give structural adjustment a human face. But, although these institutions had appropriated the concepts and principles of AD (popular participation, empowerment, etc.) they could not propose an alternative model. Rather, what emerged was a rehabilitated and dressed-up form of the same neo-liberal model of SAP, somewhat akin to the "renovation" that took place to produce "the new world order."

However, the application of the neo-liberal recipe generated such a crisis that a series of proposals called not for its renovation, but for a more radical overhaul, and even from some quarters, its abandonment. The social and political base of this more radical response was found in a great unfurling of community-based or -directed social organizations associated with the reconstruction of civil society. The critical factor in this reorganization was the growth of a complex network of NGOs, many of which had, in fact, offered themselves to institutional authorities as mediators with community grassroots organizations. For example, an NGO forum on the promotion of rural development held in October 1996 in Tepic, Mexico, resolved to create a network of civil support organizations on the basis of experiences in states such as Chiapas and Oaxaca, where over 2,000 NGOs had been identified. It is estimated that there are over 10,000 NGOs in Mexico. They proliferated in the 1980s because, as conference representatives noted, "the people no longer want to obey and just be quiet" (*La Jornada*, October 24, 1996: 42). That is, these NGOs were formed to mobilize popular discontent, and, as we will see, to channel it.

To help oppressed people awaken and find their voice, NGOs were formed not just in Mexico, but all over the region. The aim was to "support the people" as "new social subjects in the bosom of the society" and "stimulate the processes of gestation and consolidation of their collective asocial identities" (Schuldt, 1995: 70).

Governments in the region, together with financial and other institutions tied to neo-liberal policies, turned to the NGOs because they were capable of mediating relations with the base organizations and opening up channels for popular participation in public policy.[4]

In turn, many of these NGOs worked with agencies of the central government, foundations, and donor institutions to seek funding to provide marginalized and poor communities compensatory services to alleviate the impacts of the adjustment process. This relationship of solidarity and association ("partnership") constitutes the axis of the World Bank's new approach—the new paradigm, as it is widely referred to in UN agencies, such as the International Fund for Agricultural Development (IFAD).

Subsequent proposals from the NGO sector take a number of forms, but their essence is that the development has to be community-directed and -based; that is, development should be both local and create the necessary conditions for empowering communities, constituting them as collective social subjects.

This approach is expressed in the search for what has been labelled community economic development (CED). Forms of this approach are abundant, and in many places CED has been institutionalized as the dominant and principal policy. In its institutional form, CED requires a policy of political and economic decentralization, understood by Ronald Reagan among others as the devolution of government to the local authorities and "the people." Since it was widely institutionalized in the 1980s, CED has been promoted as a small business enterprise strategy, with the private sector viewed as the motor or creative force of the development process through entrepreneurship and generating jobs and income.

However, in spite of the vast array of CED projects and proposals implemented all over the world, no systematic comparative evaluations of the strategy and its associated models exist. The precise conditions needed to implement the strategy, and its effectiveness and viability as a national strategy, remain unclear.

Aside from CED (which is essentially a strategy implemented from above, within the apparatus of government, and from the outside, with the support of the community of international financial and donor institutions), the NGO sector has generated a great variety of ideas but no specific models for an alternative community-based and -directed form of development. Insofar as they constitute a movement, NGOs are generally aligned in opposition to neo-liberalism and are active participants in the search for AD. One exemplar of these proposals is the Alternative Strategy for Economic Development, elaborated in September 1995 by the Civic Alliance, an amalgam of 53 social organizations in Mexico, together with seven other NGOs. The strategy was elaborated on the basis of some 425,000 signatures collected in support of the Referendum for Freedom, convoked in June of the same year, and the first National Congress to Condemn the Economic Policy of the Mexican Government. In 1996, the EZLN on its own and independent of this development summoned a series of Encounters against Neo-liberalism and for Humanity (Democracy) for same purpose: to encourage and give form to a widespread disillusionment and dissent and to a diffuse politics of resistance and opposition to neo-liberalism. Their aim was to transform this intellectual and political energy into concrete alternative proposals. But can community-based development projects be translated into a viable national development strategy? The outcome is uncertain, but will be closely monitored and awaited with interest.

NEW CLASS MOVEMENTS IN THE COUNTRYSIDE

The double discourse and opportunism of many leaders of organizations on the left has caused both confusion and absolute distrust within the political class and its political instrument of choice—the political party, which, as Max Weber pointed out, is an organization that pursues power. In this context, many citizens have abandoned the class struggle to devote themselves to the problems of their daily life, seeking to survive the conditions created by neo-liberalism and simply make a living (often in the informal sector, which may mean the streets and, possibly, criminal behaviour). Some intellectuals, armed with a postmodernist perspective, have seriously misinterpreted this trend as the emergence of new social subjects and new social movements based on the politics of everyday life and social identity—of gender, of ecology, of ethnicity—and, by the same token, the end of class politics.[5]

Notwithstanding the twofold tendency that many people have to escape from politics into the problems of managing their everyday life under neo-liberalism while electing regimes that generate these same problems, there is a growing movement of resistance and opposition to neo-liberal capitalism in many countries.

Although this politics of resistance and opposition has adopted different forms in various contexts, it undoubtedly has a class basis. In Bolivia, for example, the miners and coca producers, the teachers, and a new type of union bound to the social movements have coordinated their protest actions with an amalgam of social organizations, rather than with the parties of the left. But, more than anything, it can be seen in the struggles that are taking place in the countryside—the apparent centre of a new wave of insurgency.

An exemplar of these new class movements is the Landless Workers' Movement (MST) in Brazil, formed on a base of hundreds of organizations and hundreds of thousands of activists and supporters. The MST has created a national political debate on the land reform issue, and according to most observers, is the most dynamic and best organized social movement in the country and the region. It is also the most effective, with a consistent record of concrete achievements and successful land occupations, through which it has accumulated a huge reservoir of social forces to deploy in direct action. In

Bolivia, the closure of the mines and imports of inexpensive and contraband products have weakened the hitherto powerful mining and industrial sectors unions, organized in the form of the Bolivian Workers Central (COB). In their place, organizations of peasants, in particular the *cocaleros* (many of whom are former miners) have formed, and they are leading the struggle against neo-liberalism, with massive confrontations, marches, and general strikes that have paralyzed the country (Contreras Baspineiro, 1994). In Paraguay, the National Federation of Peasants is the principal force behind the massive mobilizations that have shaken the country, placing the land issue at the centre of the political agenda and making it the main axis of struggle against neo-liberalism (*Informativo Campesino*, April 1996, No. 91). Also in Mexico (in Guerrero, Chiapas, and Oaxaca), serious confrontations between peasant organizations and the state abound (*La Jornada*, August 10, 1996: 3; Chiapas, No. 2 [Mexico, 1996]; *La Jornada*, October 10, 1996).

Finally, in Ecuador, Colombia, and El Salvador, along with other countries in the region, the peasants have also constituted themselves as the principal subject of the class struggle against neo-liberalism. In many contexts, the peasants are of indigenous origin, giving a national and ethnic character to their struggle. However, the principal aspect of their struggle can be found in their relationship to the means of social production and the state.

In short, the epitaph given to the peasantry by analysts and historians such as Eric Hobsbawm (1984) is premature to say the least and misinformed to say more. The demographic argument about their declining numbers does not translate well into political analysis, at least with respect to Latin America. First of all, millions of families continue to live, produce, and work in the countryside: more than 6 million in the case of Mexico. Second, the urban crisis and its unemployment, under-employment, and misery do not provide a promising avenue for the peasant youth. Third, in context of the land takeovers in Brazil, Paraguay, El Salvador, and other countries, there is evidence that people are countering the traditional move from the countryside to the cities. Fourth, neo-liberal policies have battered the small producers with low prices, unequal competition, and a non-payable debt. Fifth, aside from structural considerations, a new generation of peasant leaders has emerged in recent years, and they show a marked capacity for organization, a sharp understanding of international and national politics, and a deep political commitment to changing the lives of their members.

Note that we are not speaking here of traditional peasant movements. First, in many cases, these peasants are not divorced from urban life. Some are ex-miners or workers who have been let go or fired. Others are daughters of small peasant producers who are educated at the secondary or primary level and who have joined (and sometimes lead) the movements, instead of migrating to the cities to work in domestic service. In other cases, the militants who lead the movements have a religious upbringing but have abandoned the church in the struggle for agrarian reform. The "new peasants," particularly the militants in leadership positions, often travel to cities to participate in seminars and training schools, and political discussions.

In short, although they have their roots in the land struggle and are agricultural producers, often living in land camps, many of the new peasant leaders have a cosmopolitan vision. In number and quality, these peasant intellectuals vary from country to country. In Brazil, the MST has invested considerable resources and energy in training a new leadership cadre, with hundreds of peasants annually attending their leadership training school. In other cases, as in Paraguay, Bolivia, and El Salvador, the peasant movement depends on fewer leaders, but those who are savvy.

The second critical point about these new peasant movements (NPMs) is that they are autonomous. The MST, for example, has a cordial relationship with the PT. The same applies to the relationship between the Democratic Peasant Alliance (ADC) in Argentina and the Farabundo Martí National Liberation Front (*Frente Farabundo Martí para la Liberación Nacional*, or FMLN). But the force of both movements lies in their direct struggles: land takeovers, highway blockades, sit-ins of public buildings. Their ideological discussions, as well as their strategies and tactics, remain within the movement in every case, and are not subordinated to any party line. On the contrary, these movements are giving dynamism to the political struggles of the parties on the left; that is, the agrarian struggle. At present, the NPMs are often the catalyst for protests against neo-liberalism. In Bolivia, for example, peasant organizations have broken their traditional ties with the parties and are actively debating the idea of forming their own "political instrument." In fact, the National Peasant Federation in Paraguay has done just that by launching the political revolutionary socialist movement. In Ecuador, the CONAIE has called for a new "national indigenous uprising" and has formed its own political instrument to present their own candidate in the presidential elections.

Third, NPMs are involved in direct action rather than the electoral process, as a rule. In fact, as in Chiapas, they have generally discarded it as one specific form of political action. They prefer a combined strategy of direct action and negotiations with representatives of the state. Or they prefer to coordinate actions with the unions, NGOs, and the parties in specific contexts such as coordinating a general strike or proposing a piece of legislation. They always retain control of the pace and the direction of the principal form of struggle: massive mobilization.

Fourth, NPMs are influenced by a mixture of classic Marxism and, in various contexts, by issues of gender, ecology, and, in particular, ethnicity and nationality. Particularly in Bolivia, and in Paraguay, the issues of national liberation and those of land struggle are closely tied to ethnic identity, respect for indigenous culture, the rights of indigenous peoples, and claims of national autonomy. Political debates are generally marked with the idea of the close connection between problems of class and the nation. In Brazil and Bolivia, groups within the NPMs are organized to obtain more and better positions within decision-making and power structures. They also think and work within a political framework that makes connections between the issues of class and gender, discarding any bourgeois feminist ideas about the centrality of gender or the possibility of examining it in isolation from class. They similarly discard an economistic or classist approach.

Fifth, NPMs are usually coordinated through and to a certain extent united by international organizations such as Via Campesina that debate and exchange relevant experiences of struggles—struggles that are increasingly seen as shared. An internationalist consciousness and practice is emerging from these experiences. For example, the militants of the MST in Brazil frequently meet with their counterparts in Paraguay, and to a lesser degree in Argentina and Uruguay. The same thing is happening in the Andes among the indigenous peasants of Bolivia, Peru, and Ecuador, as well as in Central America.

To summarize, the reappearance of peasant-led social movements in the 1990s is not simply a return to the 1960s and 1970s. In many cases, the successes and the failures of those years have been studied and debated in search of lessons they can provide. There are elements of continuity with the struggles of the 1960s and 1970s in the NPMs, but there are also differences in tactics, strategy, politics, and organization. The NPMs are much more conscious of the existence of a global empire of the neo-liberal policy program that is tied to the world economic order. They are also all but united in an awareness of the need to confront and oppose it: an understanding that neo-liberalism is the principal enemy and all peasants and indigenous people have a common struggle and need to join forces.

CONCLUSION

In Latin America and elsewhere, the people are at another crossroads. On the one hand are the efforts to reconstitute a system whose global expansion has transformed the economic and social conditions of the greater part of the population in its national fortresses. The system of neo-liberal capitalism has spread across the globe, but so have its internal contradictions, which are generating the possibly of a devastating economic crisis and a protracted class struggle. The politics and policies that it sustains are under severe pressures and are in decline, despite efforts to rescue it through various forms of restructuring. On the other hand, it is possible to identify a growing number and broadening range of forces of resistance and opposition.

This chapter has identified a range of responses to neo-liberalism today. Among intellectuals, there is a deep division with ideological and political dimensions. On the one hand are the efforts and proposals to soften its effects, to give it a human face, and to reconstitute neo-liberal capitalism in a different form (ECLAC). These solutions are sponsored and supported by the multilateral financial institutions. Basically, these institutions offer a limited variation on models of the roles assigned to the state and to the market. On the other side, we have identified a movement dedicated to the search for an alternative form of development. This movement is supported by a multiplicity and diversity of non-governmental and community-based organizations. We conclude that by virtue of its broad albeit heterogeneous social base, this search for alternative development offers greater possibilities for effective social change than do neo-liberal and neo-structural strategies. However, these responses to neo-liberalism are very limited in scale and scope, and have a limited capacity to generate the political conditions required for their implementation at the national level. In this respect, we put more faith or hope in the social forces projected by the left in its new formation—not as a political class or political party, but as a social movement with a broad base in the popular sectors of civil society. In this regard, we have drawn particular attention to social movements constructed and led by peasants. At present, these movements have a greater dynamism than any other, as well as the potential to unite the forces of opposition to neo-liberalism. These new emerging movements of the left are far from offering an alternative economic model to what has been defined as the new economic model. But they offer a strategy of resistance and a political perspective for a better future in a new world.

NOTES

1. As for Mexico, see the words of Michel Camdessus, General-Director of the IMF: "The IMF is preparing a program that will serve as a framework for assuring the growth of the Mexican economy during the years ahead ... as for the micro-economic details and the development priorities, they are matters well taken care of by my friends at the World Bank and the Inter-American Development Bank" (*El Financiero*, September 27, 1996).

2. In Venezuela, as in Argentina, the probable cause of a drastic fall in the value of wages and an increase in poverty, according to the minister of finance, is a marked increase in the rate of unemployment (17 to 20 per cent) and increases in the price of basic commodities (36 to 50 per cent) (*La Jornada*, October 21, 1996: 52). The minister of finance in Argentina, where unemployment hit 17.1 per cent declared in the same terms. In Mexico, the situation is the same, notwithstanding the statements by Camdessus, the US under-secretary of state, and David Rockefeller about the "positive performance" of Mexico's key macroeconomic indicators (*La Jornada*, Oct. 30, 1996) and a relatively low level of official unemployment (4 to 5.8 per cent). These cases are discussed by Petras (1997), for example, the *Movimiento Izquierda Revolucionario* in Bolivia, which in the 1980s entered into an alliance with Hugo Banzer, ex-dictator; the Socialist Party in Chile that forms part of the Christian democratic-led concertation regime; MAS in Venezuela, which is backing Caldera's Plan Venezuela de Calderas in exchange for several government posts.

3. An example of the absurdity reached in these efforts is Burbach's (1994) classification and analysis of the Zapatista social movement in Chiapas, Mexico, as "the first postmodern political movement." Holloway (2002) uses the Zapatista experience as the inspiration for his theory of a new "non-power" aproach to social change—that, in effect, change can be effected without the conquest of state power.

4. The critical role of NGOs in World Bank projects is evident in the fact that out of every five projects between the World Bank and governments of developing countries in the 1990s, two involved NGOs (Nelson, 1995). The World Bank's policy of partnership with NGOs derives from a strategic decision made towards the end of the 1980s in the context of a "new understanding" about the need to protect the vulnerable groups, particularly the poor, in the process of adjustment (*Finance & Development*, December 1992). In this regard, the Bank elaborated a consensus document in 1987, and initiated a working group of NGOs, giving them a measure of autonomy, with their own permanent representation in Geneva to give the Bank advice and consultations—and strategic albeit critical collaboration. In this regard, see Arruda (1993). Despite its relationship with the Bank, the NGO Working Group is generally guided by a search for an alternative form of development to that espoused by the Bank.

5   See, for example, the several essays compiled by Escobar and Alvarez (1992) and Slater (1985). This perspective on the new social movements of Latin America aims to move beyond this impasse and crisis. In this regard, see, inter alia, Schuurman (1993). The basis of this theoretical crisis is the impasse reached in theory and practice by the proponents of both neo-liberalism and neo-structuralism. The AD movement has its origin precisely in an effort to escape the impasse created by these lines of thought, in the form of constituting a new paradigm. On this point see, inter alia, Griesgraber and Gunter (1996). But this effort, just as similar efforts taken by proponents of diverse theories and actions in the radical political economy paradigm, signally failed to move beyond the theoretical impasse and explain the dynamics of the world capitalist system and the development process. On this entire problematic see, inter alia, Sachs (1992) and Schuurman (1993), who point towards diverse attempts to resolve the impasse related to an entirely different line of thought that denies the existence of any intelligible structure or a historic process rooted in the workings of a system.

EIGHT

Movement in the Countryside and Cities

The Latin American countryside is on the move. What was once a predominantly rural society has transformed to an increasingly urban one in terms of social production, livelihoods, living, work, and residence. Nevertheless, rural society remains on the centre stage of social change in the region. Not that the dynamics of rural social change do not affect urban society. In fact, one feature of the new social movements (NSMs) that has arisen from these changes is their intersection, if not strategic or tactical alliance, with social forces of resistance and opposition in the urban centres, particularly in zones that encompass what Mike Davis (2006) has termed "the planet of slums" (for example, El Alto in Bolivia). Behind the dynamics of these NSMs are organizations and socio-political movements of landless workers in Brazil; the *cocaleros* in Bolivia; the communities and organizations, such as CONAIE, that make up the indigenous movement in Ecuador, Bolivia, and Chiapas and beyond in Mexico; and the semi-proletarianized peasantry and its diverse accretions, in Central as well as South America.

This chapter focuses on the political dynamics of social change and national development associated with these organizations and movements. These movements exhibit or engage the most dynamic forces of social change in the region. Although viewed in their totality as "the popular movement," they are divided both in terms of the social forces they mobilize and the paths they take towards social change.

There are three basic modalities of social change and development, each associated with a distinct road that needs to be travelled. Two of these roads—electoral politics and social mobilization—are paved with state power, which is to say that in order for social change and development to occur, state apparatus needs to be captured and used. This is the central objective of what might be termed the "old politics." The third road to social change and development takes the form of "no power": local development based on the accumulation of social capital and built on a culture of solidarity and networks of reciprocal exchange that supposedly exist in communities inhabited by the rural poor.

Strictly speaking, *roads* might not be most appropriate metaphor, because the three modalities of change and development are not mutually exclusive. In practice, the diverse rural poor that make up the bulk of the population in the countryside view these roads to change as strategies that can be combined, rather than as alternative options. In Bolivia and Ecuador, for example, the struggle for social change in recent years has involved the simultaneous use of electoral politics, social mobilization, and local development. Nevertheless, we must distinguish the political dynamics associated with each of these paths to social change and analyze the associated pitfalls and outcomes. This we do with a broad-brush sweep across the region, and then we take a somewhat closer look at developments in Bolivia and, more distantly, in Ecuador. These two countries exemplify like no other the political dynamics of social change in what might be termed the era of "neo-liberal globalization." For one thing, they have given rise to some of the most dynamic anti-systemic forces of social change in the region. For another, the political dynamics of social change in these countries show the pitfalls of each of the available paths.

THE ROAD TO STATE POWER: ELECTORAL POLITICS OR MASS MOBILIZATION?

Since the Cuban Revolution in 1959, a turning point in the struggle for social change in Latin America, three waves of insurrectionary social movements have emerged, each mobilizing a certain constellation of oppositional forces, each arising in a specific conjuncture of objectively given structural conditions, and each associated with a specific subjective or political response to these conditions. The first wave of social movements hit in the 1960s, and swept across the region in the 1970s. The broad context for this wave included the following: a process of state-led economic and social development; the institutional framework of the Bretton Woods world economic order; a growing East–West cold war and ideological divide; a process of decolonization, national liberation, and social change; and the implementation of a two-pronged strategy of rural development designed to put out the fire and smouldering embers of revolutionary ferment in the countryside, executed under the US foreign policy framework of the Alliance for Progress.

MOVEMENT IN THE COUNTRYSIDE AND CITIES

This strategy, the Alliance for Progress, was formulated within the framework of a larger geopolitical project—international co-operation for development. This project, together with the very idea of development, was invented to ensure that those countries in the process of liberating themselves from the yoke of European colonialism would take a capitalist path towards nation building and economic growth—eluding thereby the lure of communism (Sachs, 1992). More specifically, especially in Latin America, the development project aimed to turn the rural poor away from radical change based on confronting the economic and political power structure; that is, to deter them from taking direct action against the owners of property capital and the state.

By the 1970s, the golden age of capitalism, an extended period of rapid economic growth, had come to an end. A system-wide production crisis had emerged, as well as a profit crunch on capital that gave rise to a class war between capital and labour, and to diverse efforts to restructure a way out of the crisis (Veltmeyer, 2005). Under these conditions, the conflict between capital and labour assumed different forms, as did the struggle for social change in Latin America.

The opposing dynamics of this struggle could be condensed in the formula "reform or revolution." In the urban centres, the struggle for social and political change was formed around the organized working class, but the politics of change, the quest for state power (or the power to influence and change government policy), took the bourgeois form of participation in the electoral process. In the countryside, however, the dominant mode of social change was to directly confront state power with collective direct action, as well as with insurrection and armed force. The state responded to the revolutionary ferment in the countryside in different ways: softly, in the form of rural integrated development, but also in the tough form of direct action against and repression of the emerging social movements, especially those that had resorted to armed force, which raised the spectre of another Cuba.

In the space of a decade at most, virtually all of these movements were destroyed or decapitated, their leadership in disarray, accommodated to the option of reform presented by the government and international co-operation for development. FARC in Colombia was one of few such organizations to survive the counter-insurgency, although others took to ground to engage in a rebuilding process. In places such as Venezuela (and in the MAS throughout the region), the Communist Party often officially eschewed or abandoned armed force as a tactical means of achieving state power and cast off the guerrilla struggle for social change. As for the groups that went to ground, very few managed to regroup and emerge as a political force. An exception here is the EZLN, which irrupted on the political stage in Chiapas at the precise point (January 1, 1994) at which NAFTA too came into effect.

In the urban centres, in the 1970s, the insurgency of the labour movement was repressed by the state, in a number of cases (particularly in the southern cone) under the aegis of a militarized and colonized state operating under the "national security doctrine" of the US government.

The 1980s gave rise to new developments—epoch-defining changes associated with the process of neo-liberal globalization that would create an entirely different context for rebuilding the popular movement and mobilizing the forces of resistance and opposition. In these new circumstances, a second wave of social movements hit Latin America, this time in the urban centres. These new movements were of particular interest to academics ensconced in their offices and attuned to cyberspace rather than the real world. As viewed by these academics, these movements were heterogeneous, without a definable class basis or orientation, and focused a on a variety of ostensibly non-class or middle-class issues, such as environmental protection, human rights violations, and women's rights, as well as a struggle for democratic representation, participation, transparency, and government accountability. As for the struggle against urban poverty, IMF mandated macro-economic policy reforms, and in the vestiges of various military regimes, it was the urban poor themselves who mobilized and took action (Petras and Leiva, 1994).

In the late 1980s, a third wave of social movements was formed in the countryside. Rooted for the most part in indigenous communities, peasant producers, and landless workers, these movements would give rise in the 1990s to some of the most dynamic forces of resistance and opposition to government policy and the underlying neo-liberal agenda. Of particular importance was the rural Landless Workers' Movement in Brazil (MST), the Confederation of Indigenous Nationalities of Ecuador (CONAIE), the *cocaleros* of Chaparé, and in a more limited regional context, the Zapatista Army of National Liberation (EZLN). For an analysis of the dynamics of these social movements, see Petras and Veltmeyer (2003, 2005).

THE DYNAMICS OF SOCIAL MOBILIZATION AND ELECTORAL POLITICS

Developments in Bolivia and Ecuador in the 1990s and beyond exemplify the dilemma of the popular movement: to opt once again for the parliamentary road to state power by using the electoral mechanism and political party as a form of political organization, or to take the revolutionary road of mass social mobilization—to confront state power with collective direct action and possibly armed force.

A review of political developments in both countries suggests a fundamental orientation to and preference for mass social mobilization and the confrontation of state power as the best way to bring about fundamental social change in government policy. In the 1990s in both Ecuador and Bolivia, a series of insurrectionary actions and mobilizations took place. The political landscape was littered with the detritus of these mobilizations, including several ousted presidents and defeated or retracted neo-liberal policies. Indigenous uprisings in Ecuador, in 1990 and then again in January 2000, gave rise to the view that the decade was a major advance for indigenous movement. In Bolivia, a similar lifting of the tide of an indigenous movement was evident, although it would take a different form.

In both Bolivia and Ecuador, the formation of an apparatus to contest national and local elections was a significant political organizational development. These were Pachakutik, an indigenous party in Ecuador,[1] and the Movement towards Socialism (MAS) in Bolivia, constructed on the model of MAS in Venezuela.

Social Change Dynamics in Ecuador

In Ecuador, the formation of Pachakutik not only provided the indigenous movement with a way to contest elections, it also divided the movement, with one group oriented towards social mobilizations and another towards electoral politics.[2] In fact, both aspects of the indigenous movement continued, with mass social mobilizations in some situations and electoral politics in others. Mass social mobilization and electoral politics were viewed as complementary rather than as alternative options. The origins of mass social mobilizations can be traced to various events, notably the mobilization that led to the February 1997 ouster of Abdala Bucaram's four-month-old government, and also to January 2000, when a quasi-revolutionary situation developed, providing conditions for a direct assault on the centre of state power.[3] Another neo-liberal regime was overthrown, albeit only temporarily (for four hours), to be replaced by a triumvirate that included Antonio Vargas, CONAIE's president at the time, and Lucio Gutierrez, a middle-ranking colonel who was part of the armed forces that supported and joined the insurrection. In fact, the uprising had several important outcomes in addition to the ousting of another head of state. For one thing, it provided the economically dominant, ruling political classes a clear signal that the indigenous movement was "on the march" and not to be denied or ignored as it had for centuries.

More significant perhaps for the lessons that it would provide was the indigenous movement's use of the electoral apparatus as an alternative way to state power. The insurrection of 2000 created conditions for a transition towards a government eventually formed by Gutierrez. By 2002, Gutierrez had gained the support of CONAIE and the indigenous movement in his personal quest for state power: they agreed to join his government in exchange for participation in it. Suffice it to say that once he became President, Gutierrez betrayed the movement by failing to fight neo-liberalism and rescinding promises to support a more popular program of changes and development. The assumption had been that with CONAIE's participation, the government would not be able to turn towards the neo-liberal model for its macroeconomic policies and that it would be compelled to respond to the popular and indigenous movement. Clearly, this expectation was not met, and the underlying trust and alliance was soon broken. It did not take long for CONAIE to come to terms with Gutierrez's embrace of Washington and the neo-liberal policy agenda, which CONAIE spent a decade of struggle mobilizing against. In September 2003, CONAIE convoked a national convention to call the Gutierrez government to account and to recall its political representatives from the government, compelling them to give up their posts and their support of the government.

For the next three years, CONAIE underwent a process of rebuilding a seriously weakened movement. Unfortunately, the leadership of the movement had not fully digested the lesson of its detour into electoral politics. In 2006, the movement participated once more in the electoral process, this time with its own presidential candidate, Luis Macas. Given the widespread racism in Ecuadorian society and the racist and classist politics of the political class, he was totally marginalized by the process. The experience was not unlike that of Felipe Quispe in Bolivia's presidential elections, although Quispe did not have anywhere near the representation that Macas had. Nor can we compare the organizational strength of Quispe's MIP (Pachakutik Indigenous Movement) with Pachakutik or CONAIE (the Confederation of Indigenous Nationalities of Ecuador). But the issue is the same: Can the indigenous movement anywhere overcome the built-in obstacles of the electoral process and avoid the pitfalls? The political dynamics of this process are constrained by certain rules and conditions that are not codified but are nevertheless operational. These rules, set by the political class, operate against the interests of the popular movement. For one thing, they prevent any substantive move towards the left and the implementation of a popular government program. But to argue this point we need to take a closer look at Bolivia.

Social Change Dynamics in Bolivia

All structures or institutionalized practices constrain, but they also provide opportunities: While they restrict the actions of some, they facilitate the actions of others. The constraints built into the structure of electoral politics—the formation and the exercise of government—clearly favour the group or the class that has encircled state power, in many cases penetrating and inhabiting it. The historical evidence is strong enough to obviate the need for much discussion. Just as clearly, those groups and classes that are excluded from the means of production and the corresponding legal and political relations (the state) are also constrained. They are not even able to benefit from the structure, even when it is opened up to popular participation, as happened under the Bolivian government of Gonzalo Sánchez de Lozada in 1994.[4] Economic and political power is founded on a certain configuration of class power, and the built-in constraints of the electoral system permit little realignment of this power. Only a very narrow range of deviation from prescribed policy is allowed. This point is clearly illustrated by political developments in Bolivia that preceded the ascent of Evo Morales (leader of the *cocalero* movement, the MAS, and the first indigenous head of state) to the presidency in 2005, as well during his tenure in power.

The developments that led up to Morales's presidency involved complex and shifting dynamics of resistance to the neo-liberal model that the previous governments had been using as a guide to national policy since 1985. The popular movement resisted the neo-liberal policy agenda in acts of protest and cycles of mass mobilization, during which there were several critical conjunctures and high points. During this protracted period of upheaval, various organizations in the popular sector of Bolivia's civil society came together, albeit in an unorganized fashion, to oppose to the government.[5] The combination of these diverse forces of resistance in this conjuncture of objective (socio-economic) and subjective (political) conditions generated what in retrospect might be viewed as a quasi-revolutionary situation that brought the popular movement to the brink of state power. However, the critical and explosive factor was the government's move to limit access to the country's vast hydrocarbon reserves of natural gas and oil, and to privatize production in the sector. The ensuing Bolivian Gas War in October 2003 mobilized some of the same social and political forces of opposition and resistance as that of the so-called water war of 2000, which was centred in Cochabamba but also engaged the popular movement in El Alto and elsewhere.[6] In the heat of the October 2003 war, the neo-liberal regime was overthrown and the country's president, de Lozada, ousted in a process of mass social mobilization. The government attempted to quell resistance through violence and brutal repression, including the murder of 67 unarmed protesters by military forces. During a subsequent gas war in May and June 2005, another neo-liberal regime was similarly overthrown.

It is evident that Evo Morales did not play an active role in the struggle of October 2003. Indeed, Morales's failure to actively engage in the popular struggle suggests that he was more concerned to preserve the institutions that he intended to use as a means of achieving state power.[7] It appears that Morales helped defuse the emerging quasi-revolution by supporting the congressional installation of Carlos Mesa as President of Bolivia. Subsequently, the forces of popular resistance and opposition were channelled into the process of electoral politics, which led predictably to a *toma de la municipalidad* (takeover of local governments) by the MAS and then to Morales's presidency.

The successful outcome of Morales's strategy to achieve state power in 2005 might be seen as a validation of electoral politics as a path towards change. But, in fact, it is not a matter of choosing one path over the other. Without the mass mobilization that preceded and haunted the elections, Morales would never have been able to scale the steps to state power. It was the force of this mobilization that paved the way for his successful use of elections as a way to state power.

The importance of mass social mobilizations in the process of social change can also be illustrated in subsequent developments, limited as they are to the year that the MAS has exercised state power (to the time of this writing). Many of Morales's supporters, as well as the Latin American and foreign left, hoped and expected that he would revert neo-liberalism and advance the popular agenda, and thereby add weight to the apparent leftist tilt of several governments in the region. After all, after centuries of class exploitation and racist oppression, Morales was the first indigenous peasant leader in history to successfully climb the steps to state power, and he did so by means of the machinery of representative democracy and electoral politics.

Notwithstanding the apparent or alleged conflicting pressures that might have narrowed Morales's political options, the test of a regime's character is not its programmatic statements but its actions—its actual, not its proposed, policies. By briefly assessing the regime's actual practice and its social impact, we can see the workings of diverse social forces and the weight of particular and conflicting economic interests behind government policy. This assessment also allows us to determine the regime's ideological orientation: the nature and limits of the social changes that it might bring about. As tentative as this exercise has to be, it is one means of determining the true nature of the Morales regime—its "socialist" character.

So what have been the government's major policy decisions and actions over its course of state power? What are the social forces behind these policies and actions? That is, to what pressures do they respond? What have been their outcomes and social impacts? Who and what groups have benefited from the government's policies and actions? And what groups and classes have borne the cost of these policies and actions? These questions, and our tentative answers to them, can be grouped according to critical policy areas: property in the means of production, finance, and access to productive natural resources.

Property in the Means of Production

State versus private ownership is the key issue in the control of available productive resources. The question in Bolivia is whether the regime is prepared to advance or to revert the privatization agenda, to re-nationalize ownership and control into the hands of the state. The actions of the Morales regime have been ambiguous. On the one hand, the government has declared that the natural hydrocarbon resources of oil and gas "belong to the people," and one of its first actions was to re-establish state ownership over these assets. The demands and pressures of the popular movement dictated this decision. It was not just a question of popular support for these policies; the government had absolutely no choice in the matter. However, when it came to the less contentious issue of extracting, processing, and exporting iron ore, which incited no such mobilizations, the government proceeded in an entirely different direction. In the case of El Mutún, the world's largest iron ore deposit, the government signed off on a contract with Jindal, an India based multinational, that had been negotiated by the previous regime—a contract that has all the hallmarks of a neo-liberal policy. It would seem that the critical factor in the government's action on the issue of privatization is the correlation of class forces and the degree of social mobilization. The social movement was solidly behind the government's policy to re-nationalize the hydrocarbon sector; indeed, it forced its hand. But the popular movement was relatively absent in the case of Mutún, although even here Morales was constrained to "report" to it—to achieve a support base for what might otherwise have been an unpopular policy. After all, the policy did run counter to the government's professed anti-privatization policy.

The government successfully eliminated potential opposition by reporting to the popular movement, a strategy that it has implemented at various conjunctures for policy announcements. For example, on August 17, 2006, two weeks after the public forum on the Constitutient Assembly and the announcement of the new agrarian reform, Morales met with leaders of 32 social organizations in the city of Cochabamba to report on the government's efforts during nearly seven months in office. In the Mutún consultation, the popular movements expressed their satisfaction with Jindal's promise, as communicated by the government, to invest over $2 billion and create 21,700 direct and indirect jobs. Of course, the precise terms of the contract were not spelled out, either in this public consultation or in subsequent public or newspaper reports.

Clearly, government policy regarding ownership and control over society's productive resources, and the role and weight of public versus private enterprise, can be taken as a measure of a government's class character, as well as the constellation of social forces behind it.

Finance

A second defining feature of a government's ideological orientation and a measure of its political meaning—the class character of the state—is finance: the source of capital used to fund the government's economic and social programs. In a capitalist state, national development is predicated on the accumulation of private capital, but in the Morales regime, perhaps it is too soon to judge. It could be argued that a year in power is not enough time to bring about a shift in the balance between private and public enterprise, and between private and public forms of capital accumulation and finance. In any case, despite the government's announcement that hydrocarbon and other such strategic natural resources belong to the people and its declared intent to nationalize production in the sector, the multinationals remain engaged in the process. Indeed, they have been invited to stay in the country and participate in the production and export process, with due guarantees that their investments will be protected. In fact, the government has not managed to achieve its stated aim of acquiring a 51 per cent ownership share in the joint venture hydrocarbon economic enterprise. Thus, the multinationals are still effectively in control and the government dependent on them to capitalize and finance operations in this strategic sector.

As for how the government finances its own operations and programs, there has also been negligible change at the level of policy. The basic source of government finance is revenue derived from taxing economic activity, and the Morales government has not introduced any measures, such as the creation of a community or popular (producers and workers) development bank that would change this. The only change has been to boost government revenues by increasing both the royalty placed on the exploitation of the country's natural resources and the tax rate on economic activity. But the lack of data makes it difficult to determine its success. The government has predicted a significant increase in government revenues from this source. But to date, there is little evidence of any shift in priorities, and it would appear that little change in policy or spending priorities can be expected in the short or immediate term.

If the government were serious about its supposed socialist agenda, then it would begin by making some move towards state control over finance, regulating if not re-statifying or nationalizing the banks and other financial institutions to create a pool of public finance. However, it appears that for the government socialism does not entail the socialization or statification of the means of production to reverse two decades of neo-liberal policy. In fact, Morales himself has defined the government's political practice and socialism to mean something quite different. "Communalism" based on reciprocity "is our political practice," he says, which not only harkens back to the utopian socialism of the nineteenth century, but also turns the government towards a participatory form of decentralized and local development advanced by de Lozada.[8]

Access to Productive Natural Resources

Another critical area for government action and policy is to improve access to society's productive natural resources, to institute what is considered a more socially inclusive form of national development. In addition to the government's move to statify ownership of natural resources in the hydrocarbon sector and to resist the privatization of water, the popular movement (not congress) has demanded land reform related to the agricultural sector. Just under 90 per cent of Bolivia's productive terrain is worked by only 50,000 families, leaving millions of Bolivians with little or no land. The government's plan is to change the laws of the National Institute on Agrarian Reform (INRA) by expropriating idle land and returning it to the Bolivian people. This plan is in response to pressures exerted by the rural poor, mostly indigenous people of the western high plains. Since these poor have no political representation in the government or the congress, except tangentially through MAS, these pressures for change and government action are exerted through the social movement; that is, social mobilization. So, how has the government responded? On August 2, 2006, Morales announced the government's new agrarian reform law, designed to modify INRA and authorizing the government to private lands found to be unproductive, obtained illegally, or used for speculation (primarily in eastern Bolivia, where most of the land is owned and worked by only 5,000 families). However, the congress, which has the authority to restrain the government beyond narrow limits of change, has invited peasant farmers, indigenous groups, and agribusiness leaders to debate the government's bill and other proposals to change the INRA.

As it turns out, Morales's bill and the government's actions fall far short of its announced agrarian revolution. Rather than fulfilling its "great desire" to expropriate private lands in the hands of "political interests and powerful families" who are well represented in congress, the government's reform consists primarily of handing out legal title to state land to individual families. (Morales kicked off the announced land reform by handing out 15 titles covering 9,600 square miles of state-owned land to poor Indians.)

The government's strategy is to use popular pressure from indigenous and union groups to press congress to vote in favour of the controversial measure. Morales used the announcement of the government's agrarian reform on August 2 to pressure congress into allowing the government to seize private lands. Morales's proposed bill would alter INRA's bylaws. Morales quotes some of the unions and indigenous leaders he's spoken to: "[I]f they don't change the INRA law in order to expropriate idle lands and return them to the Bolivian people, then what good is the congress? ... If they don't change the INRA law, the congress should shut down." But of course this is not in the cards. Moreover, the government in fact has distributed very little land, acting within the strict confines of legislative power, which, unlike executive or presidential power, reflects the strength of the propertied class, the very same powerful families and interests that Morales identified as a fundamental obstacle in any reform process. As a result, the government's actions fall far short of its announced agrarian revolution. Rather than expropriating the land that the government itself recognizes to be in the hands of political interests and powerful families who are well represented in congress, much of the land that is targeted for reform belongs to the state and is located in the fertile eastern lowlands; that is, it requires colonization but little change or reform.

THE DEVELOPMENT PATH TO CHANGE

Bolivia (along with other states in Latin America) might well have been dubbed as developmental until the mid 1980s, in terms of both the weight and role of the public sector in the process of national development. But in 1985, Bolivia took a neo-liberal direction with the institution of a radical program of structural reforms in national policy. Has the Morales government made any moves to reverse this direction, towards either a developmental or a socialist state? It would appear not. To date, the government has made no moves whatsoever to challenge the existing structure of economic or political power—to change the pillars of the neo-liberal capitalist state. Not even its privatization policy for the hydrocarbon sector, forced upon the government by the popular movement, has reverted the existing class structure of property in the means of social production. There has been no announcement of any intent to re-socialize national production. To date, there have been no far-reaching structural changes in national policy, not even in regard to social programs of human resource development, such as education, health, and social security. The government's social policy continues to operate within the parameters of the sustainable human development model introduced, with international co-operation, by the previous de Lozada regime.

The road to social change in Bolivia and elsewhere in the region has generally detoured through the state apparatus, via the dynamics of mass mobilization and electoral politics. However, over the years a no-power approach to social change has emerged through the development programs and projects of those co-operating in international development. The explicit aim of these programs and projects was to provide the rural poor with an alternative to the growing pressures for more radical change and the confrontational politics of the social movements. Although this no-power road to social change was paved in the 1960s in response to the threat presented by the Cuban Revolution, the dynamics of neo-liberal structural reform in the 1980s created the conditions for a new regional front on the battleground of social change.

This front might well have been named "The Quest for Another Development"—development initiated from within and below, localized and community-based, participatory and human in form, and sustainable: "sustainable human development," in the language of its architects.

Although experiments with "another development" could be found all over the region, it was Bolivia in the late 1980s that provided the architects of this new offensive against the forces of social change with their most useful testing ground. Here, they could search for the policy measures and workable strategies needed to bring about a process of alternative development. The first step in the process was to design an appropriate institutional framework for the new development policy.

Based on information provided by the Danish Association for International Development, the resulting development plan specified three strategic considerations. To advance these considerations, the government's economic team (headed by de Lozada, Minister of Planning at the time) entered into a series of high-level meetings with officials from the international financial community (the World Bank, the IDB, etc.), the UNDP, and representatives of the most important overseas development associations operating in Bolivia (such as USAID). These meetings extended from 1986 to 1992, months before de Lozada assumed the presidency.

The meetings were held behind closed doors and in secret. However, we have a revealing account of their proceedings by Denmark's representative of international co-operation for development. In this account, three major strategic considerations were used to establish the government's reform orientation (a fundamental legal and administrative institutionality) and specific reform measures: (i) *productivity-competitiveness* to improve the productivity of Bolivia's major economic enterprises and ensure their ability to compete in the world market; (ii) *social integration-equity* to broaden the social base of national production, improving access to means of production for diverse groups of producers beyond the small stratum of big well-capitalized enterprises privileged by, and benefiting from, neo-liberal policies; and (iii) *state action-governability* to ensure political order with as little government as possible; that is, via the strengthening of civil society and participation in public policy.

Economic and social development in the late 1980s and early 1990s was essentially state-led; that is, initiated and orchestrated by the government. At issue were a series of reforms introduced through legislation or by executive decree, designed along the lines of the UNDP's model of sustainable human development and meant to be used in the construction of de Load's Government Plan for Action (1993-96). This plan was preceded by a social strategy to support a new social policy (a poverty-targeted social emergency fund) and followed by another Plan for Action (1997-2002), which, in line with a formulation by ECLAC (1990), defined for the first time the principle of equity as a fundamental pillar of government policy.[9]

With de Load's ascension to state power, the stage was set for an alternative development approach to social change. In 1994, the De Lozada instituted legislation—the Law of Administrative Decentralization (LDA) and the Law of Popular Participation (LPP)—that would establish the institutional framework for a participatory form of sustainable human development. The left, much of it associated with the popular movement in the form of diverse political parties, was appeased in the process, as were the civic associations seeking regional or territorial autonomy, In effect, the Bolivian left interpreted the new policy measures as a response to popular pressures and demands, and in any case, they generally viewed it as an opportunity, a space within which they needed to operate. It is also evident that most of the so-formed new left were not in the least aware of the implicit deal that they had made in the process of their own conversion from political to social action: in exchange for the space the government opened up to the popular movement, the left made an agreement to pursue a non-confrontational micro-project approach to social change. This new politics (to seek change within the local spaces of the power structure rather than confronting state power) found its organizational form in the non-governmental organization, which would come to replace the political party as an agency of social change and development.

In subsequent years, Bolivia was a veritable laboratory for experimentation with diverse forms or models of alternative development, such as micro-enterprise financing (MEF), the sustainable livelihoods approach (SLA), asset-based community development (ABCD), community economic development (CED), participatory development (PD), local economic development (LED), and local human development (LHD). Besides a commitment to a non-confrontational no-power approach to social change—"social change without state power," to quote Holloway (2002), a major theorist of this new approach to politics—there are several distinguishing features of these and other such forms of "another development" that have dominated the political landscape in Bolivia and other countries (such as Ecuador) over the past decade.

One feature is a concern with mobilizing social capital, the only asset the rural poor are deemed to have ready access to, and indeed to have in abundance. The accumulation of capital, the sum total of society's wealth, assets, or productive resources in one form or another other, is regarded by theorists as the driving force of development, which is conceived of as a set of *defined improvements in socio-economic conditions* lived by a population together with *the structural changes* needed to bring about these improvements. However, improved access to natural, financial, and physical forms of capital is fraught with confrontational politics, requiring direct action by the dispossessed (the landless and those who have nothing: the proletariat) or action by the state (land reform or "authoritative asset redistribution" in SLA language and government credit).

A second feature of "another development" is its politics. The political utility of social capital, which is embodied in a culture of solidarity and its norms of reciprocity and relations of trust and social exchange, is that it does not require structural change. Rather, it entails: (i) empowerment, a change in how individuals feel about themselves when they are empowered to act on their own behalf; (ii) construction of a social economy beyond both the market and the state; (iii) active participation in decisions that relate to or affect their locality or community; and (iv) a politics of dialogue—diverse interests in concert with good governance (that is, participation of civil society in the responsibility for establishing and maintaining political order).

A third feature of "another development" is the institutional framework provided by a policy of administrative decentralization. Within this framework, the responsibility for economic and social (human or integrated) development was transferred to regional, sectional, and local governments. Bolivia transferred 20 per cent of central government revenues to the local governments to this purpose. International co-operation for this form of development was manifest in policies and program funds to enable local governments to assume the assigned role as a development agency and agent (the concept of 'productive municipality')—to assume a leadership role in the process of local development, working in tandem with other strategic partners in the process.

CONCLUSION

At this point, it is difficult to gauge the outcomes and socio-economic impacts of local development and the new politics on the process of change in Bolivia. The economic and political dynamics of social change associated with local development require a more and closer study. However, it is clear enough that the option of decentralized local development has had a major political impact on the rural poor, turning them away from the social movements and demobilizing the anti-systemic forces of resistance and opposition to government policy. Evidently, it has also helped immobilize the erstwhile political left, much of it in disarray and without any organizing and mobilizing capacity.

As for the social movements and the associated dynamics of social change, it is also evident that the popular movement both in Bolivia and elsewhere has become and remains divided between those organizations that have opted for the confrontational politics of direct action and mass mobilization, and those that have chosen the electoral and development paths to social change. In this context, the new politics of local development, like the dynamics of electoral politics, have helped demobilize the social movements and defuse pressures for revolutionary change. The non-governmental organizations, as contracted frontline agents of development, have generally and often unwittingly served as instruments of this new politics, which is designed as a way of advancing the forces of neo-liberalism and globalising capital within the new world order.

NOTES

1   Pachakutik (MUPP-NP) was conceived in 1995, but it was not until 1997 that it was given a solid organic structure with a national executive committee, provincial coordinating bodies, diverse commissions, etc.

2   Regarding the 1990 uprising, the government claimed that it was orchestrated by the political opposition, forcing CONAIE to reject participation in the electoral system. In any case, the leadership of the movement was of the opinion that the critical political dynamics of social change were to be found outside this system (Dávalos, 2004).

3   For a brief review of these and other social dynamics of the indigenous movement, see Petras and Veltmeyer (2005). In addition to the objective conditions generated by the neo-liberal policy measures associated with TROLE (Law of Economic Transformation), there were at least three other factors involved. First, there was the situation of serious discontent within the armed forces, with a group of disgruntled officers concerned about both salary and institutional integrity issues. In this situation, a group of middle-ranking officers, headed by "Lucio" (Colonel Gutierrez) entered into negotiations with Vargas, the President of CONAIE, and the *Coordinadora de Movimientes Sociales*. Secondly, the ruling class was seriously divided, unable to constitute a dominant bloc and formulate a coherent government program, with an important faction of "the [highland] oligarchy" engaged in political machinations against "the [Guayaquil] bourgeoisie," creating a favourable condition for insurrectionary action (Delgado Jara, 2000). Another critical factor in the uprising was the existence of a highly mobilized mass of social forces within the highland indigenous

peasantry in alliance with a broad coalition of urban-based popular sector organizations against the government's neo-liberal agenda.

4   This happened under the reforms instituted by de Lozada's first administration (1993 to 1997) that converted many community-based indigenous organizations into OTBS (*Organizaciones Territoriales de Base*—territorial community-based organizations) with the right of representation and participation in a series of municipal or local development plans.

5   The popular insurrections of April and September were connected to (and to some extent gave rise to) diverse political currents or tendencies within the popular movement. Five of these currents have played a particularly important role in the trajectory of the movement since 2002: (i) a current headed by Felipe Quispe Huanca, the *Aymara Maliku* (maximum authority), leader of the CSUTCB (Confederation of Peasant Workers' Unions of Bolivia) and founder of the Pachakuti indigenous movement; (ii) MIP, an intellectual and political current oriented towards *social* rather than political development—an alternative form of local and autonomous NGO-assisted development protagonized from below; (iii) a labour movement led by the *Central Obrera Boliviana* (COB); (iv) an anti-neo-liberal bloc constituted by a sector of organized labour, headed by the *fabriles* of El Paz, independent from both the system and the COB; and (v) the political current represented by Morales in the leadership of the coca-producing peasants in the eastern lowlands of Chaparé, defining the politics of an important sector of indigenous peasants. In the context of political developments in 2002, this political current became part of a larger popular movement, the defence of coca assuming the same significance as oil, gas, and water, i.e., as an issue of national unity in a popular struggle against neo-liberalism.

6   It was the government's intention to alienate the last vestige of public control over this resource that sparked a mobilization that compelled the government to reverse its decision to concede the legal right of Bechtel, the ultimate owner of the privatized *Aguas del Tunari*, to market Cochabamba's reservoir of water without regard to the needs and rights of Bolivians, particularly those in the immediate locality. The second battle in this war—a legal suit levelled against the government by Bechtel to compensate the company $25 million for its loss of anticipated revenues—is ongoing, but the first skirmish in this war was decidedly won by the people, a mass mobilization that brought together diverse sectors of the popular movement into a "Co-ordinating Body for the Defence of Water and Life." Other demands of the movement included the expulsion of *Aguas del Tunari*, a multinational company registered in the Netherlands and with divisions in the UK and the US, and ultimately owned by Bechtel, one of the largest resource-extraction enterprises in the world; the derogation of SD2029, which legalized the privatization of water, and the prevention of the export of water by *Aguas del*

Tunari by way of Chile, a venture entailing investments of $80 million and anticipated revenues of $1.2 billion, almost all of which would accrue to a multinational company.

7   By various accounts, it seems that Evo Morales's pact with Mesa in the context of post-October 2003—at least as far as Morales understood it—included a commitment to stop or limit the government's US-mandated coca eradication program ("alternative development"). In November 2004, Morales, as head of the *cocaleros* of Chaparé, negotiated a pact with the government to put an end to a resurgent mass action on the coca eradication front in the form of a temporary 4-day truce. However, a number of local peasant leaders rejected the truce, arguing that Morales's electoral ambitions were being exploited by the government and that the government in all likelihood would discard him like a used condom once his help in demobilizing direct action by the coca farmers was secured. It turned out that these leaders were correct in their assessment.

8   In an interview with *Punto Final* (May, 2003: 16–17) Evo Morales, leader of the major political force on Bolivia's left, the *Movimiento al Socialismo-Instrumento Politico para la Soberanía de los Pueblos* (MAS-IPSP), defined socialism in terms of "communitarianism." This is, he notes, because "in the aylla [the principal aymara territorial unit], people live in community, with values such as solidarity and reciprocity. This," he adds, "is our [political] practice."

9   What is understood by "equity" in this context, and the corresponding implementation measures, are not clear. In the mainstream of development thinking in the 1970s, equity meant government redistribution of market-generated incomes (via progressive taxation) in the form of social and development programs. ECLAC (1990), on the other hand, defined equity as improved access of small and medium-sized enterprises and producers to society's productive resources such as land, technology, and financial capital (credit) in order to convert these producers and enterprises into productive agents. The World Bank, however, in its 2000/01 *World Development Report* on poverty defined equity as "equality of opportunity," which does not imply active intervention by the government in the direction of improved access or income redistribution.

Glossary

Another development. See *Development, alternatives to*. Forms of development that in theory are initiated from within and below; that are socially exclusive, participatory, and empowering; human in scale and form; and sustainable in terms both of the environment and livelihoods.

Anti-globalization movement. Movement against globalization in its neo-liberal form begun in Seattle. See Klein (2001). Organizational forms of this movement include the annual World Social Forum (initially in Porto Alegre in Brazil), which brings together thousands of activists and representatives of diverse civil society organizations from across the world in search of "another world," a more humane or ethical form of globalization.

Authoritarianism. A term used by political scientists to describe non-democratic forms of governments, such as military dictatorships, capitalist states such as Korea and Taiwan, socialist one-party states such as Cuba or the bureaucratic (quasi-authoritarian) states that abound in Latin America, according to Diamond (1999).

Bretton Woods Conference. A conference held at a New Hampshire resort in 1944 at which institutions such as the World Bank and the IMF were formed. The proposed International Trade Organization was stillborn because of protectionist pressures until it finally emerged in the form of the World Trade Organization (WTO) 50 years later. In the interim, the free trade agenda was advanced via the General Agreement on Tariffs and Trade (GATT), a negotiating forum.

Capital. Wealth that begets more wealth; assets or productive resources such as land and minerals (natural capital); money available for productive investment (financial capital); machinery and physical plants, facilities, and infrastructure (physical capital); knowledge and skills generated through education (human capital); relations of solidarity and reciprocal exchange (social capital). The theory is that economic development is predicated on a process of capital accumulation, generally by means of productive investment of financial capital.

Capitalism. An economic and social system based on the wage–labour relation, the functioning of markets, the agency of the nation-state, and the institution of private property in the means of production. The system is based on the labour–capital relation and divided into two basis classes: the bourgeoisie (the capitalist class) and the proletariat (the working class). See *Social class*.

Civil society. A term, as much ideological as sociological, popularized by US political scientists in the 1980s in response to a conservative counter-revolution against the state and the forced retreat of the state from its responsibility for social welfare and economic development. It usually refers to the collectivity of institutions within society that are not controlled by the state—church groups, environmental lobbies, etc. The presence of civil society is thought to be a necessary if not sufficient guarantee of democracy. Civil society is thought to be "weak" where democracy is lacking and the poor are numerous. According to the UNDP (1993: 1): "Civil society is, together with the state and the market, one of the three spheres that interface in the making of democratic societies.... [It] is the sphere in which social movements become organized."

Class. See *Social class*. A fundamental social grouping formed in the relationship of individuals to the means of production. The two main classes of capitalist society, according to Marxist theory, are the bourgeoisie (or capitalists) and the proletariat (the workers). However, contemporary societies are characterized by a broad spectrum of social classes, a number of which occupy positions outside the "capital–labour relation" (understood in economic terms as factors of production and in sociological terms as a relationship between two classes—the capitalist and working class). Often these classes are defined not in terms of the relationship to production but in terms of the source of their income or their position in the status hierarchy of income—middle, lower, upper, etc. Also, many individuals in Latin American societies occupy a somewhat ambiguous class position, combining as they often do conditions that cut across diverse social systems of production relations. This applies, for example, to the peasantry, many of whom in fact are no longer peasants and constitute what might be termed a "semi-proletariat." It is also difficult to determine precisely the class position and situation of individuals in the burgeoning informal sector in what Davis (2006) terms the "planet of slums."

GLOSSARY

Class struggle. The functioning of capitalist societies is based on an exploitative relationship between capital and labour. In theory, when workers become class-conscious (that is, aware of this exploitation), they will enter into a relationship of conflict with capital and initiate a struggle for social change. In this context, class conflict and struggle is viewed theoretically as the fundamental agency for social change and systemic transformation.

Clientelism. A patron–client relation formed to promote political advantage in a process of electoral politics. Common practice in Latin America.

COB *(Central Obrera Boliviana).* A Bolivian central of organized workers federations and organizations. In addition to serving to advance the economic and political interests of Bolivian workers, it has played a major role in Bolivian politics over the years.

Common markets. Refers to a situation where groups of countries agree, for purposes of economic benefit, to reduce tariffs among themselves, standardize currency, accept trade arbitration, and so on in order to expand trade, reduce conflict, and improve living standards. The largest common market is the European Union (EU), which includes most of Western and Southern Europe and encompasses states in Eastern Europe. The North American Free Trade Agreement (NAFTA) aims at creating a common market between the US, Mexico, and Canada.

CONAIE *(Confederación de Nacionalidades Indígenas del Ecuador, or Confederation of Indigenous Nationalities of Ecuador).* A federated organization of diverse indigenous nationalities that has led the struggle in Ecuador against the neo-liberal policies of diverse governments. Through several uprisings and social mobilizations, it has been able to arrest the implementation of some neo-liberal policies, scuttle the globalization agenda of the government, and bring about the ouster of several presidents of the country.

CUT *(Central Unica dos Trabalhadores).* A workers central in Brazil, representing millions of organized workers but closely tied to the government. Like so many labour confederations in Latin America, especially in Mexico and Argentina, CUT is a willing victim of the government's corporatist or tripartist policies designed to control the labour movement and accommodate its leadership. In June 2006, the lack of independence of CUT and its inability to advance the labour movement led to the creation of an alternative labour confederation, CONLUTE, which also brought together dissidents from the governing Workers' Party (PT).

Debt/deficit. Loans and debt remain concentrated in middle-income countries of East Asia and Latin America. In

171

1981, over 70 per cent of outstanding debt was owed by just 10 countries, and just 3 countries (Argentina, Brazil, and Mexico) accounted for almost one-half). In 1974, the total external debt of all developing nations was US$35 billion. In 1981 it reached US$751 billion. By the early 1990s it was estimated to be US$1,945 billion.

Democracy. A form of government based on the rule of "the people" (the *demos*) and respect for constitutional law; the mechanism of party politics and free elections; and the principles of universal suffrage, representation, and accountability. In practice, the idea of democracy takes a liberal or bourgeois form associated with a parliamentary or presidential system set up by a multi- or two-party system. Thus, Cuba, whose government is democratically elected in a one-party system based on constitutional law, universal suffrage, and voting by secret ballot—a system in which each community and workplace is able to freely elect its government and legislative representatives and in which the Communist Party, assigned an ideological rather than an electoral function (it is forbidden by law to participate in the electoral process)—is often regarded (wrongly, one might add) as non-democratic.

Democratization. Ostensibly a process associated with a transition from an authoritarian form of government such as a military or class dictatorship; or a process leading to more democracy, however defined. In Latin America, especially in the southern cone of South America, virtually every democratic government in the 1960s and 1970s gave way to a military dictatorship or a presidential form of capitalist authoritarianism. In the 1980s, this process was reversed, leading to "re-democratization" characterized by a return to a civilian regime based on respect for constitutional law and use of the electoral mechanism of multi-party politics. In the 1990s, the fragile democracies so reconstituted were confronted, and in some contexts threatened, by the emergence of what might be termed "social democracy"—antisystemic social movements rooted in the popular sector of civil society and opting to bring about social change by means of social mobilization rather than party politics.

Deregulation (of capital, labour, and product markets). A neo-liberal policy promoted by the Washington Consensus, which has as its aim greater access to markets, including financial markets.

Developing countries. A group of countries, once 77 in number (the group of 77) but which now constitutes 120, referred to as "Third World" or "the South." In the 1970s, under conditions of a system-wide producton crisis, a few of these developing countries became industrialized—the newly industrializing countries. Industrialization,

GLOSSARY

capitalist development, and modernization were—and still are—viewed as the structural prerequisites of economic and social development, joining the club of rich industrialized countries that make up the OECD (the Organization for Economic Co-operation and Development).

Development. A defined set of improvements in the living standards and socio-economic conditions of the population, together with the structural changes needed to bring about these improvements. So defined, development takes diverse forms: economic, social, and political. Indicators range from an increase in a country's gross national product or per capita income, a decrease in the number and percentage of individuals and households below the poverty line, and improvement in the literacy rate and/or longevity, to an expansion of choice in people's lives.

Development, alternatives to. See *Another development*. Alternative forms of development to those using the dominant economic model and theorizing within the box of mainstream development thought and practice. At times proposals for another development verge on arguments about the need for an alternative *to* development (that is, anti- or post-development). One anti-development network is the International Network for Cultural Alternatives to Development at Centre Interculturel de Montreal (*www.world-culture-network.net*).

Development (capitalist) and democracy. A highly contentious relationship that has been conceptualized in different ways. Some see development and capitalism as intrinsically connected in the form of the free market and free elections, with economic liberalization leading to political liberalization or vice versa. Others see economic and political liberalization, or democracy and capitalism, as a marriage of convenience or concerted interests, as likely to lead to authoritarianism as democracy. In practice, both capitalism and socialism can be combined with democracy or authoritarianism.

ECLAC *(Economic Commission for Latin America and the Caribbean).* A United Nations agency based in Santiago, Chile, and associated with Latin American structuralism and neo-structuralism, a school of thought that has made a significant contribution to both development theory and policy. Economists and sociologists at ECLAC have led the debate against liberalism and neo-liberalism over the years. See its journal CEPAL Review.

Economic restructuring. The practice of US capitalism and its institutions, including Wall Street, the IMF, the World Bank, and the World Trade Organization with the object of expanding its control over the economies of the developing countries, including the former socialist countries. This practice had its origins in the mid 1970s. Trade and financial liberalization are fundamental to its success. Countries that succumb to it abandon autonomous development models, such as import substitution industrialization (ISI), and embrace foreign investment.

EZLN *(Ejército Zapatista de Liberación Nacional, or Zapatista army of National Liberation)*. A group of indigenous peasants in Chiapas, a state in the south east of Mexico. Erupting on the political stage on January 1, 1994, the day that NAFTA was scheduled to take effect, the EZLN (the Zapatistas) has turned out be the archetype of a new social movement that has resonated across Latin America and the world. It has even been viewed as the first postmodern movement in history (Burbach, 1994) and, more controversially, as an examplar of the new politics—a road to change that eschews the quest for state power (Holloway, 2002).

Foreign direct investment (FDI). A form of capital associated with the operations of the transnational (or multinational) corporations that dominate the world economy. Until the 1980s, the inflow of this form of capital and the operations of these corporations were regulated by national governments in the recipient countries in order to ensure that some benefits, such as technology transfer or employment of local labour, would accrue to the recipient country, or to protect its sovereignty, national labour standards, and the environment. In the early 1980s, however, the attitude of many Third World states towards foreign investment shifted, and private investment, particularly in the form of FDI, became more welcome. When and where FDI was not welcome, the globalization strategy and the structural adjustment program of the World Bank came into play, in effect forcing governments in the developing countries to open up their economies to the forces of the world market and to deregulate the inflow of private capital.

Free trade (laissez-faire/liberal). See *Neoliberalism*. A reassertion of neo-classical economic theory in the context of a proposed new world order designed to liberate the "forces of economic freedom" from the constraints of government intervention. It became increasingly popular in the 1980s and 1990s in the form of the new economic model of world capitalist development. In 1994, the World Trade Organization (WTO) was created (replacing the GATT) in order to advance the policy of free trade. Many critics of the WTO argue that what is needed is "fair trade" rather than "free trade," in that the latter is generally advanced by the rich industrialized countries such as the US in their economic interest and *only* when in their interest.

GLOSSARY

GATT *(General Agreement on Tariffs and Trade)*. An international agreement drawn up before most colonial countries were decolonized, or the civil war in China had ended, which attempted to establish rules for the global marketplace, dominated from the outset by the US. The GATT charter was signed by 23 countries, of which 2 were in the Third World, and came into effect in January 1948. With a secretariat in Geneva and a set of rules governing negotiations over tariffs, by the early 1990s GATT had 109 members, including all of the OECD as well as the majority of developing countries.

Global governance. See *Governance*. The idea of a set of standardized practices emerging on a world scale, as effected by some remote, invisible, and perhaps disinterested world authority. Actually, global *anything* is only guaranteed by the co-operation of the most powerful states, and these must include the US. Global governance is the pursuit of national interest by other means; so is any form of international order.

Globalization. A process (or project; an ideology) designed to integrate economies all over the world into a single system based on the dynamics of capitalist development, and in which capital and the international trade in goods and services are freed from the regulatory restraints of national governments. A highly contentious project in its neoliberal form and economic dimension—financial and trade liberalization. As for its associated interconnectedness of societies and cultures all over the world; its dramatic shrinking of time and space; and its ability to increase the share and the global flow of information and knowledge, facilitated by rapid changes in information technology, the process is also fraught with controversy but with much less opposition and resistance. The literature on globalization in its multiple dimensions and diverse dynamics is voluminous but see Petras and Veltmeyer (2001) and Bowles and Veltmeyer (2007).

Governance. A neologism of the 1980s extensively used by political scientists working in the area of development. Rules of procedure and regulation designed to maintain order, or political order, without or with as little government as possible; that is, engaging non-state institutions or civil society in the process of maintaining order.

IDB *(Inter-American Development Bank)*. One of the World Bank affiliated financial institutions that operates in Latin America ostensibly to promote economic development. Similar institutions have been formed and operate in other regions of the world economy.

Ideology. A set of ideas or beliefs that is used not to describe or explain but to mobilize action in a desired direction. The concern of an ideologue (a conscious agent) is to advance not knowledge but the economic or political interests of the social group or class with whom he or she identifies or is associated. Political ideologies are normally categorized in terms of their orientation towards social or political change. In these terms the dominant ideologies are as follows: liberalism, a (centrist or reformist) belief in the need for reform and the possibility of change in the direction of individual freedom and equal opportunity; socialism, a (leftist or radical) belief in the need for equality and substantive change or systemic transformation; and conservatism, a (rightist or reactionary) concern for order, to restore or establish order, in the belief that change is neither progressive nor liberating but destabilizing and productive of chaos.

IGO *(International Governmental Organization)*. Organizations such as the International Labour Organization (ILO), created in 1919, and the International Court of Justice, created in July 2002. In 1909, there were 37 such organizations; by the mid 1990s, 260. This increase is taken as evidence of globalization. The US routinely denounces these organizations as impeding its sovereignty.

ILO *(International Labour Organization)*. Originally founded in 1919 at the same time as the League of Nations (superseded by the UN), the ILO became a specialized agency of the UN in 1946. Its main concerns are international labour standards, including child labour, slavery, and human rights.

IMF *(International Monetary Fund)*. Founded, with the World Bank, at Bretton Woods in 1944, the IMF was designed to assist countries in temporary balance of payments difficulties and conceived as a bulwark against a return of the cycle of depression and war. It was also meant to manage the world's currency system, and in this capacity it helped maintain economic stability in the capitalist system in the 1950s and 1960s. But in the 1980s and 1990s, by advocating the deregulation of capital markets, it contributed substantially to economic instability, even helping to provoke the Asian financial crisis. In 1983, when the Mexican government announced that it was unable to service payments on its accumulated external debt, the IMF began to concert its economic stabilization policies with the structural adjustment policies of the World Bank, using debt and developing countries' need for access to capital as a lever to impose an adjustment to meet the requirements of the new world economic order. Although ostensibly a multilateral institution like the World Bank, and customarily headed by a European, the IMF is essentially run by the US Treasury. MIT economist Rudi Dornbusch: "The IMF is a tool of the US to pursue its economic policy offshore." Historian Chalmers Johnson has called it "an institutional surrogate of the United States government" and "a covert arm of the US Treasury" (Johnson, 2000: 5, 210). Greider, (1997: 281-82) has called it "a paternalistic agent of global capital" charged with the responsibility of "enforcing debt collection, supervising the financial accounts of poor nations, promoting wage suppression and other policy nostrums, preparing the poorer countries for eventual acceptance by the global trading system."

Imperialism. A doctrine and practice of some states based on the belief in the right to rule and the perquisites of state power, and the dream of world domination. It has a long historical pedigree, but within the world capitalist system, it has been associated with Pax Britannica, the rule of Great Britain over much of the world as of the late-nineteenth century and well into the twentieth century. After World War II, the dream of world domination and the state policy of world domination were taken over by the United States. Imperialism as the projection of state power, takes multiple forms: economic, political, and military. It is argued that both development and globalization can be viewed and best understood as disguised forms of imperialism.

Imperialism, US. The projection of state power by the US in diverse forms—economic, political and military—aimed at hegemony over the world economy. Since the end of the World War II, the US has pursued a foreign policy that to all intents and purposes has been governed by this dream of world domination. In the 1990s, a group of neo-conservative policy advisors close to the White House (and with the presidency of George W. Bush) designed a blueprint for US world domination. This document, the Project for a New American Century, included plans for gaining control over oil fields and to attack Iraq and Afghanistan, long before 9/11. With the added complement of Condoleezza Rice, co-author of the Defence Guidance Planning (DGP), a document that outlined the need for the US to assert its power unilaterally in the service of global American Empire, the neo-conservative noose around the neck of US foreign policy was tightened.

Informal sector. The part of any economy that is unmeasured and therefore not regulated or taxed. Comprising all sorts of micro-enterprises and irregular or marginal economic activities on the streets of the urban economy in many Latin American cities and the big urban centres of other developing societies, this informal unstructured sector often amounts to one-half of the economically active population. The social dynamics of informal sector economic activity and conditions are carefully researched and analyzed by Mike Davis (2006) in the context of a process of rapid urbanization and capitalist development in developing countries all over the world.

International Forum on Globalization (www.ifg.org). An alliance of 60 anti-globalization organizations in 25 countries that grew out of the Battle of Seattle. Its main concern is the effect of global capitalism and particularly the role of the IMF, World Bank, and WTO.

ISI (import substitution industrialization). In Latin America, ISI (a variant of Keynesianism), originated with the problems of the Depression wherein the larger economies of the continent, unable to export in order to pay for their imports, turned to producing their own manufactured goods. ISI thus became the dominant economic strategy in Argentina, Brazil, Chile, and Mexico from the 1930s to the 1970s. It was characterized economically by the erection of protectionist barriers and the payment of subsidies to domestic producers. In the 1980s, it was declared to be dead by the forces of international financial capitalism in league with their local delegates.

Liberalism. An ideology focused on the belief that social change and economic progress in the direction of greater individual freedom and equality of opportunity are necessary and possible. It is characterized by an orientation towards action by individuals and institutional reform rather than collective action and systemic transformation, the goal and mobilizing vision of a more radical ideology (e.g., socialism).

Liberalization, economic (trade and finance). Since the mid 1980s, trade liberalization has been undertaken universally among developing countries. Liberalization has taken the form of opening up markets (i.e., removing protectionist impediments), privatizing public enterprises, and making foreign firms welcome.

Macroeconomic stability. The condition that structural adjustment programs are supposed to guarantee. It includes, especially, currency stability.

Market. A site where goods are bought and sold. Markets are normally embedded in other social and economic institutions and constructed and protected by states. As argued by Karl Polanyi in what remains the most important book written on the functioning of the market (2001: 139-40), "The road to the free market was opened and kept open by an enormous increase in continuous, centrally organized, and controlled interventionism." Property rights lie at the foundation of any market, while law and order shapes them. In the 1970s and 1980s, neo-liberals argued that a return to markets (that is, *laissez-faire*, which diminished the role of the state) would revive lagging Third World economies. This belief in the magic of the market, which encourages possessive individualism, selfishness, and greed, is at the heart of the neo-liberal ideology and economic doctrine.

GLOSSARY

Market friendly. A term coined by Lawrence Summers and used by the World Bank for its development dogma; that is, an environment that maximizes private sector growth through macroeconomic stability, free trade, and private sector investment.

MERCOSUR *(Mercado Commun del Cono Sur).* Common market of the South. Members include Brazil, Argentina, Uruguay, and Paraguay.

Model. A simplified theoretical representation of a complex reality. Unlike a theory, the purpose of which is to explain, a model serves as an aid to analysis, helping to identify the most critical variables and links so as to make analysis and theory construction possible. An example of a model is the idea of the world economy as a "system," a set of interconnected structures with a centre and periphery whose function and evolution are governed by laws that affect countries depending on their position or structural location.

MST *(Movimento dos Trabalhadores Rurais Sem Terra, or Movement of Rural Landless Workers).* A powerful movement of landless workers in Brazil, founded in the 1980s. The MST has been leading the struggle for improved access to land and land reform. The context for this direct action movement is one of the most inequitable land tenure systems in the world, leaving over a million rural producers landless or near landless.

Multinational Corporations (MNCs). Firms with offices and production facilities in more than one country. The operations of MNCs are key to understanding economic globalization since they account for about two-thirds of world trade, with about a third of world trade being intra-firm between branches of the same company. In 1998, there were 53,000 worldwide (up from 35,000 in 1992) with 450,000 foreign subsidies selling $9.5 trillion of goods and services across the globe. The hundred largest MNCs control about 20 per cent of global foreign assets and account for about 30 per cent of total world sales of all MNCs. They employ around six million workers worldwide. A small number of MNCs dominate world markets for oil, minerals, foods, and other agricultural products and services.

NAFTA *(North American Free Trade Agreement).* Born of an agreement signed in 1993 between US, Canada, and Mexico to allow free trade, NAFTA came into effect as of January 1, 1994, when the EZLN in the south east of Mexico (Chiapas) erupted on the world political stage. The spokesperson of the Zapatistas Subcomandante Marcos defined NAFTA as the "death sentence" of the indigenous communities and their economy.

NEM *(New economic model).* See *Neo-liberalism* and SAP. On the NEM in Latin America see Bulmer-Thomas (1996).

Neo-classical economics. An approach to economics focusing on individual and group choice based on the assumptions that individuals are free to choose, are oriented towards a rational calculation of self-interest, tend to maximize "utility" (benefits to themselves or profit), and have perfect information regarding their options. Neo-classical economics is conventionally dated from William Stanley's *Theory of Political Economy* (1871), Carl Menger's *Principles of Economics* (1871), and Leon Walras's *Elements of Pure Economics* (1874-1877). Despite widespread criticism that its assumptions do not in any way describe the real world, mainstream economics today is largely neo-classical in its assumptions, at least at the microeconomic level.

Neo-liberalism. An economic doctrine that rose to prominence in the 1970s and which repudiates the role of the state in the economy, preferring to leave the economy in the hands of the market. The greatest architects or priests of neo-liberalism were the economists Milton Friedman, Fredrick von Hayek, and Adam Smith. Although neo-liberal policy "holds sway because it serves the interests of powerful groups, its effective operation depends upon its widespread ideological acceptance" (MacEwan, 1999: LL). For a history, see Susan George *Une courte histoire du néo-libéralisme (www.attac.org)*. A signal that neo-liberal ideology had reached a high point came in the World Bank's *World Development Report* of 1991 that argued taxes and protection produced inequality in Latin America and that open markets would end this: "When markets work well, greater equity often comes naturally." A tenet of neo-liberalism is that problems such as informalization, low income and poverty, and unemployment are the result of state intervention in the economy and the resulting distortion in the normal workings of the free market.

Neo-structuralism. Structuralism as a form of analysis takes certain forms (see *Structuralism*). One form, termed "Latin American structuralism," is associated with the United Nations Economic Commission for Latin America and the Caribbean (ECLAC). The theory advanced by economists and sociologists at ECLAC is that the world capitalist economic system is structured so that countries at the "centre" (in western Europe, North America, and Japan) reap all or most of the benefits of economic growth at the expense of countries on the "periphery" (in Latin America, Asia, and Africa). In the 1970s, this notion of a world economic system with a centre–periphery structure came under attack, leading to a revised or new form of Latin American structuralism (see Sunkel, 1993) that takes into account new developments.

GLOSSARY

New paradigm. See *Paradigm*. As of the mid 1980s, the World Bank and other agencies of the UN system and international development associations have turned away from forms of development based on the agency of the state and the market and the accumulation of financial and physical capital, and have moved towards local or community-based forms of development based on the accumulation of social capital. This is seen by many as a new paradigm in that it is initiated from below and within rather than from above and the outside.

New social movement. See *Social movement*. A type of social movement that emerged in Latin America in the 1980s that is characterized by heterogeneity, a concern for a wide range of socio-economic, cultural, and political issues (e.g., identity) rather than strictly class issues (e.g., land, land reform, wages, and exploitative relations and conditions).

New world order. A neologism popular in Washington in the early 1980s and a precursor to the idea of political and economic globalization.

NGO *(non-governmental organization).* First established in the 1960s in the form of private voluntary organizations (PVOs), NGOs serve a range of contradictory purposes, some charitable, some political. Often they are supported by governments and therefore serve not to promote change but to sustain the existing order. The World Bank, in its untiring attempts at co-option, claims to favour them as instruments of good governance. Indeed, a number of NGOs serve the World Bank and promote anti-state and pro-market policies. NGOs are mainly centred in the West and are sometimes criticized as being part of a system of foreign domination—as agents of imperialism.

OECD *(Organization for Economic Cooperation and Development).* The club of rich industrialized nations formed and organized in 1968. Basically, North America, Western Europe, and Japan.

Paradigm. An overarching framework of basic assumptions and a world view that determines the structure (inner form and outer limits) of thought and practice concerning an area of scientific study. For its classical formulation see Kuhn (1996). See *New Paradigm*.

Poverty. A condition defined by deprivation and the inability of households to satisfy the basic needs of its members. The basic indicator of poverty is low income. According to the World Bank, the global poor are those who earn less than US$2 a day (US$1 for the destitute or absolute poor). However, there are also non-income conditions of poverty such as lack of schooling, poor health and vulnerability to disease, food insecurity and malnutrition, poor life chances, and very limited capacity to make life choices.

Poverty alleviation. Having done so much to increase Third World poverty, the IMF in the 1990s joined the World Bank in its war on poverty, putting poverty back on the agenda and seeking ways to alleviate it.

Privatization. The policy and practice, universally supported by neo-liberal regimes, of taking publicly owned assets and publicly controlled services (railways, airlines, prisons, hospitals, water supplies, road maintenance, garbage collection) and selling them off to private investors at a loss.

Populism. A form of development theory and practice associated with the idea that small is beautiful (more human in form); the virtues of small-scale enterprise and balanced rural–urban development. In Latin America, populism refers rather to a form of politics and policies that appeal to the populace (the popular sector) against the entrenched interests of the oligarchy and the political elite.

SAP *(structural adjustment program).* The practice, initiated and supported by the International Monetary Fund and the World Bank, of making loans on the basis of conditionalities that include enforced retrenchment and the opening of markets and currencies to foreign capital. By cutting wages, SAPs supposedly reduce aggregate demand and thus inflation. Following from recession, which is intentional, comes macroeconomic stability and then growth and greater equality. In effect, SAPs lead to greater income inequality, but the theory is that this inequality functions as an incentive, a motivating device that accelerates growth in the short and medium term, but in the long term, the workings of the free market will bring about an automatic levelling in the distribution of income and wealth.

Social capital. See *Capital.* Social capital refers to the capacity of the poor to form networks of solidarity based on relations of trust and reciprocal exchange (rather than money). Within the new development paradigm, it is argued that capital so defined, as an asset that the poor have in abundance and sustained by a culture of solidarity and a community spirit, can generate a process of self-development; that is, improvements and changes initiated from within and below, by grassroots organizations in local communities.

Social class. A form of organization based on the relationship of individuals to production, a relationship that defines two basic classes: the owners of the means of production and the direct producers or the working class (those who are dispossessed from any means of production and thus forced into a relationship of dependence on, and exploitation by, the economically dom-

GLOSSARY

inant ruling class). Capitalist societies are based on the labour-capital relation, a relation that defines the existence of the bourgeoisie (the capitalist class) and the proletariat (the working class).

Social liberalism. An ideology and policy regime characteristic of Latin American governments in the 1990s. It is based on an effort to move beyond the Washington Consensus on neo-liberal macroeconomic structural reforms in national policy by giving structural adjustment a human face. The paradigm of this model is *Solidaridad* in Mexico and, more generally, the policies implemented most effectively by Chile in the 1990s. It is characterized not only by a new social policy (investing in the poor, building their human and social capital) but also by an expanded role for the state in the economy. The theoretical foundation of social liberalism is neo-structuralism, a development theory formulated by economists associated with ECLAC. See Sunkel (1993).

Social movement. A form of popular organization concerned with bringing about social change by means of social mobilization of the forces of resistance against government policy, the state, and the system behind it, and, in the Latin American context, neo-liberalism, globalization, and US imperialism. In Latin America, at least three waves of social movements, based on the agency of working class and peasant organizations and indigenous communities, have been identified.

State. A complex of political institutions that include the government in its various divisions and levels (the executive); an administrative, regulatory, or bureaucratic apparatus (the institutional structure of the economic and social programs established by the government); the legislature (the lower and upper houses of parliament or the congress and senate); the judiciary, and the security or repressive apparatus (the police and the armed forces). In its structure, it is distinguished from civil society in its many forms of organization. The actual role of the state, and its relation to civil society, is very dynamic and adaptive to changing conditions. It requires a contextualized empirical and sociological analysis.

Structuralism. See *Neo-structuralism.* A form of analysis with diverse forms, including Marxism, characteristic of social science and based on the notion of a "system" (a set of interrelated structures). A "structure" refers to an institution (a standardized way of doing things) or to identifiable limits in the variation of observable social relations or social phenomena. Structures, it is thought, set limits to how people think and act. Structuralists assume that the working of a system at the level of any one of its structures (economic, social, political, etc.) effects individuals (or countries) according to their location or position. These affects are objective (rather than subjective) in that they do not depend on the meanings that individuals might assign to them or interpret. Some structuralists assume that a system in one or more of its structures is not only limiting but totally determinant in its effects, allowing no margin of manoeuvre of individual freedom to act or think. Most structuralists, however, merely believe that individuals (or countries) are not free to choose and act, but that their actions have to take into account pre-existing conditions not of their choosing. In the 1980s, this type of analysis, in all of its forms, was subjected to criticism and rejected by advocates of post-structuralism (or postmodernism) who believed in the power of ideas and the freedom of individuals to act any which way.

Sustainable livelihoods approach (SLA). A form of another development. Promoted by Robert Chambers (1983, 1997) and other exponents of a people-centred approach towards development. It is predicated on the need to sustain not only the environment but rural livelihoods.

USAID *(United States Agency for International Development)*. A bilateral aid organization that, like the Canadian International Development Agency (CIDA), is part of a project of international co-operation for the economic and social development of economically backward countries in the Third World. Like many other international development associations (ODAs), it provides both emergency relief and development (i.e., technical and financial) assistance to these countries.

Washington Consensus. A consensus of the US Treasury, the IMF (of which the US Treasury is the largest shareholder), the World Bank, and US investment bankers that is the source of the dogma that minimum government and free markets are achievable and desirable throughout the world and that finance capital should be globalized. This consensus reflects the most powerful segment of the US ruling class. The Washington Consensus was codified by John Williamson (1990) of the International Institute for Economics.

World Bank (www.worldbank.org). Motto: Our dream is a world without poverty. For 50 years, the World Bank has been the arbiter of development. Its annual publication, *World Development Report*, establishes the priorities, the terminology, the concepts, and the questions around which all questions of development are formulated. Created, with the IMF, at the Bretton Woods Conference the World Bank had as its original mission the financing of the reconstruction of Western Europe and Japan. Implicit here was the maintenance of the world economic order, the institutional framework for a global process of capitalist development into which all countries would be inserted. Its first task

GLOSSARY

accomplished, the World Bank began to finance Third World development.

World Development Report. Produced by the World Bank since 1990, the reports frame the continuing debate on development and the ongoing war waged against poverty (against the poor, some critics have added).

WTO *(World Trade Organization).* An American-dominated organization that ostensibly seeks to remove obstacles to global free trade. Established in 1994, it is the successor to the General Agreement on Trade and Tariffs (GATT). Some of its successes include getting Third World countries to sign the following: trade-related investment measures (TRIMS), which prevent them from using trade policy as a means to industrialize; trade-related intellectual property rights (TRIPS), which gave high tech transnational corporations like Microsoft the right to monopolize innovation in the knowledge-intensive industries and has given bio-tech firms like Novartis and Monsanto the rights to privatize past research and development; and agreement on agriculture (AOA), which opened the markets of developing countries to highly subsidized agricultural transnational corporations and destroying or seriously undermining smallholder agriculture in many places.

Bibliography

Abers, R. (2000). *Inventing Local Democracy: Grassroots Politics in Brazil*. Boulder CO: Lynne Rienner.

Alvarez, S. (1993). "'Deepening' Democracy: Popular Movement Networks, Constitutional Reform, and Radical Urban Regimes in Contemporary Brazil." pp. 191–221 in Fisher, R. and J. Kling, eds., *Mobilizing the Community: Local Politics in the Era of the Global City*. London: Sage.

Amador, F. (1990). *Un siglo de lucha de los trabajadores en Nicaragua*. Managua: Centro de la Investigación de la Realidad de América Latina.

Amalric, F. (1998). "Sustainable Livelihoods, Entrepreneurship, Political Strategies and Governance." *Development*, 41 (3): 31–44.

Amin, S. (1976). *Unequal Development*. New York: Monthly Review Press.

Azpiazu, D. (1996). "Elite empresaria en la Argentina. Terciarización, centralización del capital, privatización y beneficios extraordinarios." *Documento de Trabajo*, No. 2 del Proyecto Privatización y Regulación en la Economia Argentina, Area de Economia y Tecnologia de la FLACSO/SECYT/CONICET, Buenos Aires.

Azpiazu, D. and E.M. Basualdo. (1999). "Las privatizaciones en la Argentina. Concentración del poder económico e imperfecciones del Mercado." *Revista Oikos*, 111 (8). Buenos Aires.

Arruda, M. (1993). "NGOs and the World Bank: Possibilities and Limits of Collaboration." mimeo (17 pp.). Geneva: NGO Working Group.

Atria, R., M. Siles, M. Arriagada, L. Robison, and S. Whiteford, eds. (2004). *Social Capital and Poverty Reduction in Latin America and the Caribbean: Towards a New Paradigm*. Santiago: ECLAC.

Bakx, K. (1988). "From Proletarian to Peasant: Rural Transformation in the State of Acre, 1870–1986." *Journal of Development Studies*, 24 (2). January.

Ballón, E. (1986). *Movimientos sociales y democracia: la fundación de un nuevo orden*. Lima, DESCO.

Baron, S., J. Field, and T. Schuller, eds. (2000). *Social Capital: Critical Perspectives*. Oxford: Oxford University Press.

Barry, T. (1987). *Roots of Rebellion: Land and Hunger in Central America*. Boston: South End Press.

Bartra, R. (1976). "¡Si los campesinos se extinguen!" *Historia y Sociedad*, No. 8. Winter.

Basualdo, E. (2001). "Concentración y centralización del capital en la Argentina durante la década del noventa. Una aproximación a través de la reestructuración económica y el comportamiento de los grupos económicos y los capitales extranjeros." Buenos Aires: FLACSO/Universidad Nacional de Quilmes/IDEP.

Bebbington, A., et al. (2006). *The Search for Empowerment: Social Capital as Idea and Practice at the World Bank*. Bloomfield CT: Kumarian.

Behrman, J., A. Gaviria, and M. Székely, eds. (2003). *Who's In and Who's Out: Social Exclusion in Latin America*. Washington DC: Inter-American Development Bank.

Beltran, F. and J. Fernández. (1960). *¿Donde va la reforma agraria Boliviana?* La Paz: Talleres Gráficos Bolivianos.

Benner, C. (1995). "Labor Markets and Employment Practices in the Age of Flexibility: A Case Study of Silicon Valley." *International Labour Review*, Vol. 136, No. 1.

Bessis, S. (1985). "De la exclusion sociale à la cohésion sociale." Síntesis del Coloquio de Roskilde, World Summit for Social Development. Copenhagen, Denmark. March.

Blaikie, P. (1985). "Why Do Policies Usually Fail?" in *The Political Economy of Soil Erosion in Developing Countries*. London: Longman.

Blair, H. (1995). "Assessing Democratic Decentralization." A CDIE Concept Paper. Washington DC: USAID.

Blanco, H. (1972). *Land or Death: The Peasant Struggle in Peru*. New York: Pathfinder Press.

Boisier, S. (1987). *Ensayos sobre descentralización y desarrollo regional*. Santiago: CEPAL-ILPES.

Boisier, S. et al. (1992). *La descentralización: el eslabón perdido de la cadena transformación productiva con equidad y sustentabilidad*. Santiago: Cuadernos de CEPAL.

Boom, G. and A. Mercado, eds. (1990). *Automatización flexible en la industria*. México: Ed. Limusa Noriega.

Borja, J. (1989). *Estado, descentralización y democracia*. Bogotá: Foro Nacional por Colombia.

———. (1987). *The Decentralization of the State, Social Movements and Local Management*. Santiago: FLACSO.

Bourdieu, P. (1986). "The Forms of Capital." In Richardson, J.G., ed., *Handbook of Theory and Research*. New York: Greenwood.

Bowles, P. and H. Veltmeyer, eds. (2007). *What Is Globalization?* Vol. 1. *Critical National Perspectives*. Vol. 2. *Critical Regional Perspectives*. Basingstoke (London): Palgrave Macmillan.

Brass, T. (2000). *Peasants, Populism and Postmodernism: The Return of the*

BIBLIOGRAPHY

Agrarian Myth. London and Portland OH: Frank Cass Publishers.

———. (1991). "Moral Economists, Subalterns, New Social Movements and the (Re) Emergence of a (Post) Modernised (Middle) Peasant." *The Journal of Peasant Studies*, 18 (2).

Brenner, R. (1998). "The Economics of Global Turbulence." *New Left Review*, 229, May/June.

Bromley, D. (1989). "Property Relations and Economic Development: The Other Land Reform." *World Development*, 17.

Bryceson, D.F., C. Kay, and J. Mooi, eds. (2000). *Disappearing Peasantries? Rural Labour in Africa, Asia and Latin America*. London: Intermediate Technology Publications.

Bulmer-Thomas, V. (1996). *The New Economic Model in Latin America and Its Impact on Income Distribution and Power*. New York: St. Martin's Press.

Burbach, R. (1994). "Roots of the Postmodern Rebellion in Chiapas." *New Left Review*, 1 (205).

Calderón, F. (1995). *Movimientos sociales y política*. Mexico: Siglo XXI.

Calderón, F., ed. (1989). *Descentralización y democracia: Gobiernos locales en America Latina*. Santiago: CLACSO/SUR/CLUMT.

Calderón, F. and E. Jelin. (1987). *Clases y movimientos sociales en América Latina. Perspectivas y realidades*. Buenos Aires: Cuadernos CEDES.

Camargo, J.M., et al. (1995). Stability, Growth, Modernization and Pervasive Flexibility: A Feasible Combination? Santiago de Chile: ILO.

Camargo, M. and M. Neri. (1999). *Emprego e productividade no Brasil na decada de noventa*. Santiago de Chile: CEPAL.

Campbell, C. (2001). "Putting Social Capital in Perspective: A Case of Unrealistic Expectations?" pp. 1–10 in Morrow G., ed. *An Appropriate Capitalisation? Questioning Social Capital*. Research in Progress series, Issue 1, October. London School of Economics, The Gender Institute.

Campbell, C., R. Wood, and M. Kelly. (1999). *Social Capital and Health*. London: Health Education Authority.

Cancian, F. (1987). "Proletarianization in Zinacantan 1960–83." in Maclachan, M., ed. *Household Economies and Their Transformation*. Lanham MD: University Press of America.

Candia, J.M. (1996). "Empleo Precario y Conflicto Social. ¿Nuevas Formas de Organizacion Popular." *Nueva Sociedad*, No. 142, Marzo–Abril.

Castel, R. (1995). Les Metamorphoses de la question sociale. Paris: Fayard.

Cernea, M., ed. (1991). *Putting People First: Sociological Variables in Rural Development*. Washington/Oxford: IBRD/OUP.

Chalmers, D., et al., eds. (1997). *The New Politics of Inequality in Latin America*. Oxford: Oxford University Press.

Chambers, R. (1997). *Whose Reality Counts?* London: IT Publications.

———. (1983). *Rural Development: Putting The Last First*. New York: Longman.

Chambers, R. and G. Conway. (1998). "Sustainable Rural Livelihoods: Some Working Definitions." *Development,* 41 (3), September.

Chotray, V. (2004). "The Negation of Politics in Participatory Development Projects, Kurnool, Andhra Pradesh." *Development and Change,* 36 (2).

Cibils, A., M. Weisbrot and D. Kar. (2000). *Argentina Since Default: The IMF and the Depression.* Washington DC: Center for Economic and Policy Research.

Coleman, J.S. (1988). "Social Capital in the Creation of Human Capital." *American Journal of Sociology,* 94: S95-120.

Collins, J. and J. Lear. (1995). *Chile's Free Market Miracles: A Second Look.* Oakland CA: Food First.

Contreras Baspineiro, A. (1994). *La Marcha Historico.* Cochabamba: CEDIB.

Cotler, J. (1978). *Clases, estado y nación en el Perú.* Lima: Instituto de Estudios Peruanos.

Crabtree, J. (2003). "The Impact of Neo-Liberal Economics on Peruvian Peasant Agriculture in the 1990s." pp. 131-61 in *Latin American Peasants,* Brass, T., ed., London: Frank Cass.

Crouch, C. and A. Pizzorno. (1978). *Resurgence of Class Conflict in Western Europe Since 1968.* London: Holmes & Meier.

Cypher, J. (2005). "Poverty (Mexico)." pp. 281-83 in Herrick, J.M. and P.H. Stuart, eds. *Encyclopedia of Social Welfare History.* London: Sage Publications.

Dandler, J. (1969). *El Sindicalismo Campesino en Bolivia.* México: Instituto Indigenista Interamericano.

Dataluta—Banco de dados de luta pela terra. (2002). *Assentamentos rurais.* Sao Paulo: UNESPI/MST.

Dávalos, P. (2004). "Movimiento indígena, democracia, Estado y plurinacionalidad en Ecuador." *Revista Venezolana de Economía y Ciencias Sociales,* 10 (1). Enero-Abril.

Davis, M. (2006). *Planet of Slums.* London: Verso.

———. (1984). "The Political Economy of Late-Imperial America." *New Left Review,* 143 (Jan.-Feb.).

De Janvry, A. (1981). *The Agrarian Question and Reformism in Latin America.* Baltimore OH: Johns Hopkins University Press.

De la Garza, E. (1994). "Los sindicatos en America Latina frente a la estructuración productiva y los ajustes neo-liberales." *El Cotidiano,* No. 64, 9-10, Mexico.

De la Rocha, S. (1994). "Renda e pobreza nas metrópoles Brasileiras." pp. 121-46 in L.C. de Queiroz Ribeiro and O.A. dos Santos Junior, eds. *Globalizacao, fragmentacao e reforma urbana: O futuro das cidades Brasileiras na crise.* Rio de Janeiro: Editora Civilizacao Brasileira.

De Walt, B. and M. Ress. (1994). *The End of Agrarian Reform in Mexico: Past Lessons and Future Prospects.* San Diego: Center for US-Mexican Studies.

Deininger, K. (1998). "Implementing Negotiated Land Reform: Initial

BIBLIOGRAPHY

Experience from Colombia, Brazil and South Africa." pp. 116–25 in *Proceedings of the International Conference on Land Tenure in the Developing World with a Focus on Southern Africa*, January 27–29, University of Cape Town.

Delgado Jara, D. (2000). *Atraco bancario y dolarización*. Quito: Ediciones Gallo Rojo.

Diamond, L. (1999). *Developing Democracy: Towards Consolidation*. Baltimore: John Hopkins University Press.

Dunkerley, J. (1992). *Political Suicide in Latin America*. New York: Verso.

———. (1984). *Rebellion in the Veins: Political Struggle in Bolivia 1952-82*. London: New Left Books.

Durston, J. (1999) "Building Community Social Capital." *CEPAL Review*, 69: 103–18.

ECLAC—Economic Commission for Latin America and the Caribbean. (2003). *La inversión extranjera en América Latina y El Caríbe*. Santiago: ECLAC.

———. (1990). *Productive Transformation with Equity*. Santiago: ECLAC.

———. (1998). *Social Dimensions of Economic Development and Productivity: Inequality and Social Performance*, No. 56 Productive Development Series. Santiago: ECLAC.

Escobar, A. (1992). "Reflections on 'Development': Grassroots Approaches and Alternative Politics in the Third World." *Futures*, 2495.

Escobar, A. and S. Alvarez, eds. (1992). *The Making of Social Movements in Latin America: Identity, Strategy and Democracy*. Boulder CO: Westview Press.

Escoral, S. (1996). "Clarificando os conceitos: desigualdade, pobreza, marginalidade, exclusao. O que significa exclusao social?" Mimeo., 28 pp.

Esteva, G. and M.S. Prakash. (1998). *Grassroots Post-Modernism*. London: Zed Books.

Evans, P. (1979). *Dependent Development: The Alliance of Multinational, State and Local Capital in Brazil*. Princeton University Press.

Feder, E. (1971). *The Rape of the Peasantry: Latin America's Landholding System*. New York: Doubleday & Company, Inc.

Fedozzi, L. (1994). "Poder local e governabilidade: O caso de Porto Alegre." Proposta 22 (62): 23–29.

Figueiras, O. (1999). "O Campo em Chamas." *Sem Terra*, April–June.

Fine, B. (2001). *Social Capital versus Social Theory: Political Economy and Social Science at the Turn of the Millennium*. London and New York: Routledge.

Fogel, R.B. (1986). *Movimientos Campesinos en el Paraguay*. Asunción: Centro Paraguayo de Estudios Sociológicos (CPES).

Foley, M.W. (1991). "Agrarian Conflict Reconsidered: Popular Mobilization and Peasant Politics in Mexico and Central America." *Latin American Research Review*, 26 (1).

Freund, P. (1995). *Health, Illness and the Social Body*. Englewood Cliffs NJ: Prentice-Hall.

Garcia Delgado, D., et al. (1989). *Descentralización y democracia: Gobiernos locales en America Latina*. Buenos Aires: FLACSO.

Ghimire, K.B., ed. (2001). *Land Reform and Peasant Livelihoods: The Social Dynamics of Rural Poverty and Agrarian Reform in Developing Countries*. London: ITDG.

Gómez Solórzano, M. (1992). "Las transformaciones del proceso de trabajo en gran escala internacional." In Morales, J., ed. *La reestructuración industrial en México*. Mexico: IIE, UNAM; Editorial Nuestro Tiempo.

Gonzalez Amador, R. and R. Vargas. (2005). "Baja pobreza rural pero crece desigualdad." *Demos, Desarrollo de Medios*, S.A. de C.V., August 25.

Gould, J. (1983). "El trabajo forzoso y las comunidades indígenas nicaragüenses" in Brignoli, H.P. and M. Samper, eds. *El café en la historia de Centroamérica*. San José: FLASCO.

Goulet, D. (1989). "Participation in Development: New Avenues." *World Development* 17 (2): 165–78.

Greider, W. (1997). *One World, Ready or Not: The Manic Logic of Global Capitalism*. New York: Simon & Schuster.

Guimarães, R. (1997). "The Environment, Population and Urbanization" in R. Hillman, ed. *Understanding Contemporary Latin America*. Boulder CO: Lynne Rienner.

———. (1989). *Desarrollo con equidad: ¿un nuevo cuento de hadas para los años de noventa?* LC/R. 755. Santiago de Chile: CEPAL.

Gwynne, R. and C. Kay, eds. (1999). *Latin America Transformed*. New York: Oxford University Press.

Harris, J. and P. de Renzio. (1997). "Policy Arena: 'Missing Link' or Analytically Missing? The Concept of Social Capital: An Introductory Bibliographic Essay." *Journal of International Development*, 9 (7): 919–37.

Harris, J. (2001). *Depoliticising Development: The World Bank and Social Capital*. New Delhi: Left Word Books.

Harris, R.L., A. Winson, F. Mallon, R. Galli, A. de Janvry, L. Ground, and R. Montoya. (1978). "Peasants, Capitalism, and the Class Struggle in Rural Latin America (Part II)." *Latin American Perspectives*, 5: 4: 71–89.

Heath, D.B. (1969). *Land Reform and Social Revolution in Bolivia*. New York: Praeger.

Helmore, K. and N. Singh. (2001). *Sustainable Livelihoods: Building on the Wealth of the Poor*. West Hartford CT: Kumarian Press.

Hobsbawm, E. (1984). *The Age of Extremes: A History of the World*. New York: Pantheon.

Holloway, J. (2002). *Change the World without Taking Power: The Meaning of Revolution Today*. London: Pluto Press.

Horton, L. (1998). *Peasants in Arms: War and Peace in the Mountains of Nicaragua, 1979–1994*. Athens: Ohio University Center for International Studies.

Huizer, G.. (1973). *Peasant Rebellion in Latin America*. London: Penguin Books.

BIBLIOGRAPHY

IDB—Inter-American Development Bank. (1998). *Economic and Social Progress in Latin America: Facing Up to Inequality.* New York: IDB

IFAD—International Fund for Agricultural Development. (2001). *Strategy for Rural Poverty Reduction in Latin America and the Caribbean.* <www.ifad.org>.

ILO—International Labour Organization (2000). *World Employment Report.* Geneva: ILO.

Jacobsen, N. (1993). *Mirages of Transition: The Peruvian Altiplano, 1780–1930.* Berkeley CA: University of California Press.

Jazairy, I., M. Alamgir, and T. Panuccio. (1992). *The State of World Rural Poverty.* London: Intermediate Technology Publications (for IFAD).

Johnson, C. (2000). *Blowback: The Costs and Consequences of American Empire.* New York: Owl.

Kapstein, E. (1996). "Workers and the World Economy." *Foreign Affairs,* Vol. 75, No. 3.

Katz, F. (1988). *Riot, Rebellion, and Revolution: Rural Social Conflict in Mexico.* Princeton NJ: Princeton University Press.

Katz, J., ed. (1996). *Estabilización macroeconómica, reforma estructural y comportamiento industrial. Estructura y funcionamiento del sector manufacturero Latinoamericano en los años 90.* Buenos Aires: Alianza Editorial.

Kay, C. (2000). "Latin America's Agrarian Transformation: Peasantisation and Proletarianisation" in Bryceson, D.F.,
C. Kay, and J. Mooi, eds. *Disappearing Peasantries? Rural Labour in Africa, Asia and Latin America.* London: Intermediate Technology Publications.

———. (1989). "Rural Development: From Agrarian Reform to Neoliberalism and Beyond." in Gwynne, R. and C. Kay, eds. *Latin America Transformed.* New York: Oxford University Press.

———. (1982). "Achievements and Contradictions of the Peruvian Agrarian Reform." *Journal of Development Studies,* 18 (2).

———. (1981). "Political Economy, Class Alliances and Agrarian Change in Chile." *The Journal of Peasant Studies,* 8 (4).

Kearney, M. (1996). *Reconceptualizing the Peasantry.* Boulder CO: Westview Press.

Klein, N. (2001). "Reclaiming the Commons." *New Left Review* 9, May/June: 81–89.

Knack, S. (1999). "Social Capital, Growth and Poverty: A Survey of Cross-Country Evidence." *Social Capital Initiative Working Paper 7,* World Bank, Social Development Department, Washington DC.

Korten, D. (1995). *When Corporations Rule the World.* Hartford CT: Kumarian Press.

———. (1990). *Getting to the 21st Century: Voluntary Action and the Global Agenda.* Hartford CT: Kumarian Press.

Kuhn, T.S. (1996). *The Structure of Scientific Revolutions.* Chicago: The University of Chicago Press.

Laclau, E. (1989) "Politics and the Limits of Modernity." in Ross, A., ed. *Universal Abandon? The Politics of Postmodernism.* Edinburgh: Edinburgh University Press.

Landim, L. (1988). "Non-Governmental Organizations in Latin America." *World Development*, 15 (Supplement): 29-38.

Laurelli, E. and A. Rofman, eds. (1989). *Decentralización del Estado: Requerimientos y políticas en la crisis.* Buenos Aires: Ediciones CEURI.

LeGrand, C.C. (1983). *From Public Lands into Private Properties: Landholding and Rural Conflict in Colombia, 1870–1936.* Ann Arbor: University Microfilms.

Lehmann, D. (1978). "The Death of Land Reform: A Polemic." *World Development*, 6 (3).

Leiva, F. and R. Agacino. (1995). *Mercado de trabajo flexible, pobreza y desintegración social en Chile. 1990–1994.* Santiago: Editorial Arcis.

Leiva, F. and J. Petras, with H. Veltmeyer. (1994). *Democracy and Poverty in Chile.* Boulder CO: Westview Press.

Lesbaupin, I. (2000). *Poder local X Exclusão social.* Petrópolis: VOZES.

Lesser, E. (2000). "Leveraging Social Capital in Organizations." pp. 3–16 in *Knowledge and Social Capital: Foundations and Applications.* Boston: Butterworth-Heinemann.

Liamzon, T. et al., eds. (1996). *Towards Sustainable Livelihoods.* Rome: Society for International Development.

Lindqvist, S. (1979). *Land and Power in South America.* Harmondsworth: Penguin.

Lora, G. (1964). *La Revolución Boliviana.* La Paz: Difusión SRL.

Loveman, B. (1976). *Struggle in the Countryside: Politics and Rural Labor in Chile, 1919–1973.* Bloomington IN: Indiana University Press.

Lozano, C., et al. (2006). *La dueda interna se acentua: ingresos, salarios y convenios colectivos en Argentina.* Buenos Aires: Gobierno de Argentina.

MacEwan, A. (1999). *Neo-Liberalism or Democracy: Economic Strategy, Markets and Alternatives for the 21st Century.* London: Zed Books.

———. (1981). *Revolution and Economic Development in Cuba: Moving Towards Socialism.* New York: St. Martin's Press.

Mahoney, J. (2001). *The Legacies of Liberalism: Path Dependence and Political Regimes in Central America.* Baltimore: Johns Hopkins University Press.

Malloy, J.M., and R.S. Thorn, eds. (1971). *Beyond the Revolution: Bolivia Since 1952.* Pittsburgh PA: Pittsburgh University Press.

Max-Neef, M. (1986). *La economia descalza.* Montevideo: Editorial Nordan Comunidad.

Max-Neef, M., A. Elizalde, and M. Hopenhayen. (1965). "Desarrollo a Escala Humana: una opcion para el futuro." *Development Dialogue*, numero especial, Fundación Dag Hammarskjold.

BIBLIOGRAPHY

McGowan, D. (2000). *Deraiiing Democracy: The America the Media Don't Want You to See*. Monroe ME: Common Courage Press.

Midlarsky, M. and K. Roberts. (1995). "Class, State and Revolution in Central America: Nicaragua and El Salvador Compared." *Journal of Conflict Resolution*, No. 29, June.

MST, Direcion Nacional. (1991). *Como Organizar a la Masa*. Sao Paulo: MST.

MST, Setor de Documentação do SN da CPT Nacional. (2002). Sau Paulo: MST.

Narayan, D. (2002). *Empowerment and Poverty Reduction: A Sourcebook*. Washington DC: World Bank.

Nascimento, E. (1994). "Hipoteses sobre a nova exclusao social: dos excluidos necessarios aos excluidos desnecessarios." Cuadernos do CRH, Salvador, (21): 29-47, jul.-dez.

North, D. (1990). *Institutions, Institutional Change and Economic Performance*. Cambridge MA: Cambridge University Press.

O'Donnell, G., and P.C. Schmitter. (1986). *Transitions from Authoritarian Rule: Tentative Conclusions about Uncertain Democracies*. Baltimore: John's Hopkins University Press.

Oakley, P. (1991). "The Concept of Participation in Development." *Landscape and Urban Planning*, 20: 115–22.

Olave, P. (1994). "Reestructuración productiva bajo el nuevo patrón exportador." In Arancibia Córdova, J. ed. *América latina en los ochenta: reestructuración y perspectivas*. México DF: IIEC-UNAM.

Ominami, C., ed. (1986). *La tercera revolución industrial, impactos internacionales el actual viraje tecnológico*. Mexico: RIAL-Anuario-Grupo Ed. Latinoamericano.

Orlove, B.S. and G. Custred, eds. (1980). *Land and Power in Latin America: Agrarian Economies and Social Processes in the Andes*. New York: Holmes and Meier Publishers.

Parpart, J. and H. Veltmeyer. (2004). "The Dynamics of Development Theory and Practice: A Review of Its Shifting Dynamics." *Canadian Journal of Development Studies*, XXV (1). Special Issue.

Patomäki, H. and T. Teivainen (2004). *A Possible World: Democratic Transformation of Global Institutions*. London: Zed Books.

———. (1997a). "MST and Latin America: The Revival of the Peasantry as a Revolutionary Force." *Canadian Dimension*, 31 (3). May/June.

Paugam, S. (1994). *Les disqualifications sociales*. Paris, PUF.

———. (1997b). "The Resurgence of the Left." *New Left Review*, 223: 17–47.

Paugam, S., ed. (1996). *L'exclusion. L'Etat des savoirs*. Paris: Ed. La Découverte.

Petras, J. and S. Arellano-Lopez. (1997). "Non-Government Organisations and Poverty Alleviation in Bolivia." pp. 180–94 in Veltmeyer, H. and J. Petras, *Neoliberalism and Class Conflict in Latin America*. London: MacMillan.

Petras, J. and F. Leiva. (1994). *Poverty and Democracy in Chile*. Boulder CO: Westview Press.

Petras, J. and H. Veltmeyer. (2005). *Social Movements and the State: Argentina, Bolivia, Brazil, Ecuador*. London: Pluto Press.

———. (2004). "Whither Lula's Brazil? Neoliberalism and Third Way Ideology." *Journal of Peasant Studies*, 31 (1). October.

———. (2003). "The Peasantry and the State in Latin America." pp. 41–82 in Brass, T., ed., *Latin American Peasants*. London: Frank Cass & Co. Also in *Journal of Peasant Studies*.

———. (2002). *Argentina: Entre la desintegración y la revolución*. Buenos Aires: Editorial La Maza,

———. (2001). *Unmasking Globalization: The New Face of Imperialism*. London: Zed Books; Halifax: Fernwood Books.

———. (2000). *Brasil de Cardoso: Expropriação de un pais*. Petrópolis: VOZES.

Pochmann, M. (1999). *O trabalho sob fogo cruzado*. Sao Paulo: Contexto.

Pochmann, M., et al. (2004). *Atlas da exclusâo no mundo*, 5 vols. Sao Paulo: Cortez Editora.

Polanyi, K. (2001). *The Great Transformation: The Political and Economic Origins of Our Time*. Boston MA: Beacon Press.

Portes, A. (1998). "Social Capital: Its Origins and Applications in Modern Sociology." *Annual Review of Sociology*, 24: 1–24.

Portes, A., ed. (1989). *The Informal Economy: Studies in Advanced and Less Developed Countries*. Baltimore: Johns Hopkins University Press.

Portes, A. and P. Landolt. (1996). "The Downside of Social Capital," *The American Prospect*, 7 (26), May/June: 18–21, 94.

Poulantzas, N. (1978). *Political Power and Social Classes*. London: Verso.

Pozzobon, M.R. (1997). *Desafios da gestao municipal democratica: O caso de Porto Alegre (1992–96)*. Porto Alegre: CIDADE.

PREALC—Programa Regional de Empleo de America Latina y el Caríbe. (1993). *PREALC Informe*. Santiago: ILO-PREALC

Pritchett, L. (2006). "The Quest Continues." *Finance & Development*, 43 (1). March: 18–22.

Putnam, R.D. (2000). *Bowling Alone: The Collapse and Revival of American Community*. New York: Simon & Schuster.

———. (1993). *Making Democracy Work*. New Jersey: Princeton University Press.

Putnam, R.D., ed. (2002). *Democracy in Flux: The Evolution of Social Capital in Contemporary Society*. Oxford: Oxford University Press.

Rao, V. (2002). "Community Driven Development: A Brief Review of the Research." Washington DC: World Bank.

Razeto, L. (1993). *De la economia popular a la economia de solidaridad en un proyecto de desarrollo alternativo*.

Santiago: Programa de Economía del Trabajo (PET).

———. (1988). *Economía de solidaridad y mercado democratico*, Vol. III. Santiago: PET, Academia de Humanismo Cristiano.

Rhaman Khan, A. (1993). *Structural Adjustment and Income Distribution: Issues and Experiences*. Geneva: ILO.

Rodgers, G., C. Gore, and J.B. Figueiredo, eds. (1995). *Social Exclusion: Rhetoric, Challenges, Responses*. Geneva: International Labour Organisation.

Rohter, L. (2000). "Is the Economy Brighter? Brazil's Leader Faces Wage Demands." *The New York Times*, November 30.

Rondinelli, D.A., J. McCullough, and W. Johnson. (1989). "Analyzing Decentralization Policies in Developing countries: A Political Economy Framework." *Development and Change*, 20 (1): 57–87.

Rondinelli, D.A., J.R. Nellis, and G.S. Cheema. (1983). "Decentralization in Developing Countries: A Review of Recent Experience." *World Bank Staff Paper*, No. 581. Washington DC: World Bank.

Rubio, M. (1997). "Perverse Social Capital: Some Evidence from Colombia." *Journal of Economic Issues*, 321 (3).

Roque, A. and S. Corrêa. (2001). *Guia del Mundo*. Montevideo: Institute del Tercer Mundo.

Sachs, I. (1995). "Searching for New Development Strategies: Challenges of the Social Summit." *Economic and Political Weekly*, July 8.

Sachs, W. (1992). *The Development Dictionary: A Guide to Knowledge as Power*. London: Zed Books.

Saxe-Fernández, J. (2002). *La Compra Venta de México*. Mexico: Plaza Janes.

———. (1994). "The Chiapas Insurrection: Consequences for Mexico and the United States." *International Journal of Politics, Culture and Society*, Vol. 8. No. 2.

Saxe-Fernández, J., J. Petras, O. Nuñez, and H. Veltmeyer. (2001). *Globalización, imperialismo y clase social*. Buenos Aires and Mexico City: Editorial Lumen.

Schuldt, J. (1995). *Repensando el Desarrollo: Hacia una Concepción Alternativa para los Paises Andinos*. Quito: Centro Andino de Acción Popular (CAAP).

Schuurman, F., ed. (1993). *Beyond the Impasse: New Directions in Development Theory*. London: Zed Books.

SEADE/DIESE. (2000). *Pesquisa de Emprego e Desemprego: Indicadores Selecionados*. Sao Paulo: Marzo.

Sen, A. (1989). "Development as Capability Expansion." *Journal of Development Expansion*, No. 19: 41–58.

Silberschneider, W. (1993). *Democracia e participacao politica: O Partido dos Trabalhadores e o Conselho Municipal de Orcamento na Administracao Chico Ferramenta (1989–1992)*. Master's Thesis, Sociology, Universidade Federal de Minas Gerais.

Slater, D. (1994) "Power and Social Movements in the Other Occident: Latin America in an International

Context." *Latin American Perspectives*, 21(2): 11–37.

———. (1985). *New Social Movements and the State in Latin America*. Amsterdam: CEDLA.

Solow, R. (2000). "Notes on Social Capital and Economic Performance." In Dasgupta, P. and I. Serageldin, eds., *Social Capital: A Multi-Faceted Perspective*. Washington DC: World Bank.

Stedile, J.P. (2000). Interview with James Petras, May 14.

Stiefel, M. and M. Wolfe. (1994). *A Voice for the Excluded: Popular Participation in Development: Utopia or Necessity?* London and Atlantic Highlands NJ: Zed Books and UNRISD.

Sunkel, O. (2003). *Development from Within: Toward a Neostructuralist Approach for Latin America*. Boulder CO: Lynne Rienner.

Thiesenhusen, W. (1995). *Broken Promises: Agrarian Reform and the Latin American Campesino*. Boulder: Westview Press.

Thiesenhusen, W., ed. (1989). *Searching for Agrarian Reform in Latin America*. Winchester MA: Unwin Hyman.

Thiesenhusen, W. (1995). *Broken Promises: Agrarian Reform and the Latin American Campesino*. Boulder: Westview Press.

Thorpe, A., et. al. (1995). *Impacto del ajuste en el agro Hondureño*. Tegucigalpa: Posgrado Centroamericano en Economia de la Universidad Nacional Autónoma de Honduras.

UNCTAD—United Nations Conference on Trade and Development. (2001). *World Investment Report 2001: Promoting Linkages*. New York and Geneva: United Nations.

UNCTAD. (1998). *World Investment Report 1998: Trends and Determinants*. New York and Geneva: United Nations.

UNDP—United Nations Development Programme. (2003). *Human Development Report 2003: Millennium Development Goals*. New York/Oxford: Oxford University Press.

———. (1990, 1992, 2001, 2002). *Human Development Report*. New York: Oxford University Press.

———. (1996). "Good Governance and Sustainable Human Development." Governance Policy Paper. <http://magnet.undp.org/policy>.

———. (1993). *Cooperation for Development: Bolivia Report*. La Paz: UNDP.

UNICEF. (1989). *Participación de los sectores pobres en programas de desarrollo local*. Santiago: UNICEF.

United Nations, Department of Economic and Social Affairs. (2005). *The World Social Situation: The Inequality Predicament*. UNESCO, New York.

US Census Bureau (2002). US Direct Investment Position Abroad on a Historical Cost Basis. Washington DC.

United States, Department of Commerce. (1994). *U.S. Direct Investment Abroad*. Washington DC: Bureau of Economic Analysis, October.

UNRISD—United Nations Research Institute for Social Development. (2000). "Civil Society Strategies and Movements for

BIBLIOGRAPHY

Rural Asset Redistribution and Improved Livelihoods." Geneva: UNRISD.

Vasapollo, L. (2003). *Il piano inclinato del capitale. Crisi, competizione globale e Guerra*. Rome: Jaca Books.

Veltmeyer, H. (2005). "Development and Globalization as Imperialism." *Canadian Journal of Development Studies*, Vol. XXVI (1): 89–106.

———. (1997a). "Decentralisation as the Institutional Basis for Participatory Development: The Latin American Perspective." *Canadian Journal of Development Studies*, XVIII (2).

———. (1997b). "New Social Movements in Latin America: The Dynamics of Class and Identity." *The Journal of Peasant Studies*, 25 (1).

Veltmeyer, H. and A. O'Malley. (2001). *Transcending Neoliberalism: Community-Based Development*. West Hartford CT: Kumarian Press.

Veltmeyer, H. and J. Petras. (2000). *The Dynamics of Social Change in Latin America*. London: Macmillan Press.

———. (1997). *Economic Liberalism and Class Conflict in Latin America*. London: MacMillan Press.

Vergara, P. (1996). "In Pursuit of Growth with Equity." *NACLA Report on the Americas*, XXIX, 6, May/June.

Vilas, C. (1995). *Between Earthquakes and Volcanoes: Market, State and Revolutions in Central America*. New York: Monthly Review Press.

Walton, J. and D. Seddon. (1994). *Free Markets and Food Riots: The Politics of Global Adjustment*. Oxford: Blackwell.

Wheelock Román, J. (1975). *Imperialismo y dictadura: crisis de una formación social*. Mexico City: Siglo Veintiuno Editores.

Wilber, C. and K. Jameson. (1975). "Paradigms of Economic Development and Beyond." In Wilber, ed., *Political Economy of Development and Underdevelopment*, 4th ed. New York: McGraw-Hill.

Williamson, J., ed. (1990). *Latin American Adjustment. How Much Has Happened?* Washington DC: Institute for International Economics.

Woolcock, M. and D. Narayan. (2000). "Social Capital: Implications for Development Theory, Research and Policy." *The World Bank Research Observer*, 15 (2). August.

Woolcock, M. (1988). "Social Capital and Economic Development: Towards a Theoretical Synthesis and Policy Framework." *Theory and Society*, 27: 151–208.

World Bank. (2004a). *Operationalizing Pro-Poor Growth*. Washington DC: World Bank.

———. (2004b). *Partnerships in Development: Progress in the Fight Against Poverty*. Washington DC: World Bank.

———. (1998). *Assessing Aid. What Works, What Doesn't, and Why*. New York: Oxford University Press.

———. (1996). *Including the Excluded: Ethnodevelopment in Latin America*, Vol. 1. Washington DC: World Bank.

———. (1990, 1997, 2000, 2002). *World Development Report*. Oxford: Oxford University Press.

———. (various years). World Development Report. Oxford: Oxford University Press.

Xiberras, M. (1996). *Les théories de l'exclusion*. Paris: A. Colin.

Zamora, R. (1995). "Foreword" to *Free Trade and Economic Restructuring in Latin America*, eds. Rosen, F. and R. Ardaya. *La construcción municipal de Bolivia*. La Paz: Strategies for International Development.

Index

Abers, Rebecca, 78, 79, 82, 83
Acción Catolica, 51, 53, 53n5
Afghanistan, 22, 26
Africa, 12, 17, 18
Agenda Venezuela, 134
agricultural restructuring, 40–41, 119–22, 158
Alliance for Progress, 24, 50, 53n5, 150–51
Alliance for the Countryside, 41
Alternative Strategy for Economic Development, 141
Amaru, Túpac, 111, 125
American Century, 22–23
Amplio, Frente, 133
another development (AD), 31, 34, 42–43, 52, 138–39
   in Bolivia, 162–63
   features of, 43–47, 55–57, 98–101, 163–64
   social capital and, 60, 163–64
Argentina, 14, 17, 27
   class struggle in, 86
   elections in, 133, 134, 136
   income in, 16, 95, 107n13
   labour laws in, 87
   land reform in, 122
   neo-liberalism in, 73
   social exclusion in, 91, 93
   social movements in, 8, 131, 144
   urbanization of, 114
Asia, 17, 18, 25
asset-based community development (ABCD), 163
Atorga Lira, Enrique, 40

Bachalet, Michelle, 136
banks, 20–23, 29n5, 40, 45, 121–22, 125, 126
Batista, Fulgencio, 112
Belém Novo, 77

Bolivarian Revolution, 131–32, 134
Bolivia, 17, 76
   coca farmers in, 120, 132, 142, 143, 149, 152, 155, 166n5, 167n7
   decentralization in, 157, 164
   development politics in, 162–63
   elections in, 9, 133, 136, 154–57
   financial policy in, 157–58
   insurrection in, 150, 151, 153, 154, 165n3
   land reform movement in, 113, 125, 159–61
   neo-liberalism in, 73, 161
   new social policy in, 35, 97
   social change in, 150, 155–57
   social liberalism in, 36–37
   social movements in, 128, 131, 132, 142–45, 149
Bolivian Gas War, 132, 155–56
Bolivian Workers Central (COB), 143
Borda, Fals, 99
Brazil, 14, 27, 86
   development advances in, 75–78
   economic growth in, 73–74, 90, 106n5
   elections in, 132–33, 135
   imperialism in, 24
   income in, 75, 91–92, 94–95
   labour laws in, 87
   land reform movement in, 113–14, 115, 121–22, 124–26
   military dictatorships in, 72–75
   municipal governments in, 75–78
   non-governmental organizations in, 76–77
   participatory budgetary process in, 71, 74–78
   political/economic history of, 72–74
   social exclusion in, 91, 92–93

social movements in, 8, 142, 144–45, 149, 152
social programs in, 107n12
repression in, 118–19
urbanization of, 114–15
Bretton Woods, 23–24, 28n1, 150
British Empire, 19
Bucaram, Abdala, 131, 153
Bush Administration, 22–23, 26, 117–18

Caldera, Rafael, 133, 134
Camdessus, Michel, 35, 95, 147n1, 147n2
Campbell, C., 63–66
Canadian International Development Agency (CIDA), 51
Candia, José Michael, 137
capital
   access to, 98
   accumulation/centralization of, 13, 15–16, 56
   inflows and outflows of, 21–23
capitalism
   in development theory, 42
   golden age of, 7–8, 24, 151
   labour vs., 15
   in new economic model, 8, 13, 88
   politics and, 58, 60–61, 88, 158–59
capitalist class, 15–17, 19, 32, 66–67, 119
Cárdenas, Cuauhtémoc, 135
Cardoso, Henrique Fernando, 73–74, 77, 79, 81, 84, 87, 90–95, 107n12, 119, 126, 133, 135
Castro, Fidel, 113
Catholic Action, 51, 53n5
Chambers, Robert, 102
change. See social change
Chavez, Hugo, 27, 131–32, 133, 134, 136
Chiapas, 140, 143–45, 147n3, 149, 151. See also Zapatista Army of National Liberation (EZLN)
Chile, 14, 24, 47, 76, 85
   elections in, 134, 136
   land reform movements in, 115
   neo-liberalism in, 24, 73
   neo-structuralism in, 49
   new social policy in, 35, 38–39, 97
   poverty in, 97, 115–16, 85
   social liberalism in, 36
China, 17, 21, 25, 26–27
Chotray, V., 66
cities, 32, 88, 94, 114, 116–17, 123, 143, 151, 152
Civic Alliance, 141

civil society, 8, 50–52, 71, 74, 81, 98, 139. See also non-governmental organizations (NGOs); social movements
civil society organizations (CSOs), 60
class
   capitalist/propertied, 15–17, 19, 32, 66–67, 119, 160
   middle, 15, 16, 32, 134
   political power and, 155
   struggle, 58, 85, 95, 112, 117, 121, 125, 138, 142–46, 151
   working, 15–17, 32, 85–87
class identity, 63
clientelism, 65, 76, 78–82
client states, 20, 24, 25
cold war, 12, 150
Collor, Fernando, 73, 93
Colombia, 24, 51, 125, 143
common identity, 61–63
communism, 81, 151
communitarianism, 159, 167n8
community, 43–45, 56, 59, 62–63, 102
community economic development (CED), 141
comparative advantage, 14
Concertación Party, 134
Confederation of Indigenous Nationalities of Ecuador (CONAIE), 124, 128, 144, 149, 152–54, 165n2
Confederation of Peasant Workers' Unions of Bolivia, 166n5
consciousness raising, 51, 53n6
conselhos populares, 80–81, 83
co-operatives, 45, 99–100
corporations, 15–16, 20–22, 26, 72, 166n6
crime, 33, 92
Cuba, 24, 50, 109–10, 113, 120, 124, 127, 150, 151, 161

Dag Hammarskjold Foundation for Alternative Development, 42, 138–39
Danish Association for International Development, 162
da Silva, Luiz Inácio (Lula), 73, 74, 119, 124, 128, 133, 135, 136
debt, 8, 16, 25, 41, 48, 50, 90
debt crisis, 13–14, 89, 93, 107n12, 127
decentralization, 14
   in Brazil, 74–78
   of decision making, 34, 44, 50, 80–81, 96, 104
   of government, 38, 60, 71, 74–78, 78, 164
   pitfalls of, 82

INDEX

in social liberalism, 36–37
decolonization, 150–51
de Janvry, Alain, 118
de Lozada, Gonzalo Sanchez, 36, 155, 156, 159, 161, 162, 166n4
democracy, 9, 51, 59–62, 80
Democratic Peasant Alliance (ADC), 144
Dependency theory, 42, 53n3, 139
deregulation, 14, 15, 21, 25, 115
de Souza, Betinho, 95
development, 7–9, 43–47
    alternative, 34–35, 42–50. *See also* another development (AD)
    as economic growth, 41–42
    history of, 12–13, 31, 56
    international, 50–52, 151
    limitations of, 146
    municipalization of, 9, 75–78
    new economic model as, 19
    non-governmental organizations and, 50–52
    participatory, 58, 71–74, 101, 138–42
    social capital and, 58, 67–68
    social change through, 149–50, 161–64
    in social liberalism, 36
De Walt, Billie, 116
Dominican Republic, 24
downsizing
    of government, 15, 33, 59, 61, 87–88
    of social programs, 32, 33, 61, 95
    of workforce, 90–92
Durston, John, 63–64, 65, 69
Dutra, Olivio, 82

economically active population (EAP), 16
economic growth, 13–14, 17, 48
    in Brazil, 90, 106n5
    as development, 41–42, 56
    of golden age, 151
economics
    of imperialism, 19–22
    macro-, 8, 17, 25, 48, 68, 84, 152
economy of solidarity, 96
Ecuador
    agricultural restructuring in, 122
    elections in, 9, 133, 153–55
    land reform movement in, 124
    political action in, 153
    social change in, 150, 153–55
    social movements in, 128, 131, 143, 144, 152
education, 33, 34, 38, 56, 91, 92, 97
El Barzón, 123

elections, 8–9, 131–36, 144–45, 152–61
El Salvador, 143, 144
employment, 34, 89, 91, 137
empowerment, 37, 39, 42, 56, 58, 66, 100, 164
    social, 102, 104, 121
encomienda system, 111–12
environment, 44, 46, 138, 145
equity, 48–49, 89, 167n9
ethnicity, 63, 66, 67, 138, 145
Europe, 12, 19, 25, 26, 85
Evans, Peter, 72

Farabundo Marti National Liberation Front (FMLN), 144
farmers, 8, 9, 40–41. *See also* land reform; peasants
Fedozzi, Luciano, 76
financial policy, 158–61
Fine, Ben, 57, 61
foreign aid, 20, 23, 24, 50–52
foreign direct investment (FDI), 21–23, 72
formal sector, 88–89, 91, 137
Fourth World, 18
Franco, Itamar, 73
free trade, 136
Freire, Paulo, 52, 53n6
Fujimori, Albert, 134
Fund for Solidarity and Social Investment (FOSIS), 35, 38–39

Garcia, Alan, 133
gas and oil industry, 27, 132, 155–59, 166n5
gemeinschaft, 63
gender, 34, 44, 66, 67, 128, 137, 145, 152
General Agreement on Tariffs and Trade (GATT), 28n1
gesellschaft, 63
globalization, 7, 15, 150, 152
    in development, 46–47, 55–56
    multinational corporations and, 15–16
    in new economic model, 18–19
    resistance to, 25, 33–34
    social capital and, 55
golden age of capitalism, 7–8, 24, 151
government, 17, 101. *See also* state
    downsizing of, 15, 33, 59, 61, 87–88
    financial policies of, 158–61
    local, 74–75, 79–81, 157, 164
    military, 8, 14, 24, 72–76, 136
    participatory, 71–83
    resource ownership and, 159–61
    in structuralist model, 13
Government Plan for Action, 162–63

grassroots organizations, 43, 61
Guatemala, 24, 65
guerrilla movements, 24, 51, 116, 151
Guevara, Ché, 116
Guimarães, Roberto, 99
Gutierrez, Lucio, 153, 154, 165n3

Hayek, Friedrich, 14
health care, 33, 34, 38, 56, 91, 92, 97
Hobsbawm, Eric, 116, 143
Honduras, 115
Humala, Antauro, 134
Human Development Report 2001 (UNDP), 104
human rights, 24, 138
hydrocarbon industry, 27, 128, 132, 155–59, 166n5
hyperinflation, 17

imperialism
  economics of, 19–22
  history of, 12, 19–20
  new economic model as, 19–20
  non-governmental organizations and, 52–53
  politics of, 22–27
  of United States, 19–27
import substitution industrialization (ISI), 47
income. *See also* wages
  decreasing, 92–93
  distribution of, 17–18, 31, 86, 93–97, 107n10
  in least/most developed countries, 17–18
indigenous peoples, 44, 64, 137
  in Bolivia, 155–56
  in Ecuador, 153–55
  landlessness of, 110–11, 122
  political movements of, 8, 9, 52, 117, 124, 128, 141, 145, 149, 153
industrialization by export promotion (EPI), 47–48
inequality, 65–66, 86, 91, 93, 100
inequality predicament, 18, 27
inflation, 13, 15, 17, 89, 135
informal sector, 88, 91. *See also* social exclusion
Institutional Revolutionary Party, 135
Instituto del Tercer Mundo, 94
insurrections, 153–55, 166n5
integrated rural development, 50–51
Inter-American Development Bank (IDB), 28, 33, 59, 64

international development agencies (IDAs), 50–52, 52
International Financial Institutions (IFIS), 14–15, 20, 26, 34, 52, 98
International Fund for Agricultural Development (IFAD), 67, 140
International Institute on Agrarian Reform (INRA), 160
International Labour Organization (ILO), 88
International Monetary Fund (IMF), 8, 17
  history of, 12–13
  policies of, 14–15, 35, 49, 87, 107n12
  protest against, 26, 33
International Trade Organization (ITO), 28n1
investment, 21–23, 26–27, 56, 72
Iran, 27
Iraq war, 22, 26
Israel, 22
Italy, 75–76

Japan, 25

Kay, Cristóbal, 116, 118
Kennedy, John F., 24
Keynesianism, 48
Kirchner, Néstor, 133, 136

labour. *See also* working class
  adjustment programs and, 88–89, 91–93
  conditions of, 92–95
  division of, 14, 31
  family, 88–89
labour laws, 87–89
labour movement, 7–8, 16–17
  peasants groups and, 120
  suppression of, 24, 85–103, 152
laissez faire. See neo-liberalism
land. *See also* land reform
  expropriation of, 125
  occupations of, 109–14, 118, 122, 125–29, 144
  ownership of, 36, 98, 104, 113, 115, 126, 159–61
  titling of, 122, 125
land banks, 125, 126
landlessness, 109–17, 149, 164
Landless Workers Movement (MST), 109, 119, 124, 142–43, 152
land reform, 104, 109–10, 118
  in Bolivia, 159–61
  death of, 110, 116, 118
  history of, 111–13
  market-assisted, 121–23

INDEX

in Mexico, 40–41
occupation tactic for, 109–14, 118, 122, 125–19, 144
peasant-initiated, 123–26
social movements and, 128
state-led, 118–20
Law of Administrative Decentralization (LAD), 36, 163
Law of Economic Transformation (TROLE), 165n3
Law of Popular Participation (LPP), 36–37, 163
least development countries (LDCs), 17–18
Lehman, David, 115–16
Lesser, Eric, 64
liberalization, 14, 115
liberal theory, 12–13
liberation theology, 51, 53n5
local economic development (LED), 163
local government, 74–81, 157, 164
local human development (LHD), 163
local sector, 9
    in alternative development, 44–47, 55–59
    businesses and markets in, 86, 88
    social capital and, 58
London School of Economics (LSE) Gender Institute, 62–66
Lopez Portillo, Mexico, 33
Luce, Henry, 22

Macas, Luis, 154
macroeconomics, 8, 17, 25, 48, 68, 84, 152
Making Democracy Work (Putnam), 57, 59–62
Marcos, Zapatista, 18, 28
markets
    global, 15
    invisible hand of, 35, 95
    land reform and, 121–23
    local and regional, 45
    regulation of, 97
Marshall, Alfred, 14
Marx, Karl, 12, 58, 66, 110
Marxism, 42, 145
Mauss, Marcell, 65
Menem, Carlos, 87, 93, 134
Mesa, Carlos, 156, 167n7
Mexico
    Chiapas region, 140, 143–45, 147n3, 149, 151
    elections in, 9, 134–35
    labour laws in, 87
    land issues in, 41, 113, 122, 123, 124
    new social policy in, 35, 39–41, 97

privatization in, 22, 29n5, 40
social liberalism in, 36
social movements in, 8, 33, 128, 131, 140, 141, 143
wealth in, 16, 93, 107n10, 147n2
micro-enterprise financing (MEF), 163
micro-enterprises, 88–89
micro-projects, 9, 40
middle class, 15, 16, 32, 134
military dictatorships, 24, 72–76, 136
military force, 20, 24, 26
Morales, Evo, 132, 136, 155–61, 167n7, 167n8
most developed countries (MDCs), 18
Movement toward Socialism (MAS), 132, 134, 153, 155, 156
multinational corporations, 15–16, 20–22, 26, 72, 166n6
municipal government, 74–81, 157, 164
Mutún, El, 157–58

National Action Party, 135
National Confederation of Agricultural Workers (CONTAG), 126
National Congress to Condemn the Economic Policy of the Mexican Government, 141
National Federation of Peasants, 143
National Institute of Colonization and Agrarian Reform (INCRA), 126
National Peasant Federation, 144
neo-liberalism, 11–12, 27–28, 150, 152
    in alternative development, 48
    in Brazil, 73–74
    decline of, 25, 27, 95, 139
    ECLAC alternatives to, 47–50
    impacts of, 15–19, 37
    imperialism and, 19–27
    policies of, 12–19, 33, 86–95
    in political parties, 132–35
    popular participation and, 43–44
    resistance to, 8, 25
    three pillars of, 95–96
neo-structuralism, 35–36, 43–44, 47–50
new economic model (NEM), 19–20, 41, 55–56
newly industrializing countries (NICs), 13, 25, 50, 139
new paradigm, 28, 31–52, 55–56, 68, 104, 139, 140
new peasant movements (NPMs), 142–46
new social movements (NSMs), 137–38, 148n5, 149
new social policy (NSP), 34–35, 38–41

205

Nicaragua, 115
non-governmental organizations (NGOs)
   control of, 26, 76–78, 147n4
   in development programs, 39, 44, 50–52, 138–42
   growth of, 8, 52, 76
   role of, 52–53

Obredor, López, 135
Official Development Aid (ODA) organizations, 121
oil and gas industry, 22–23, 27, 132, 155–58, 166n5
Orçamento Participativa, 78, 80, 81, 83
Organization for Economic Cooperation and Development (OECD), 51
ownership
   of land and resources, 58, 98, 104, 113, 115, 126, 159–61
   state vs. private, 157–59

Pachakutik Indigenous Movement, 154, 166n5
Pachakutik, 153, 154, 165n1
Paraguay, 124–25, 143–45
participation, 43–45, 70n2, 164
   in Brazil, 71, 74–78
   problems with, 77–78, 99–101
   social capital and, 59, 66
   in social liberalism, 36–37
   as transformative, 96–97, 100
participatory budgetary process, 71–83
participatory development (PD), 58, 72–79, 101, 138–42, 164
Party of the Democratic Revolution, 135
peasants. See also rural sector
   disappearance of, 116–17
   land reform movements of, 110–13, 116, 123–26
   relationship of, with state, 119
   social movements of, 121, 128, 143–44, 152
   types of, 120
People's Assembly, 75
Peru, 8, 14, 17
   agricultural restructuring in, 123
   elections in, 9, 134
   land reform movement in, 125
   neo-liberalism in, 73
Petras, James, 22, 117, 118
Pinochet regime, 36, 115, 119
Plano Real, 135
political parties, 137, 142, 144. See also individual parties

political power. See also elections; government
   another development and, 164
   class and, 155
   in land reform, 121
   psychological power vs., 66
   social capital and, 58, 62
   social change and, 104, 149–50
politics
   of adjustment, 60
   of imperialism, 22–27
popular councils, 75, 80–81
Porto Alegre, Brazil, 34, 75, 78–80, 132
Poulantzas, Nicos, 78
poverty, 16, 86, 106n7. See also income
   in Argentina, 95
   in Brazil, 91–95
   in Chile, 97, 115–16
   debt crisis and, 14
   extreme, 34, 35, 37, 95, 101, 115
   in Mexico, 16, 93, 107n10, 147n2
   neo-liberalism and, 17–19, 32–33, 123
   new social policy and, 37–41
   rates of, 17–19, 94, 115, 123
   rural, 32, 67, 94, 115–16, 123
   social capital and, 67–68
   social exclusion and, 91
   urban, 94, 152
poverty line, 67, 94, 95
power-sharing, 104
Prestes, Luis Carlos, 112
private enterprise, 14
private voluntary organizations (PVOs), 50–51
privatization, 14, 15, 134
   of banks, 22, 29n5, 40
   in Bolivia, 132
   in Brazil, 73
   of gas and oil, 132, 155–57
   under new economic model, 21–22
   poverty and, 115
   of public works, 21–22, 33
   of social programs, 38
   of water, 33, 132, 156, 159, 166n6
Procampo, 41
Productive Transformation with Equity (ECLAC), 96–97
productivity, 48, 88–89, 164
   crisis of, 151
   downsizing and, 91–92
   natural resources and, 159–61
Project for a New American Century, 23, 29n6
property, 119, 157–58. See also ownership

INDEX

protest movements, 33, 132–33, 136–37
public works, 21–22, 33
Putnam, Robert, 57, 59–62, 64

Quispe, Felipe, 154, 166n5

Razeto, Luis, 96, 99
Reagan Administration, 141
reciprocity, 56–57, 59
Referendum for Freedom, 141
Regional Employment Program of Latin America and the Caribbean (PREALC), 88, 99
resources, ownership of, 58, 98, 104, 113, 126, 159–61
Ress, Martha, 116
revolution, 9, 50–51, 53n5, 110, 112–13
  Bolivarian, 131–32, 134
  Cuban, 109–10, 120, 124, 127, 150, 161
  Mexican, 112
  reform or, 151
  repression of, 151
Revolutionary Armed Forces of Colombia (FARC), 24, 26, 128, 151
rural sector
  land ownership and, 109–27, 112–13
  migration to cities of, 116–17, 149
  poverty in, 16, 32, 67, 94, 115–16, 123
  social capital in, 163–64
  social movements in, 8, 9, 142–46, 143
Rural Workers Movement (MST), 80, 125, 126, 127, 128, 144

Sachs, Ignacy, 18, 46
Sachs, Jeffrey, 95
Sachs, Wolfgang, 31, 42
Salinas de Gortari, Carlos, 35, 39–41, 95
Samper, Ernesto, 133, 134
Sarney, José, 73
satellite states, 20, 24
savings, 13, 56
self-capacitation, 52, 66
Sen, Amartya, 70n1, 106n7
Sierra Leone, 93, 94
slavery, 110–11
Slim, Carlos, 135
slums, 33, 114, 149
Smith, Adam, 14
social capital, 55–59, 61, 65, 68–69
  democracy and, 59–62
  development and, 67–68
  inequality and, 65–66
  in land reform, 121
  mobilization of, 163–64
  poverty and, 67–68
  socio-economic status *vs.*, 65–66
  in sustainable livelihoods approach, 102–4
  weaknesses of, 57–60, 62–69
Social Capital Initiative (SCI), 69
social change
  development policies and, 161–64
  electoral process as, 152–61
  no-power approach to, 161, 163
  three modalities of, 149–50
social consensus, 36
social debt, 90
Social Development Summit, 38
social empowerment, 102, 104, 121
social exclusion, 67, 85–103, 105n1
  neo-liberalism and, 86–95
  six pillars of, 90–92
  sustainable livelihoods approach and, 101–2
social investment funds (SFIs), 38–39
socialism, 12l, 13
  in Bolivia, 157, 159, 163, 167n8
  in political parties, 132–35
Socialist Party of Chile, 134
social liberalism, 31–37, 61, 139
social mobilization, 151–53. *See also* social change
social movements, 127–29
  in Argentina, 8, 131, 144
  in Brazil, 8, 142, 144–45, 149, 152
  in Bolivia, 128, 131, 132, 142–45, 149
  in Ecuador, 128, 131, 143, 144, 152
  history of, 136–38, 150–51
  in Mexico, 8, 128, 131, 143
  new, 137–38
  repression of, 151–52
social programs
  cuts to, 32, 33, 61, 95
  informal sector and, 88–89
  privatization of, 38
  social exclusion and, 91, 92, 97
Solidaridad, 35, 39–41
solidarity, 59, 62–63, 138–42, 164
  dependence of, 32–33
  economy of, 96
  of rich and poor, 36, 95–96, 104
  social change and, 150
Somoza, Anastasio, 112
Soros, George, 95
squatters, 114
state, 7. *See also* government

207

as agent of modernization, 13
in another development, 34
land reform and, 118–20, 121
repression by, 119–20, 126, 127, 137, 156
retreat of, 52
social change without, 162–63
visible hand of, 35, 95
Stédile, Pedro, 125
Stiglietz, Joseph, 95
street workers, 85
structural adjustment, 8
with a human face, 32–38
poverty and, 86–87
social impacts of, 90–92
structural adjustment program (SAP), 8, 11, 14–19, 124, 139–40
structuralism, 13, 31, 35–36, 43–44, 47–50, 53n4, 56
subsidies, 15, 26, 32, 119, 134
Support Project for Small-scale Producers of Zacapa and Chiquimula (PROZACHI), 64, 65
sustainable human development, 67, 161, 162
sustainable livelihoods approach (SLA), 85, 101–04

technology, 45, 87, 88, 89, 90, 92, 98
Thiesenhusen, William C., 125
third sector, 51, 60
third way, 61–62, 73
Tonnies, Ferdinand, 63
Torres, Camilo, 51
trickle-down theory, 48
Trujillo, Rafael Leónidas, 112

underclass, 18–19
unemployment, 89, 91, 92
Unified Workers' Confederation (CUT), 83
unions. *See* labour movement
United Nations, 8, 18–20, 36
United Nations Centre for the Study of Transnational Corporations, 15
United Nations Conference on Trade and Development (UNCTAD), 15–16, 21
United Nations Development Programme (UNDP), 18, 59, 85, 162
United Nations Economic Commission for Latin America and the Caribbean (ECLAC), 35, 47–50, 59, 67, 71, 73, 96–98, 163
United Nations Research Institute for Social Development (UNRISD), 99–100

United States
capital accumulation of, 19–20
foreign policy of, 20
imperialism of, 19–27, 72
manifest destiny ideology in, 19–20
national security doctrine of, 152
power of, 20–25
resistance movements against, 26–27
United States Agency for International Development (USAID), 50–51, 162
urbanization, 149
urban sector, 33, 88, 94, 114–15, 123, 143, 151, 152
Uruguay, 14, 136

Vargas, Antonio, 153, 165n3
Vargas, Getulio, 112
Vatican, 51, 53n5
Venezuela
elections in, 9, 133, 134, 136
land reform in, 122
social movements in, 131–32, 151–52
unemployment in, 147n2
Via Campesina, 145

wages. *See also* income
decreasing, 13, 17, 18, 86, 88–90, 92
minimum, 89–90, 94, 95
Washington Consensus, 8, 11, 12, 21, 38, 67, 73
water, 33, 132, 156, 159, 166n6
wealth. *See also* income; poverty
distribution of, 31, 35
net movement of, 21–23
Weber, Max, 142
welfare. *See* social programs
Williamson, John, 11
Wolfowitz, Paul, 23, 29n6
Workers' Party (PT), 71, 73, 74, 78–83, 119, 124, 128, 132–36
working class, 15–17, 32, 85–87. *See also* labour
World Bank, 8, 9, 17, 20, 28n1
Brazil and, 77
development programs of, 51, 139–40
economic policies of, 14–15, 19, 35, 98
history of, 12–13
income distribution and, 67, 68, 94–95, 101, 139
labour laws and, 87
land reform and, 121–22
non-governmental organizations and, 76–78, 147n4
protest against, 26, 33

INDEX

social capital and, 57, 59, 60, 64
social policies of, 36, 37, 49, 97
World Bank Partnership Program, 77
World Social Forum (WSF), 34, 105n3
World Summit for Social Development, 94
World Trade Organization (WTO), 12–13, 26, 28

Zamora, Ruben, 136
Zapatista Army of National Liberation (EZLN), 117, 124, 128, 141, 147n3, 152
Zedillo, Ernesto, 29n5, 37, 87, 93